Madeira

Alex Liddell was born in Glasgow in 1934. He pursued an academic career as a university lecturer in philosophy and politics until 1987 after which he became a wine investment advisor working in Europe between 1987 and 1991. He is the author of *Port Wine Quintas of the Douro* and contributor to the *1997 Oz Clarke's Wine Guide*. He has a lifelong interest in madeira and fortified wine.

FABER BOOKS ON WINE
Series Editor: Julian Jeffs

Bordeaux (new edition) by David Peppercorn
Burgundy (new edition) by Anthony Hanson
French Country Wines by Rosemary George
Haut-Brion by Asa Briggs
Sauternes by Stephen Brook
Sherry (new edition) by Julian Jeffs
The Wild Bunch by Patrick Matthews
The Wines of Alsace by Tom Stevenson
The Wines of Australia (new edition) by Oliver Mayo
The Wines of Greece by Miles Lambert-Gocs
The Wines of the Loire by Roger Voss
The Wines of New Zealand by Rosemary George
The Wines of the Rhône (new edition) by John Livingstone-Learmonth
The Wines of South Africa by James Seely

of related interest:
Superbooze 1998: The Definitive Guide to Supermarket Drink
by Tom Stevenson
To Your Good Health!
by Tom Stuttaford

MADEIRA

ALEX LIDDELL

faber and faber

LONDON · BOSTON

First published in 1998
by Faber and Faber Limited
3 Queen Square London WC1N 3AU

Typeset by RefineCatch Limited, Bungay, Suffolk
Printed in England by Clays Ltd, St Ives plc

A CIP record for this book
is available from the British Library
ISBN 0-571-19097-9

2 4 6 8 10 9 7 5 3 1

To my very good friend Dieter Bohrmann,
who shares my love of madeira,
without whose generous help and encouragement
this book would not have been written.

Contents

CONTENTS

Acknowledgements

I have many people to thank for the help which they gave me in the preparation of this book.

First and foremost, I wish to express my thanks to Belmagri SA for making a generous financial grant towards the costs of publishing this book. I also wish to acknowledge and tender thanks for help received from the following: Artur de Barros e Sousa, Lda; H. M. Borges, Sucrs., Lda; Henriques & Henriques Vinhos, SA; Madeira Wine Co., SA; Pereira d'Oliveira (Vinhos), Lda; Silva Vinhos, Lda; Vinhos Barbeito (Madeira), Lda; Vinhos Justino Henriques, Filhos, Lda; the Instituto do Vinho da Madeira, which kindly provided hospitality; the Serviços de Produção Agrícola of the Direcção Regional da Agricultura; the Direcção Regional de Estatística; and the Direcção Regional de Turismo.

Many individuals very kindly gave me unstintingly their time, their knowledge, and often their hospitality. Amongst these I should particularly like to thank the following: Francisco Albuquerque, Ferdinando de Bianchi, Richard Blandy, João Brazão, João Brito, João César, John Cossart, Sigfredo da Costa Campos, Ivo Couto, John Crook, Isabel Dantas, Luisa Dias, David Fairlie, Manuel Eugénio Fernandes, Mário Fernandes, Manuela de Freitas, Ricardo de Freitas, Patrick Grubb, Duncan McEuen, João Pedro Marques, Anthony Miles, Artur and Edmundo de Olim, Aníbal and Luís d'Oliveira, Constantino Palma, Américo Pereira, João Abel Santos, Catherine Scott, Henrique Seabra, Susan Seldon, Duarte da Silva, Jacques Faro da Silva, James Symington and Alberto Vieira.

I wish to thank the following for having allowed me to quote from books of which they own the copyright, or from manuscripts in their possession: Richard Blandy, Blandy's Madeiras, Lda, John

Cossart, Christie's of London, Ricardo de Freitas, William Leacock, the Madeira Wine Company, and Susan Seldon.

I should especially like to thank Ernest Halberstadt, who read through drafts of Chapters 10 and 11, and who saved me (a non-chemist) from some blunders. Julian Jeffs, the editor of the series of which this book forms a part, and John Cossart read through the entire first draft of this book. They gave me much helpful advice and saved me from some stupid errors. I am greatly in their debt, but I need hardly add that the opinions expressed in this book are my own, and that Julian Jeffs and John Cossart do not necessarily agree with any of them: indeed, they sharply dissent from some of them.

Preface

———

'I know of no wine of its class that can beat Madeira when at its best
. . . In fact, I think Madeira and Burgundy carry combined intensity
and complexity of vinous delights further than any other wines.'[1]
Such is the glowing eulogy penned by George Saintsbury in his
Notes on a Cellar-Book. Yet it has to be admitted that, in the century which has elapsed since these words were written, the reputation of madeira has not just diminished amongst amateurs of wine:
it has all but totally disappeared.

The first madeira I ever tasted was a Cama de Lobos 1789,
which I purchased only because its date, shared with the French
Revolution, fired my romantic imagination and excited my curiosity. How, I wondered, could a wine from the eighteenth century
possibly have survived into the twentieth? This was in 1958, when
I was up at Oxford, and I had found it on a list of old vintage
madeiras offered for sale by Avery's, the long-established Bristol
wine merchant. I have the original invoice in front of me as I write.
It cost £3.75 a bottle, which was an immense sum for me in those
days, but curiosity prevailed over financial caution. In fact, for good
measure I bought *two* bottles, just in case I enjoyed it.

I shall never forget the ravishment of that first taste. Its powerful
and explosive attack, rich complexity of flavour, rapier-like dry finish, and long, intense aftertaste were quite beyond anything I had
hitherto experienced. I was hooked for life – and rapidly invested in
three more bottles, one of which still remains in my cellar.

I even had the impertinence to write to Avery's to ask how they
could be sure that the date of the wine was really 1789. How much
less alluring, I insinuated, if it had happened to be 1788. The terse,
slightly rebuking reply merely stated that 'it was in cask from
1789 until early in the present century when it was transferred into

demijohns from which it was bottled, as we say, a year or so ago'.[2] How, the letter seemed to say, could you doubt the word of a firm such as ours? We have a reputation to maintain.

So began the fascination which madeira has had for me over the last forty years. I am in no doubt that Saintsbury is correct. At its best – which is an important qualification – madeira makes a statement about the vine which is almost unparalleled. Every serious wine lover owes it to himself to discover its delights. If I can communicate some of my own enthusiasm for madeira and thereby bring into the fold those of my readers who do not yet know that they have been missing one of the world's great wine experiences, I shall be well satisfied. Despite my enthusiasm, however, my book is far from being uncritical; some of my friends on the island may even think it goes too far in the opposite direction. Sadly, although the fortunes of madeira, like port, have always been subject to fluctuating fashions of taste, the decline of madeira in the twentieth century has been partly a self-inflicted injury.

I first went to Madeira a quarter of a century ago, in 1973. The island, and to some extent the wine, were both very different in these days. That was before the 1974 revolution, still referred to today by many older people as 'the times of misery'. Poverty was rife and, in the north of the island, people without shoes were a not uncommon sight. Much of the cheaper madeira was of deplorable quality, and almost entirely made from the hybrid vines which are now banned.

The visitor to Madeira as the century nears its end finds a very different situation. The entry of Portugal into the EU has, within the past ten years, provided considerable aid for development of the infrastructure, and this is now rapidly transforming the island. Tourism, the mainstay of Madeira's economy, has increased by 75 per cent during this period.[3] With hotel and time-share building proceeding apace, it looks set to increase further with the extension of the airport to accommodate jumbo jets. There has been enormous development to the west of the capital, Funchal, new fast roads have made communication quicker and easier, and a general air of prosperity is starting to prevail.

Within the same period there have also been encouraging changes in the wine scene. As recently as 1992, in a book about Portuguese wine, an English writer painted a bleak picture for the future of the island's wine industry and warned, with considerable justification, that 'it looks as though madeira could be facing terminal decline'.[4] Not all the reasons for gloom have yet been dispelled, but this present book, even if sometimes critical, is far from being an obituary notice. Indeed, the portents for the future are now distinctly brighter.

There are few books exclusively about madeira, and in English there have been none in print for several years now. Noël Cossart's *Madeira* remains fascinating and unbeatable for its wealth of personal reminiscence and the authoritativeness which comes from having spent a lifetime in the trade. I gladly acknowledge my own inevitable and considerable indebtedness to such a rich source of information. But Cossart retired from the wine trade a quarter of a century ago, and some of what he wrote about the production of madeira was already out of date when his book first appeared in 1984. Since then the pace of change has accelerated as much for madeira as for other things, and an up-to-date book is now more than ever necessary.

The first part of this book is concerned with the history of the wine and its trade. The sources for such a history are extensive, and happily they are now beginning to attract the attention of scholars. I have had to rely mainly on secondary sources, and my use of primary materials in a book of this scope has, of necessity, had to be very limited. However, Dr Alberto Vieira has completed a proper, detailed history of madeira, and this will shortly be published, with a large photographic record of the trade, on CD-ROM in both Portuguese and English. I fully acknowledge my debt to his source book of documentary material on the history of the wine, and his courtesy in answering my many questions. Professor David Hancock, of the Department of History at Harvard, is shortly to publish a book on the central importance of madeira in the development of the British North American colonies, and this will plug another gap in our knowledge. My own contribution, within the confines of a general book on madeira, is necessarily comparatively brief, but I believe that it sheds some new light on certain aspects of the wine's history.

I have made extensive use of guidebooks and reports published by visitors to Madeira up to the end of the nineteenth century. These visitors were not for the most part specialists in wine matters. They were often reliant on what others told them, and doubtless made mistakes about some of the information they were given.

Moreover, this was the age of plagiarism and much has simply been diligently copied from earlier publications – even word for word! Such sources, therefore, have to be used with caution. Nevertheless, I have used as much direct quotation as possible in Part I of the book, in the belief that the words of those who lived through historical events can often bring them to life for the reader as no later commentator can.

Inevitably, a book of this sort has to contain a number of statistics which can easily prove wearisome to the reader. Those which relate to the geology and climate of the island I have put in an appendix. Lists of export totals are likewise tedious, but general trends are interesting. I have therefore adopted and extended a graphical form of representation used by Lemps in his book *Le Vin de Madère* – and hereby make grateful acknowledgement of the fact – to display exports from Madeira for the last two centuries, and this also appears as an appendix.

A note on spelling conventions and terminology

'Madeira' with an upper-case M refers to the island, and with a lower-case m refers to the wine.

Câmara de Lobos and Cama de Lobos are alternative names for the same place. I have preferred the former, except when referring to wine originating from Câmara de Lobos, which by tradition seems always to be called Cama de Lobos.

I have relied on the context to make it clear when I am referring to a grape variety and when I am referring to the wine which is made from it. However, there are alternative correct spellings in Portuguese of some of the grape varieties. Thus we have *malvasia* and *malvazia*. Nowadays, the former is most often used to refer to the grape, whilst for many years the latter has been used as the spelling for the wine. Nobody seems to know why this is so, but I have adopted the same convention. Other alternative spellings are *jacquet* and *jacquez,* and *sercial* and *cerceal*. I have chosen the former in both cases.

I use Portuguese spelling in preference to anglicized versions for two of the wines, although there is nothing wrong with these in context. Thus I refer to Boal rather than to Bual, and to Malvazia rather than to Malmsey, except in quotations or when shippers have used the anglicized form on their labels.

Sercial, Verdelho, Boal and Malvasia used to be called the *castas nobres*, or noble varieties. This phrase, although convenient, is now old-fashioned. I have, therefore, adopted the following terminology:

Classical varieties: meaning Sercial, Verdelho, Boal and Malvazia.

Traditional varieties: meaning these four varieties and, additionally, Terrantez and Bastardo.

In Portuguese all syllables and vowels are pronounced. The stress invariably falls on vowels with accents, failing which on the penultimate vowel.

Introduction

═══

Madeira (meaning 'wood' in Portuguese) is the largest island in a small archipelago of the same name in the Atlantic Ocean. This Portuguese possession is situated on the parallel 33°N – which puts it on roughly the same latitude as Casablanca and Bermuda – and is 796 km west of the coast of north Africa. The island is 57 km long (east–west) and, at its broadest, 23 km wide (north–south), with a total area of 736.8 square km. This makes it comparable in size to Rhodes or Minorca.

Porto Santo, the only other populated island of the archipelago, is 36 km north-east of Madeira and is much smaller, being 12 km long by 7 km wide. The remaining islands consist of two groups, the Desertas and the Selvagems, which are now designated as bird sanctuaries.

Madeira rarely fails to charm its visitors. It has an equable sub-tropical climate, year-round sunshine and is justly famous for its profusion of flowers. The island is also renowned for its spectacular scenery, ranging from alpine splendour at its mountainous centre and a corniche road along its northern cliffs, to a desolate plateau reminiscent of Dartmoor and pine forests reminiscent of Scotland. Madeira was once the exclusive destination of the wealthy, who came by sea, either for health reasons or simply for relaxation, but since 1965 air travel has made it accessible to a wider range of visitors and tourism has become its principal economic activity. Funchal, the capital, has up to now been the main focus of tourist development, the rest of the island having managed to preserve much of its tranquil simplicity. But as the twentieth century nears its end the pace of change has accelerated sharply, and one senses that Madeira may soon lose the atmosphere of time-forgotten remoteness which many consider to be its principal attraction.

Madeira's reputation as a destination for travellers goes back to the late eighteenth century, but the fame of its wine goes back even further, to the late fifteenth century, not long after the island was colonized by Portugal. For centuries the production of wine was its principal activity, and one might say that the history of the wine and of the island are to that extent the same.

PART I

The History of the Wine

I

Early History

Discovery, colonization and land tenure

According to what was for long the accepted story, Porto Santo was 'accidentally' discovered in 1418 by João Gonçalves Zarco, Bartolomeu Perestrelo and Tristão Vaz Teixeira, who were all in the service of Prince Henry the Navigator, the Portuguese Infante. Two years later, in 1420, Zarco and Teixeira 'ventured' 37 km beyond Porto Santo to investigate a dense, dark cloud on the horizon, and thereby discovered Madeira. A more romantic story gives the credit to an Englishman, Robert Machin, cast ashore on the island whilst eloping with a fellow countryman's wife!

The truth seems to be much more prosaic. Madeira and Porto Santo appear named as such, often with the Desertas and the Selvagems too, in numerous fourteenth-century maps, such as the Medici Atlas (1351), the chart attributed to the Pizzigani brothers (1367), the Catalan planisphere of Abraam Cresques (1375), the Solleri chart (1385) and the Pinelli chart (1390). Thus, according to recent informed historical opinion,[1] there appears to be no doubt that Madeira was discovered, nobody knows by whom, well before 1420. It was shortly after 1420 – 1425 is given as the official date – that the colonization of Madeira and Porto Santo started. Prince Henry appears to have taken the initiative in this, and official authorization was given to Zarco on 1 November 1430 by Prince Henry's father, King João I, to divide up and allot the lands of the archipelago for settlement.

The settling of the islands was in fact in the hands of the three 'discoverers', who became captains of the areas (captaincies) they administered. Teixeira became captain of Machico and the east of the island; Perestrelo became captain of Porto Santo; and Zarco was

3

appointed captain of Funchal and the west of the island. (Caniço in the south and Porto Moniz in the north marked the boundary between the two Madeiran captaincies.) Each of the captains leased land to others according to a system of *sesmaria*, under which the grantees – mainly aristocrats, wealthy foreign venturers and the occasional bourgeoisie – had to undertake to develop the land productively within a specified period during which they paid no rent, but after which they entered into full possession of it. The obligations of *sesmaria* were usually discharged by importing large numbers of African and Arab slaves. This system lasted until 1501, after which land could only be acquired by purchase, leasehold, inheritance or dowry, and this tended to concentrate property ownership in the hands of the aristocracy, rich foreigners (as much through marriage as purchase) and bourgeoisie who had prospered during the initial period of development.

These began to consolidate their position by establishing entails (*morgados*), which ensured the inheritance of land and property on the basis of primogeniture. This was the foundation on which the most powerful families on the island amassed and maintained their fortunes, and at one stage it was estimated that two-thirds of the land of the entire archipelago was held in entail under the *morgado* system.[2] Although modified from time to time, this remained the real basis of land tenure until it was abolished in 1863,[3] but its effects persisted even after this, and were only finally removed as one of the results of the 1974 revolution.[4]

On to this structure of land tenure was grafted a system of tenancy called *contrato de colonia* (colonial contract), whereby the landlord owned the land but the tenant owned any improvements he had made which added value to the land, including a house if he built one. The landlord would provide or share with the tenant the costs of working the land, and in return would receive a proportion, generally a half, of the value of the crops produced. The contract passed from generation to generation, and in practice the system proved to be remarkably stable. It still exists. However, the right of the tenant to buy the freehold of his land was established in 1976. This has not only greatly reduced the number of surviving colonial contracts, but has finally undermined what remained of the system of *morgados*.

Early development and trade

The first colonists were members of the Portuguese nobility who brought with them labourers and artisans mainly from northern Portugal.[5] Wealthy and entrepreneurial adventurers from other parts of Europe (Italians, Flemish, French and Castilians – and a single Scotsman by the name of Drummond, who was a nephew of King Robert III and cousin to James I) soon followed, encouraged by special privileges designed to exploit their connections with potential export destinations. The island was covered with dense forest and the centres of population were established in areas close to the south coast, first at Machico, then at Funchal, gradually spreading westwards along the south coast. The forest had to be burned to provide arable land, and initially subsistence crops of grain and vines were planted, with sugar cane – planted speculatively for the first time beyond Europe – as a potential export. The rough terrain was adapted for agriculture by terracing the slopes of hills, and by 1461 a system of *levadas*, or irrigation channels, which has been consistently extended into our own day, had been constructed.[6] Spring water from the central heights of the island is diverted into collecting channels which are fed, through successive stages, into increasingly larger and more important channels, often carved out of the living rock and routed through tunnels. The *levadas* descend in altitude by very gradual degrees, and eventually provide water for crops (and drinking).

Farming prospered, and we know that Madeira was already exporting sugar, grain, wine and timber to the Portuguese mainland, to African markets, and to the Gulf of Guinea by 1461.[7] The land, enriched by the burning of the forests, was incredibly fertile. Sugar cane found new markets in northern Europe and the Mediterranean, and by 1466 it had become the principal crop, to the detriment of grain, which then had to be imported. Production grew with amazing and accelerating rapidity from the middle of the fifteenth century until it peaked in 1506, and brought correspondingly increased levels of prosperity to the settlers.

The first wine

We do not know for certain which vines were first planted, but it seems reasonable to suppose that the first settlers brought with them the varieties already established in the Minho and other parts of northern Portugal from which they came. One reason for so thinking is that the traditional method of cultivation in Madeira, using trellises to support the vines, is remarkably similar to that still used in the Minho for *vinho verde*. Both in northern Portugal and in Madeira until earlier in this century, an alternative method of support was to grow vines up trees and, indeed, occasional survivals of this tradition can still be found. It seems likely, therefore, that the settlers at first grew for their own consumption what they had been used to back home.

Fairly early on, however, Malvasia was introduced to the island. Alvise da Mosto, a Venetian navigator who visited Madeira around 1450, published an account of his voyages in 1507. His report is interesting: 'Really very good wines are produced here for a new colony, and they are so plentiful that there are sufficient for those on the island and they even ship them abroad. Amongst the vines the Lord [Prince Henry] ordered the planting of plots of Malvasias, which he sent for from Candia, and which are doing very well. And the country being so good and fertile, the vines almost produce more grapes than leaves, and the bunches are very large, of the length of two, three and, I venture to say, even of four palms, which is the most beautiful thing in the world to see. Black grapes without pips are here hanging on pergolas in complete perfection.'[8]

It is remarkable that wine was already being exported within about twenty-five years of the establishment of the colony, and the productivity of the vines is astonishing. It is implied that there are several varieties, though Malvasia is singled out – the mention of a specific variety is rare for this period. We are evidently concerned here with Malvasia Cândida, Cândida being a corruption of Candia, the capital of Crete (also known as Heraklion). Prince Henry may well have planted this variety speculatively (like the sugar) as a potential export because, it is said, he wished to compete with the wines from the eastern Mediterranean, of which Venice had at the time a virtual monopoly. Whether the cuttings came specially from Crete is, perhaps, another matter. It is thought that the vine had already been established in Portugal before it came to Madeira,[9] so this may simply be a colourful embellishment.

How extensive the export of wine was at this time we have no means of telling. Although sugar clearly remained the dominant commodity throughout the century, wine exports probably grew as the vineyards themselves increased in number. We do know, however, that in 1461 some islanders petitioned for exemption from taxes on their exports of wine, sugar, wood and cereals; and in 1485 the island Council imposed another tax on wine exports to meet its revenue needs.[10] As the century neared its end, however, the most significant event for the future export of madeira was certainly the discovery of America by Christopher Columbus, who had himself stayed in Funchal for some time in 1478 while negotiating a purchase of sugar, and who later married the daughter of Bartolomeu Perestrelo, the first captain of Porto Santo. His house in Porto Santo is open as a museum.

The sixteenth century

By 1514 the population had reached 5,000 – not including the slave population, which some thought was large enough to constitute a risk to security. Meanwhile, Funchal prospered and had been raised to the status of a city in 1508. The customs house had been founded in 1477,[11] and banking and money-lending flourished. Despite the problems of communication between the centres of population – the only way was by sea – an elaborate customs and fiscal system operated. There were eight parishes on the south coast and one on the north. A new society, with the same social stratification as that of the mainland, had been created.

The position of foreign merchants, whose community was dominated by Italians, had been equivocal in the second half of the previous century. The strong competition, especially with regard to sugar, which they offered to native merchants led to restrictions being placed on their residential status and their trading rights. Slowly their situation was regularized, and by a decree of 22 March 1498 foreigners were again permitted to establish permanent residence on the island.[12] Giovanni Baptista Lomelino, whose descendants were to establish an important madeira shipping firm, arrived in Madeira in 1476.[13] At the beginning of the sixteenth century even more Italians settled on the island. A list of the 173 most important families on the island at this period includes 56 of foreign origin.[14] It was not, however, until the end of the century that we can record the first English merchant, Robert Willoughby, who arrived about 1590. He was known to the Portuguese as Velovi.

Amongst the new Italian settlers was Simão Acciaioly, who

arrived in 1515. He is credited with having introduced Malvasia Babosa, another variety of the grape, which now seems to be virtually extinct on the island. The Madeiran Acciaiolys were a branch of the powerful Florentine Acciaiolis (as the name was originally spelled), noted bankers and the builders of the Castello di Montegufoni, famous as the Italian home of Sir Osbert Sitwell. The last members of the Acciaioly family have now left Madeira, but Oscar Acciaioly, who died in 1979, was a madeira shipper who specialized in the Scandinavian market.

Between 1502 and 1503 sugar production was almost double that of the previous year,[15] but after 1506 it began to diminish. This was the start of a long decline caused by over-production, soil exhaustion, pests and plant disease, the increasing cost and scarcity of slaves, and finally, towards the end of the century, the *coup de grâce* – cheaper competition from Brazil. Faced with these crises, many cane fields were converted to vineyards, and wine, finding new markets in the Americas and West Indies, increasingly became the island's main export. By 1537 it was being imported into England.[16]

We have two specific references to Malvazia during the century. In 1530 Madeira was visited by another Venetian, Giulio Landi, who comments in his *La Descrittione de l'isola de la Madera*, published in 1574, that Madeira 'produces a large amount of wine of all sorts; but for the most part they are big wines, and white, and similar to the Roman *greco*.[17] It also produces Malvazia, but not yet in much quantity; and it is reputed to be better than that from Candia. And because those on the island are not used to drinking wine, they sell it to merchants; who then take it to Iberia and to other northern countries.'[18] Landi appears to indicate that, just as wine was overtaking sugar as the island's principal export, its celebrity was also increasing.

Another Italian traveller, Pompeo Arditi, visited Madeira somewhat later, in 1567. In his *Viaggio all'isola di Madera e alle Azzore*, published in Florence only in 1934, he wrote: 'The whole island makes a large quantity of wines which are considered most excellent and very similar to the *Malvasia* from Candia'.[19] Compared with Landi's comment about the Malvazia being 'not yet in much quantity', Arditi's phrase 'large quantity' might suggest that its production had greatly increased in the intervening thirty-five years. It may have done, but it is important to put this in the context of

Landi's remark about wine 'of all sorts', mainly white, *and* of Malvazia. Malvasia Cândida never was, then or later, the principal grape variety in Madeira in a quantitative sense. As we shall see, commentators from the sixteenth century onwards remarked as often on the small production and scarcity of Malvazia as they did on its excellence. The scarcity of genuine Malvasia Cândida today is only an intensification of a situation which has always existed.

A third visitor, named Lopez, briefly remarks in 1588 that 'wine groweth in great abundance in Madeira, yea, and in my opinion the best in the world, whereof they carry abroad great store into divers countries, especially into England'.[20]

By the end of the century Madeira had a physiognomy remarkably like today's. Twenty-six more parishes had been created, but only seven of them were on the north coast.[21] The population of Funchal had swelled to around 10,000, while Santa Cruz and Machico had 4,000 and 3,000 inhabitants respectively.[22] Even the disposition of the vineyards, which is known to us from a chronicle called *As Saudades da Terra* by Gaspar Fructuoso (published only in 1873), is not so very different from that of the twentieth century.[23]

There is a problem about how to interpret what Fructuoso tells us. Apart from Malvazia he talks of *vidonhos*, and through the mists of history we cannot say whether Fructuoso intended to indicate by this word another variety of grape, or a type of wine, or was referring to grape varieties in general. The issue is a complex one which is fully discussed in Appendix 6, to which the reader is referred for further information.[24] So as not to complicate the following discussion unduly, the word is left untranslated.

Fructuoso, who died in 1591 in the Azores, where he had lived for many years, wrote his chronicle towards the end of his life. The information he gives us about the vineyards, which is interwoven with a topographical description of the island, probably relates to a period at least ten years earlier – say, around 1580. Not only is it rich in detail, but he even discusses the quality of the various wines. But however interesting his account is to the specialist, to quote it extensively would be wearisome to the reader unfamiliar with the island – although virtually all the rivers and places mentioned by Fructuoso are readily identifiable by the same names today.

The tour starts in the east and goes westwards along the south coast of the island. Between Machico and Funchal, Fructuoso mentions the following locations of vineyards: Machico itself (where 'they say that the wine is the worst in the whole island, and as such very little is loaded [exported]'); the Porto de Seixo river (with 'many Malvasia vines and *vidonhos* which are better than those of Machico'); Santa Cruz; the Boaventura river; Gaula (with 'many vineyards of Malvasias and many other *vidonhos*'); the Porto Novo river ('the wines from which are very good for loading, and where there are fine Malvasias, the best on the island, and other *vidonhos* from which they make more than 300 pipes of wine each year'); and Caniço. In and around the city of Funchal, Fructuoso specifies the Santa Luzia river[25] ('above which they make 400 pipes each year of extremely good wine'); the Água de Mel river; the Church of Nossa Senhora de Calhau beside the João Gomes river ('above which there are many vineyards of Malvasias and *vidonhos* from which they make 200 pipes of wine each year'); and the São João river ('above which there are many vineyards which give more than 200 pipes of good wine each year').

West of Funchal, Fructuoso notes the Acorridos river, just east of Câmara de Lobos ('above which there are many vineyards of Malvasias and good *vidonhos*'); Câmara de Lobos; and 'a league from Câmara de Lobos is the quinta of Luís de Noronha [which] has few vineyards, being on high ground, but along the seaboard the same Luís de Noronha has a *fajã* with a large orchard and very valuable mature vines which give 40 to 50 pipes of Malvazia every year'.[26] Then come Campanário (which has 'grazing grounds, and wheat and rye crops, because the hill-folk are more given to rearing cattle than to cultivating vines'); the Melões river; Ribeira Brava (where 'the wine is not as good as it is at Funchal'); the Tábua river (where 'the wine is similar to that of Ribeira Brava'); Ponta do Sol (where 'the wines are not as good as those of Funchal'); and, north of Ponta do Sol, Calcanhos.[27] Further west the main crop seems to be sugar cane, though Fructuoso makes a passing mention of vines at the property of João Rodrigues Castelhano a league from Calheta, and at Jardim do Mar. On the north coast, vines are mentioned in connection with Seixal, São Vicente (where they are plentiful), and Ponta Delgada. Only São Jorge 'has many vines producing good wine for loading'.[28]

This remarkable and detailed account not only gives us a clear picture of the extent of the vineyards, but also enables us to make a calculation of the amount of wine produced. Simply adding the specific amounts mentioned by Fructuoso gives us a total of 1,150 pipes, most of which we must assume to have been exported. To this has to be added the production of the other areas he mentions. If we assume that this was at least half as much again, we arrive at a figure in excess of 1,700 pipes. Given that another historian has estimated that the average amount of wine exported each year in the first decade of the seventeenth century was 2,000 pipes,[29] and assuming that in the final twenty years of the fifteenth century there may have been some expansion of the vineyard area to meet growing export demand, this figure does not seem too implausible.

The character of the wine

What was the madeira of this period actually like? Some writers have speculated about whether it was a dry or a sweet wine. One suspects from the distinction made between Malvazia and Vidonho that the latter was probably drier than the former. But how sweet was the Malvazia? Because we are used to thinking of it as the sweetest of all madeiras, the idea that it may once have been dry initially strikes us as ludicrous. We must remember, however, that at this time the modern technique of stopping the fermentation of the wine by adding alcohol, thereby preserving some of its natural sugar, was not employed in Madeira, so fermentation would be allowed to come to a natural end.

So far as I know, right down to the end of the seventeenth century Malvazia is never described by those who mention it as a *sweet* wine: they always call it a *rich* wine. It is conceivable, therefore, that Malvazia had a perceived sweetness arising from the intense fruit character of the grape, rather as some dry Muscats can seem to be sweet, or as a Gewürztraminer can be rich. This view has as a representative Noël Cossart, who states that 'the Malmsey of that time was unfortified, and probably fermented right out'.[30]

The contrary view is based on the favourable comparisons of madeira made in the fifteenth century with the wines traded from the east through Venice, which are usually accepted as having been sweet. Moreover, the wine of Madeira was competing in a market dominated by sack from Spain and the Canaries, and some authorities, such as Julian Jeffs, assert that 'sack was always classified as a sweet wine'.[31] He points out that methods of sweetening wines after fermentation had 'long been known' and claims that Elizabethan sack was 'certainly fortified'. However, there is no specific reason for thinking either that post-fermentation sweetening was applied to madeira, or that it was ever fortified at this date, though this would certainly have helped to stabilize it as a sweet wine. Indeed, the fact that none of the commentators allude to such practices until the eighteenth century seems to be a sufficient reason for ruling it out.

My own view coincides with that of André Simon, who states the matter succinctly: 'There is no doubt that, originally, the word *Seck*, pronounced and soon after spelt *Sack*, was only applied to the drier wines shipped from the south of Spain; but at the close of the six-teenth and during the seventeenth century it became a generic name for all wines more or less similar, in taste and colour, to those of Jerez, whether they were actually shipped from Port St Mary, or any other Spanish or Portuguese port, or even from the Canaries and Madeira.'[32] Henderson, in his *History of Ancient and Modern Wines* published in 1824, adds a relevant observation. He says that the wines called *Sack* 'probably first came into favour in con-sequence of their possessing greater strength and durability, and being more free from acidity, than the white wines of France and Germany; and owed their distinctive appellation to that peculiar sub-astringent taste which characterizes all wines prepared with gypsum'.[33]

Gypsum (hydrous calcium sulphate), generally known at the time as *gesso*, was commonly used to make wines of the type classified as sack. The earliest appearance of the word in English recorded by the OED – in 1598 – relates to wine: 'Gesso when it is first put into the wine maketh it bitter'. Henderson points out that 'the Spaniards had borrowed from the Greeks the practice of adding gypsum to the must, which they afterwards improved upon . . . as to be able to excel all other nations in the manufacture of dry wines'.[34] He adds that 'burnt gypsum . . . occasions a rapid fermentation and imparts a harsh dry taste to the wine'.[35] Savary des Bruslons, in his *Diction-naire du Commerce* published in 1723, remarks that old madeiras are better 'than in their first year, because of a bitter and hot taste which only dissipates with time'.[36] Gypsum has, of course, always played a part in the making of sherry; and, anticipating a little, gypsum is frequently mentioned between the seventeenth and nine-teenth centuries in connection with the fermentation of madeira.[37] The use of gypsum in making madeira (and at times as a clarifying agent) therefore appears to have been standard practice for several hundred years. It is no longer used as a matter of course, but is still used from time to time.[38]

My view therefore, following Simon and Henderson, is that sack was predominantly a dry wine. Most discussions of the nature of madeira at this time have, I believe, failed to make a proper distinction between Malvazia and Vidonho. Vidonho (or Vidonia, as it came to be called) was a sack-like dry wine; Malvazia was a rich wine. Even if the Malvazia was fermented out, the grapes, which may (according to some)[39] have been left to become semi-raisins, would have had such a high sugar concentration that the residual sugar content of the wine would have remained quite high. The wine may not have been entirely stable, giving rise to the risk of secondary fermentations, and, as we shall see in the next chapter, there do appear to have been problems of this sort with Malvazia. Croft, in 1787, goes so far as to call it 'an unfermented wine' which 'would not stand [keep] in the English climate without passing the line, or undergoing a long sea voyage'.[40]

Madeira wine, at the end of the sixteenth century, clearly had much in common with the wines of the Canaries and almost certainly had a similar character. Malvazia was probably a rich, sweetish wine with a perceived fruitiness; Vidonho (or Vidonia) was certainly dry, probably rather astringent, rather alcoholic and warming – in short, more akin to sack than was Malvazia.

2

Madeira Comes of Age

The seventeenth century

Only from the middle of the seventeenth century do we begin to have (incomplete) customs house records of the duty-paid exports of wine from the island. The Funchal customs registers for 1650 indicate that 2,405 pipes of wine paid duty; those for the first nine months of 1682 give a total of 3,410 (or, in annual terms, 4,546 pipes); in 1699 a total of 5,483 pipes was recorded.[1] However, since Portuguese ships enjoyed the privilege of shipping duty-free, these totals must be considerably less than the amounts actually exported, which again must be less than the amount of wine actually made. Duncan, in his book on seventeenth-century Atlantic trade, attempts to extrapolate from these and other sporadic reports about the activities of Portuguese shipping to speculative global totals for annual exports, such as 3,500 pipes for 1650 and 6,500 pipes for 1699.[2] These, in my view, have to be taken with extreme caution. Shipping must have been considerably disrupted during the Anglo-Portuguese naval war of June–December 1650, and it is impossible to know how this is reflected in the customs house figures for that year. Nor do we know whether there was a large or small harvest, always a crucial factor. Hence the duty-paid total for this year cannot plausibly be used, in conjunction with other arbitrary assumptions, to estimate the normal year-upon-year average for the middle of the century.[3]

We do, as it happens, have two independent estimates of production for this period, both astonishingly high. Christopher Jeaffreson, a young Englishman travelling to his estate in St Christopher's (St Kitt's) in 1676, reports that 'some years twenty-five thousand pipes of wine' are produced.[4] In 1689 the traveller

14

John Ovington tells us that 'Twenty Thousand Pipes of Wine, by a modest Computation, may be reckoned the Annual Increase of the Grapes ... Eight Thousand are thought to be drunk upon the Island, three or four are wasted in Leekage, and the remainder is Transported, most of it to the *West Indies*, especially to *Barbadoes*, where it is drunk more liberally than other *European* Wines'.[5] Subtracting the amounts for local consumption and ullage gives us 8,000–9,000 pipes for export, which does not seem to be modest at all. In fact, I find it unbelievably high. So, as we cannot assess Ovington's accuracy, the most we can say with confidence is that by the end of the seventeenth century exports of wine had grown to something well in excess of 6,000 pipes, and that this must represent something like a threefold expansion of trade over the course of the century.

It is interesting to note commentators' remarks on the small amount of wine consumed on the island and on the sobriety of its inhabitants. Landi gives us one explanation: 'Amongst them the drinking of wine, old men apart, is a shameful thing; especially for the young men and the women. The reason is that they believe that those women who drink wine must be of little honesty. The young men abstain from drinking wine so as not to offend the ladies, to whom the smell of wine is displeasing.'[6] A century later, John Ovington provides a more intriguing speculation: 'The Venereal Excesses to which they are strangely addicted, with the immoderate heat of the place, would be apt to put Nature under various disorders. Therefore Men of the greatest Consequence and Fortune, (whether it be that Sobriety might render them more Spruce and Amorous for the Exercise of Love, or that they are bred up in an Antipathy to that gross and scandalous Vice of Drunkenness,) seldom exceed the allowable bounds of Drinking.'[7]

The British commercial presence in Madeira, initiated by Robert Willoughby in the 1590s, started slowly. Of the eighteen foreign merchants registered in the customs house records for 1620, only three were British. During the middle of the century, from 1638 until 1682, the principal merchant (amongst foreigners and Portuguese alike) was Richard Pickford, and from this period until the end of the century another fifteen names were added to the British contingent.[8] The 1687 customs register records about eighty names, but according to Duncan, the most important import-export business was confined to about thirty of them, of which eight or nine might be said to have been both wealthy and powerful. Of these thirty merchants, about two dozen were foreign and just short of half were British. One of them, John Carter, became the first British consul in 1658, but the most famous of the British merchants – on account of the fact that a large section of his business correspondence has been published – is William Bolton, who arrived in Madeira in 1676.[9] These merchants were prosperous and enjoyed a luxurious lifestyle. Ovington says they 'imitate the *English* way of Living in their City and Country Houses; and wearied with the Town, divert themselves in their Rural Plantations' where he discovered 'the Hills were all cover'd with Vines, and the Valleys with ripe Grapes, which yielded us a fragrant smell from the fruitful Vineyards whither soever we turn'd our Eyes'.[10]

The influx of the British appears to have been closely connected with the development of colonial markets in America and also with trading concessions made to British merchants. From 1580 until 1640 Portugal was under the domination of Spain, whose kings had also been the kings of Portugal. During this period English and Dutch trade prospered at the expense of Portuguese trade, and many of Portugal's overseas possessions changed hands. The conclusion of the brief Anglo-Portuguese war in 1650 brought about a 'favoured nation' treaty in 1654, by means of which King João IV, to limit further territorial aggrandisement at Portugal's expense, accorded concessions to British merchants resident in Portugal and Madeira. The British Factory, an association of British merchants, was probably started about 1658. The trading position of these merchants was further reinforced in 1663 – after the restoration of the monarchy in Britain and the marriage of Charles II to Catherine of Braganza – when, under the Staple Act, Madeira and the Azores were exempted from the prohibition in the 1660 Navigation Act against the export of any goods to English colonies except in English ships directly from English ports.[11] This concession gave the British merchants in Madeira a virtual monopoly of the trade with the West Indies and the American plantations, and compensated for the fact that Brazil, which had hitherto been the most important market for madeira, declined in importance from this date onwards.

These traders were effectively general brokers whose prosperity depended upon the importation of all manner of goods as much as it did on the export of wine. Indeed, if Bolton is representative, they did not warehouse the wine they exported, but obtained it from 'the natives' as required in settlement of credit for imported goods already supplied:[12] 'Nor, indeed, would it be any Prudence in us to buy before hand, not knowing how or when any ships may come, and the Keepeing of wine is very chargeable: it quickly makes them very deare.'[13]

As the markets in the Indies and Americas opened up, a triangular trade between Madeira, the New World and Britain or continental Europe became general, including the transshipment of goods from the British and Portuguese colonies back to Europe. Thus English textiles, pickled herring, butter and cheese, American wheat and cereal crops, Newfoundland and New England salt fish, Portuguese olive oil, spices, cheese and sausages – together with a huge assortment of raw materials such as metals, ship's chandlery, materials for defence, household articles and furniture – were all imported. On the export side, wine was far and away the most important commodity, amounting to perhaps as much as 95 per cent of the total.

The wine

During the seventeenth century we find the wine being classified in various ways. At the beginning of the century, for example, the price paid to growers for their ordinary wine was fixed in October each year, after the harvest, by the council. In 1625 the price paid to growers made a distinction between the grapes grown on the middle slopes and upwards (*meias terras para cima*) and those grown on the middle slopes and downwards (*meias terras para baixo*), the price of the latter being 20 per cent higher than that of the former. Devaluation of the currency, however, reduced this differential to less than 8 per cent by 1667.[14]

In 1650 the customs house distinguished between *vinhos melhores* (better quality wines) and *vinhos mais baixos* (lower quality wines). To what extent this mirrored the previous distinction is not clear. The former were shipped mainly to the Portuguese mainland and to Brazil, and had a (customs) estimated value of 8 réis per pipe.[15] The latter went to Barbados and English plantations, having an estimated value of 6 réis per pipe. Duties reflected this differential, being 888 milréis and 666 milréis per pipe respectively.[16] In 1667, however, this duty differential vanished, and by 1670 the distinction between the two markets had also vanished. Indeed, more and more of the better wines began to find their way to America. The prices realized by merchants generally seem to have run 20–40 per cent ahead of the customs house estimates. In the 1670s the prices were depressed, but from 1682 until the end of the century the increased trade with British colonial markets gave them a considerable boost. Thus in this period ordinary wine increased in price by 50 per cent, and Malvazia by 71.5 per cent.

Malvazia, as much because of its rarity as its quality, always commanded a higher price than the ordinary wines. In 1650, while the better-quality wines were estimated at 8 réis by the customs, Malvazia was estimated at 9 réis. Of the 2,405 pipes of wine exported in 1650, 1,540 pipes were better-quality wines, 778 pipes were of the lower quality, and only 87 pipes were Malvazia – that is, 3.6 per cent of the total quantity and 5–6 per cent of the total value. This may be a rogue figure, however, if the production of Malvazia in 1650 was abnormally low; in 1699, Bolton loaded 158 pipes of Malvazia in one day, which is over 80 per cent more than the recorded total of shipments for 1650.[17] Even making allowance for the growth of the vineyards in the half century since 1650, this seems an extraordinary difference.

The Bolton letters yield a miscellany of information. Apart from giving us a graphic picture of the vicissitudes of a merchant's life (including the risk of summary arrest and deportation), we learn from Bolton that back-loading – that is, shipping wine back to Madeira – from the West Indies was becoming common.[18] This was the start of *vinho da roda*, the custom of sending madeira on a voyage to the tropics and back again for the express purpose of improving it. He also indicates that one shipment of 100 pipes of wine came, 'except some Pipes that are always forced upon us by the Governours of this Place', from a single vineyard.[19] This comment seems to indicate that there was something like a quota system in existence to ensure that some wines (perhaps inferior ones) eventually got shipped. But it also indicates that there were already some very large single vineyards in existence. Assuming a fairly large yield of 15 tons per hectare, a pipe capacity of 415 litres, and assuming that no more than 10 per cent of the shipment consisted of the pipes forced on Bolton, then at 850 litres of wine per ton this would give us a single vineyard with an area of more than 15 hectares – half as big again as the largest single vineyard on the island today.

Bolton refers frequently to *old wines*. These, however, were not generally much older than the previous vintage. They seem to have been slightly more expensive than *new wines* – that is, the wines of the current vintage, made in September and October, racked in January and on sale by Easter. The market price for wine was established on a supply and demand basis only after the arrival of 'the Jamaica Fleet' in April each year. Until then the wine producers held off declaring a price. If there were a lot of old wines available, this would hold down the price of the new wines. Generally, despite the higher price, the old wines would be loaded in preference to the new wines, whose sale would be proportional to the unsatisfied demand for old wines, and the scarcity of either would drive up the price as the year progressed. This picture could, however, be modified in the light of the quality of successive vintages. Sometimes Bolton describes the new wines as being 'Green and Small', but even when he says 'tis the generall Opinion that ye new wines will be very good, the best that has bin for some years', he adds that they are not the clients' first choice: 'The old wines are drawing to a Conclusion. Should ships come dropping in as they doe, shall soone be forced to load ye New.'[20]

Bolton makes three references to Vidonia. He says that the grapes are vintaged before the Malvazias and susceptible to rain prior to picking.[21] Amongst the other wines mentioned by Bolton are 'white wines' and 'tent' or 'tinto'. There are more than a dozen references to the former, which obviously formed a staple, if small, part of the trade. My surmise (explained below) is that these white wines are in fact the Vidonias referred to under a more generic name. 'Tent' or 'tinto', which was probably not yet made from Tinta Negra Mole, was a red wine used to give colour to white wines. Occasionally Bolton would ship a pipe of Tent with other wines so that the recipient could improve or adjust the colour on delivery. Once he ships a pipe 'to assist ye Poor french wines'.[22]

The character of the wine

Towards the end of the century we have reports on the wine from Sir Hans Sloane, who visited the island in 1687, and the previously cited John Ovington, who visited in 1689. What they say accords well with what we learn from Bolton, except that the Vidonias are never mentioned as such.

Sloane reports that 'the greatest part of this Island is at present planted with Vines, the Soil being very proper, for it is rocky and steep; they keep their Vines very low with Pruning, in that agreeing with the Culture of the Vines in *France*, as also in that these Wines grow on the same Soil with those most esteemed there, as the *Hermitage* Wines, which grow on the rocky steep Hills on the sides of the *Rhosne*. The Grapes are of three sorts, the White, Red and great Muscadine, or *Malvasia*; of which three the first are most plentiful, for out of the White is made the greatest quantity of Wine, which is made Red by the addition of some Tinto, or very Red Wine made out of the Red Grapes, which gives it a deeper Tincture than that of *Champagne*, and helps it to preserve it self much better. It is sufficiently known that White-Wines, generally speaking, perish very soon, and that Red ones are much easier preserved, the deeper their Tincture be . . . The Virgin Wine, or that made of the Juice running of the Husks immediately without standing or pressure, is soon ready to drink, fine, and very soon perish'd, the Husk impregnating the Wine with something equivalent to Hops in Beer . . . The *Malvasia* or Wine made from the Muscadine Grape, does not keep, but Pricks very soon, and so is made in very small quantities. The great quantity of Wine here made, is that of the White mixt with a little Tinto, which has one very particular and odd Property, that the more 'tis expos'd to the Sun-beams and heat the better it is, and instead of putting it in a cool Cellar they expose it to the Sun. It seems to those unaccustomed to it to have a very unpleasant Tast, though something like Sherry, to which Wine it comes near in Strength and other Properties. It is Exported in vast quantities to all the *West-India* Plantations, and now of late to the *East*; no sort of Wine agreeing with those hot Places like this.'[23]

Ovington tells us that 'the main product of the Island is Grapes, brought hither first from *Candy*, of which there are three or four kinds, whereof they make their Wine. One is coloured like Champaign, of little esteem; another is more strong and pale as white wine; the third sort is rich and delicious, called Malmsey; the fourth is *Tento*, equalling Tent in colour but far inferior in Taste; it is never drunk unless in other Wines, with which it is mixt to give them a Tincture, and to preserve them. And for fermenting and feeding them, they bruise and bake a certain Stone, called Jess, of which nine or ten pounds are thrown into each Pipe. The *Madeira* Wine has in it this peculiar Excellence, of being meliorated by the heat of the Sun, when it is prick'd, if the Bunghole being open'd 'tis expos'd to the Air. The product of the vine is equally divided between the Proprietor and him that gathers and presses the Grapes; and yet for the most part the Merchant is Thriving and Rich, whilst the Grape-gatherer imploy'd by him, is but Poor. Among the Merchants the *Jesuits* are none of the meanest, who everywhere contend for precedence in Fortune, as well as in place; and have here secured the Monopoly of *Malmsey*.'[24]

Sloane and Ovington are remarkably unanimous in what they say, though there are subtle differences. Both agree on classifying the wine into three types. Firstly the red, which is poor in quality, is mixed with white wine as a colorant and preservative, and (according to Ovington) is never drunk on its own. Secondly the white, which constitutes the bulk of the export wine, is tinted to a colour (darker than) champagne – at that time a still, pale-coloured wine with 'a rosy tinge' – and becomes better with heat. According to Sloane it tastes rather like sherry and is an acquired taste. Ovington tells us that a smaller quantity is not mixed with red and is stronger and paler, *like* a white wine. This, one has to presume, is the Vidonia. Thirdly the Malvazia, which Ovington describes as 'rich and delicious'; Sloane says it keeps badly, turns sharp, and is therefore not made in large quantities.

The light red wine, classified by Bolton as being of the 'comon sorts',[25] constituted the bulk of the exports. From the resemblance of its taste to sherry it is clear that it must have been slightly oxidized, and in this respect may already have had something in common with modern madeira. It was almost certainly a dry wine. André Simon, somewhat surprisingly, states that 'a smaller quantity of ordinary beverage *White Wine* was made from the *Verdelho* grape',[26] without indicating his grounds for so doing. Perhaps he is alluding to Ovington's stronger, paler white wine, but as he regarded Vidonia as a sweet wine, he would not presumably have identified this wine with Vidonia. As far as I am aware, however, there is no direct evidence to show that *Verdelho* had reached the island by this time, though this is possible and even probable.

As for the Malvazia, Sloane's comment that it does not keep contrasts unexpectedly with the comments they both make about madeira's capacity to benefit from heat, and with what we gather about its ageing potential from Bolton. It may suggest that, as a sweet wine, it had the instability of a wine which had not been completely fermented. Bolton indicates that there were problems from time to time, but not solely confined to the Malvazia. Thus in 1705 he reports that 'the last Vintage ... was small and we find a great many of the wines are turned sower, which makes the Natives on the High Ropes, not Knowing what to Demand for them'.[27] Because Sloane's comment is out of line with the other information we have, he may have been misinformed or may have misunderstood what he was told. Sloane does not comment on the quality of Malvazia, which may not be surprising in the light of what he does say. It is more surprising that Ovington does not comment either.

It is clear from what both have to say that heating the wine in the sun had already become a fairly common practice, although *vinho do sol* is a term which does not crop up until 1730.[28] Madeira's response to heat had two aspects. First, it had the ability to withstand heat, not in itself easy to explain, which is what made it, with the Azorean Pico-Faial,[29] so popular in the West Indies and the American plantations. Secondly, it actually *improved* with heat. However, it was to be another hundred years before heating the wine became part of its industrialized production process.

Ovington's mention of 'Jess' refers to the use of gesso (or gypsum) in fermenting the wine, which was discussed in the previous chapter. Bolton tells us that he made 'some white wines without Jesso which our W.B. order'd us to gett made, but not haveing heard how they prov'd, did not think it convenient to Run the Risque of makeing any more this Yeare'.[30] The use of gypsum was obviously commonplace.

It is noteworthy that by this time Malvazia was closely associated with the Jesuits. A Jesuit college was first established in Funchal in 1569. The Jesuits thereafter established a number of houses around the island, and were supported by charity, bequests and by farming the lands they came to own. The largest of these properties was Quinta Grande – 'large farm' – west of Cabo Girão, an area still in existence today. It had originally belonged to descendants of Zarco, who transferred parcels of land to the Jesuits by gift and by sale, eventually making it one of the largest single properties on the island. The Jesuits continued to run Quinta Grande until 1759, when the order was expelled from Portugal and its possessions confiscated by the Marquês de Pombal. Quinta Grande was then sold by auction to João Francisco de Freitas Esmeraldo for 140,000 cruzados (56,000 réis). The quinta was always a large vine-growing area and included the famous Fajã dos Padres, the best and most celebrated Malvasia vineyard in Madeira.[31] Ovington, in common with later travellers, claims that the Jesuits controlled the entire production of Malvazia on the island, but there is no conclusive evidence that this was ever so.

By the end of the seventeenth century Madeira was poised for the expansion of its trade. Situated on so many trading routes it enjoyed an unparalleled advantage. It produced a wine which the world was to want more and more – in such quantities, in fact, that production could not keep up with demand, and adulteration and falsification were to become almost the norm and very nearly its downfall.

3

The Eighteenth Century

The development of trade

The privileges of British merchants were generally consolidated by the Methuen Treaty of 1703, whereby Portuguese wines imported into England paid a third less duty than, for example, French wines, and English woollen textiles (the single most important British import into Madeira) were admitted into Portugal duty-free. The merchants of Oporto, however, benefited from this treaty much more than those in Madeira, for despite this concession relatively little madeira was imported into England until much later in the eighteenth century, and the concession regarding woollens was almost immediately limited when in 1712 the Portuguese government decided to impose restrictions on trade with Brazil. The main destinations of exports of madeira continued to be the West Indies, North America and, increasingly, the East Indies (including non-British possessions like Pondicherry, Bengal and Surat).[1] Exports to Europe were of secondary importance.

Details of production and export volumes remain patchy and unreliable throughout the century, with regular annual figures available only after 1798.[2] From the scant information before this it is almost impossible to judge any trends. John Atkins, visiting the island in 1721, tells us that 'their vintage is in *September* and *October* and make about 25,000 pipes'[3] – the same total given by Jeaffreson forty-five years earlier. The export total of 8,000 pipes for 1765[4] is similar to the figure given by Ovington for 1689. Cossart asserts that 'up to 1745 annual shipments averaged 7,000 pipes'.[5] All this suggests, perhaps, a rather stagnant level of production. Sporadic figures for the last quarter of the century[6] indicate that exports doubled over that period. America was still the prime market by a long way. Even during the War of Independence (1777–82), exports to America never dropped below 58 per cent, and twice exceeded 80 per cent, of all the wine exported from the island.[7]

These figures are misleading, however, if taken to indicate continuing and even increasing prosperity. Foreign wars in the second half of the century brought about a drop in the price of wine to under half of what it had been, and because Madeira had virtually a monoculture economy based on wine and was dependent on imports for three-quarters of its cereals, this drop produced serious social consequences. At this time most of the cereals required by Madeira were imported from North America. In 1757 the cereal crop had failed and in some places the peasants had had to sustain themselves by eating roots, fruit and broom (genista) flowers.[8] Later, the War of Independence further reduced the amount of cereals available for import, and the drop in the price of wine meant that only half the previous imports of cereals could be paid for out of wine revenue. The problem was exacerbated by a steep rise in the population during the second half of the century: from 51,343 in 1754 to 79,773 in 1797 (reaching 84,364 in 1803). Even before famine became manifest, the misery of large parts of the population, who were without work or the means of subsistence, had led to an attempted uprising in 1767, and in 1773 the peasants who held land by *contrato de colonia* had petitioned the king (unsuccessfully) for a fairer division of the profits from their work.[9]

Helpful visitors furnish us with their estimates of total production. They are fairly consistent, although curiously the alleged totals drop just as export volumes increase. These range from 30,000 to 35,000 pipes (10,000 being exported to Britain and her colonies) in 1768;[10] 28,000 pipes (8,000 for the island, the rest exported mainly to the West Indies) in 1772;[11] about 30,000 pipes (13,000 exported and the rest made into brandy for Brazil) in 1777;[12] between 15,000 and 25,000 pipes (up to 15,000 pipes being exported) in 1792;[13] and 25,000 pipes in 1797.[14] 13,000 pipes for export seems to be a wild overestimate. The latter figures seem more believable.

We do, on the other hand, have production figures for 1787.[15] The north produced 8,198 pipes and the south 6,833 pipes, giving a grand total of 15,031 pipes.[16] This is far from the heady 25,000 pipes mentioned by Atkins in 1721, though it does seem plausible when compared with a known export total of 10,819 pipes for 1788. It also shows that the north was considerably the larger producer of wine. As the wine from the north always had the reputation of being considerably lower in quality than that from the south, it is no wonder that this was to lead to difficulties.

Fraud and increased regulation

The global demand for madeira during the whole of the eighteenth century was greater than could be supplied from the best wines of the island alone. This led to two sorts of fraudulent practice, which were current for most of the century: the adulteration of wines on the island, and the passing off as genuine madeira of wines from other sources. The incidence of both frauds increased as trade expanded towards the end of the century, and both contributed to the slump in sales early in the following century. This situation was a constant preoccupation of the authorities and merchants for the next two centuries and led to ever-increasing regulation of the trade.

On 23 December 1724 the Funchal Senate received a petition signed by 38 merchants who, dismayed by the way that good wine was being adulterated with inferior wine from the north of the island, asked for a ban on wine produced in the north being brought to the south. This would have effectively prevented its being exported, since Funchal was the only port of embarkation. No action was taken until 9 January 1737, when in response to a petition by a merchant called Francisco Teodoro, the Senate imposed just such a restriction.[17] With no official outlet except local consumption, one wonders what the authorities expected would become of the wine from the north. Doubtless much of it was distilled into spirit. But over the next thirty years, as ways of evading the law were found, the situation deteriorated further. In 1768 the authorities were forced to take action to regulate the wine trade in a more extensive way than ever before. Two official posts were created – a Juiz de Fóra and a Presidente dos Risiduos – whose role was to prevent fraudulent practices. Then, on 11 March 1768, the Governor issued an edict which confirmed the embargo on moving wine from the north of the island to the south until after the end of May each year, and expressly forbade the mixing of wines from the two parts of the island, thereby making a simple demarcation between the two areas. Moreover, a distinction was made between the inferior wine made in the upper (northern) parts of the parishes on the south coast and the better quality wine (suitable for export) made closer to the sea in the lower parts of the same parishes, implying a secondary demarcation between north and south within the southern parishes. Most importantly, however, the thirteen articles of the edict classified the wine into three distinct qualities based on the markets for which it was destined.[18]

This remarkable document cannot fail to remind one of the Pombaline demarcation of the port-producing area of the Douro eleven years earlier, in 1757, which may well have inspired it – even if the demarcation in Madeira had neither the influence nor the permanence of its port counterpart. The classification of the wines is similar to that of the Douro, which also corresponds with the market to which the wine is destined. Unlike the Douro classification, however, no fixed prices were set for each kind of wine. There were three categories: (1) wines of the best quality intended for export to all destinations except Brazil; (2) wines of medium quality, only to be exported to Brazil or sold for the consumption of ships' crews; and (3) wine for consumption in taverns.

At the same time as the demarcation took place in the Douro, the Marquês de Pombal, partly to regulate the market and partly to limit the monopoly of English merchants, set up (in 1757) a Portuguese monopoly company called the Companhia Geral da Agricultura das Vinhas do Alto Douro. This may have inspired a move to set up a Companhia Vinícola in Madeira. On 6 May 1774 the Funchal municipal council considered a report on the advantages of such a company, but nothing appears to have become of it.

The provisions of the 1768 edict continued in force for some time. Although the threefold categorization of quality seems in practice to have been jettisoned by the end of the century, a statement by the Governor on 21 January 1821 indicates that the demarcation between wines from the north and south still held: 'The wines of Madeira have a prompt sale in Brazil, wine from the south selling at from 130 to 140 milréis a pipe, and that from the north at 50 to 60 milréis.'[19] Despite the measures which had been taken, however, wine from the north continued to find its way on to the export market. On 16 August 1785[20] further restrictions were imposed. Wine made in the north could only be moved under a local magistrate's licence, as could the wines of Ponta do Sol, Calheta and Arco and Estreito da Calheta, which it was 'absolutely prohibited' to move into parishes eastwards of them. On 16 August 1786 there was a further and more elaborate edict on adulteration and fraud, repeating the prohibition on mixing wine from the north and south within the southern parishes, with severe penalties for offenders.[21] New forms of fraud proliferated. A ruse which the growers in the north employed to make their wines look like the tinto wines of the south was to colour them with the juice of black cherries (just as elderberries were being used at the same time in the Douro to give colour to inferior port). On 27 February 1788 the Governor ordered that all black cherry trees should be grafted with red cherries (which were unsuitable for colouring the wine) or be uprooted. Anyone caught planting a black cherry tree was subject to a fine of 6,000 réis.[22] The town council had occasion to refer to this malpractice again as late as 1819.[23]

On 20 September 1710 a prohibition on the importation of foreign wines and spirits was imposed, with the aim of stopping the adulteration of madeira with inferior foreign products.[24] The idea was not only to safeguard the reputation of madeira in foreign markets, but also to keep the price high. Despite this, inferior wine was imported into Funchal from the Canaries and the Azores, then mixed with madeira and re-exported. Less easy to control was the converse of this form of fraud, whereby madeira was imported into the Canaries and other places to be mixed with the cheaper local wines and later passed off in foreign (mainly Asian) markets as genuine madeira. During the eighteenth century a wide range of (unsuccessful) controls on the size, design and marking of casks was imposed by the authorities to combat this abuse.[25] The Funchal Archive contains a list of the ships engaged in taking madeira to Tenerife for adulteration between 1784 and 1787,[26] which can only have been possible through the connivance of unscrupulous merchants. John Barrow, visiting Madeira in 1792, marvelled that 'although it is supposed that the quantity consumed in Great Britain, under the name of Madeira, is, on the least calculation, equal to the whole quantity that is exported from the island, or more than three times what is actually imported, yet it is well known that a variety of mixtures pass for Madeira, some of which are compounded of wines that never grew on the island, as those of Teneriffe, Lisbon and Xeres'.[27] Vidonia from Tenerife was about a third the cost of madeira[28] and became known as 'mock madeira'.[29] Another measure to exclude foreign wines and spirits was passed on 27 January 1789.[30]

The British influence

The British merchants dominated the commercial scene in Funchal throughout the century, acting through their commercial association, the British Factory, under the guidance of the consul. At a meeting held on 26 October 1722, twelve merchants were present. In 1771 the Factory consisted of a consul, vice-consul and twenty-two merchants, from which ten were selected to direct the business of the factory in conjunction with the consul.[31] Shortly afterwards there seems to have been an influx of traders, for between 1786 and 1790 we find thirty-five separate British firms and twenty-one individuals listed as shippers.[32] The British Factory existed until 1838, and was financed by a levy, sanctioned in 1717, on goods imported from England and on wine shipped by its members. These funds were applied to projects of benefit to its members and to the British community.

In the middle of the eighteenth century we begin to encounter names which are still to be found in the trade, the oldest firms still existing (even if in transmuted form) dating from this time.[33] Amongst these are John Leacock, Francis Newton and Thomas Gordon. Relations between the British community and their Portuguese hosts were certainly difficult for much of the time. Strains appeared when downturns in the wine trade, on which the island economy depended, brought extensive privation and misery to the peasant population. The virtual monopoly of the wine trade enjoyed by the British made them extremely powerful. When in 1722 relief had to be granted to wine producers by reducing the 10 per cent tax – the *décima* – which had long been levied on new wine, the official decree did not mince its words: 'By reason of lack of commerce on the said island and of poverty, most of its population are in a miserable state because . . . either they sell their wines to the English or they ship them to Brazil, and they get little profit from whichever of these courses they take, because the English want to wring them from them (by extortion) for very inferior prices'.[34]

Staunton, writing at the end of the century, indicates that British merchants were not averse to profitable sharp practices. He instances the commonly practised fraud of 'salt water invoices', whereby the prices paid for goods in England were increased after shipment so that even higher prices could be asked for them when they were sold on to the native Madeirans, the 'only sufferers' from this ruse.[35]

Despite the many social difficulties which the island experienced during this period, the eighteenth century is notable in the history of madeira for two technical developments which permanently changed its character: fortification and *estufagem* (from the Portuguese word *estufa*, meaning 'stove', 'hot-house' and 'green-house'). The adoption of the second practice by the merchants also brought them closer to being wine merchants in a modern sense, because instead of merely broking wine, as was common at the beginning of the century, merchants had to acquire wine in order to heat it, and then had to store it afterwards.

Fortification

We do not know for certain when the practice of fortification first began. Experiments in distilling in Madeira took place around the turn of the century, so the possibility of fortification dates from this time. Cossart mentions that a Portuguese book on viticulture published in 1720 recommended the addition of brandy to wine in order to improve it, but it is probable that the Madeira merchants learned of the advantages of fortification as a means of stabilizing wine for export from Oporto, where the practice became general around 1730,[36] or even from Spain, where it had been used for much longer. What can be asserted with confidence is that most firms appear to have been fortifying their wine by the middle of the century. Writing in October 1753, Francis Newton, who had hitherto prided himself that his wines were 'fresh and full flavoured unlike the ones laced with Brandy', was constrained to admit that 'I really impute the complaints I have had of wines to my not putting a bucket or two of brandy in each pipe as other houses do'.[37] In 1756 Michael Nowlan, an associate of John Leacock, received advice from London: 'Some Gentlemen here that are knowing in the Wine Trade assure me that if a couple of gallons of fine clear Brandy was put into each pipe of our best Wines 'twill improve them greatly. I believe that some of the Houses in Madeira use this method . . . I observe that their Madeiras drunk here in gentlemen's houses are fine pale amber colour nothing tending to a reddish.'[38] It may be that the fortification of the wine was something of a trade secret, because we find in 1771 one of the anonymous chroniclers of

Cook's first voyage round the world declaring that 'it is commonly reported that no distilled spirit is added to these wines, but I have been well assured of the contrary, and have seen the spirit used for that purpose'.[39]

It is clear from Nowlan's remark about the wine's pale amber colour that, with the start of fortification, madeira came closer to the drink we know today. Croft describes it as having 'a kernelly taste like a walnut'.[40] However, unfortified 'madeira burgundy' continued to be made for much of the next century, and fortification was not yet used to check the fermentation of the wine. It was simply an addition of spirit to the wine immediately prior to shipping, intended originally to ensure that the wine reached its destination in sound condition. According to calculations made by Noël Cossart, the wine resulting from this kind of rough and ready fortification would have had an alcoholic strength of about 15 per cent by volume.[41]

Estufagem

If fortification was common by the middle of the eighteenth century, the process of *estufagem* began only at the end of the century. However, as we know from Sloane, there was a general awareness at least as early as 1687 that the wine benefited from the heat of the sun. Croft, writing in 1787, tells us that 'in England they put [the wines] in stoves or hot-houses for the sun; in America they keep them in cisterns on the tops of the houses'.[42] The term *vinho do sol* (sun wine) was already current in the 1730s, and in the eighteenth century storehouses were built with glass roofs so that the wine could benefit from sunshine.[43] Heat was reckoned the most important element of the beneficial effect of sending madeira on long sea voyages. Many old houses in Funchal have, behind their shutters, shelves built into the sides of the window recesses, looking for all the world like small cupboards (of which the shutters are the doors). These were expressly for storing bottles of wine so that they might benefit from the heat of the sun shining in at the windows. So there is ample evidence that the wine was deliberately subjected to heat long before the invention of *estufas* enabled this to be done on a commercial scale. Jullien even reports, as late as 1816, another curious method of heating the wine, which is 'to plunge the bottles, well corked, in a trench filled with hot horse-dung, and in six months or a year the maturity, &c. of a voyage is gained'.[44] This extraordinary and highly uncommercial procedure is confirmed by Redding – although he may have lifted the information from Jullien's book.

The first recorded *estufa* was built in Funchal in 1794 by a merchant called Pantaleão Fernandes, who 'having already observed that wine is much improved by being kept in warm places, principally by being placed in the sun, heated a store containing wine from the last vintage with little stoves both night and day, and obtained an encouraging result'.[45] The invention was hailed as a way of imparting the characteristics of maturity to the wine without having to wait for it to age naturally, and as a way of achieving the effect of a *vinho da roda* without a comparable expenditure of time and money. In no time at all other merchants were building their own *estufas*.

One such was John Leacock, who explained his plans in August 1800: 'We are erecting an *Estufa* & hope to have it furnished in two or three weeks. We shall stand in need of two common *Thermometers*, *good* but the *least* expensive, in order that we may regulate the heat; we therefore beg you will send out a couple very carefully packed. We hope this new Mode of treating Wine will answer, but we have never yet heard whether any remarks have been made by the Correspondents of those who ship it – they are now common & all the Houses use *Estufas* – several of them have built them, & others put their Wine into hired *Estufas*, where they pay 5mooo p. pipe[46] for 3 Months stewing. We are not yet *perfectly* satisfied of all the Effects produced by the Application of Heat to the Wine, but think that in general they keep too fierce a degree of Heat, which keeps the Wine constantly boiling, and renders it rather insipid & weak. We are of Opinion that a more Moderate Temperature will succeed better, & shall prolong the Period to *Six* instead of Three Months as we see. However the great test will be, how it is approved by those who drink it after a Voyage. Certainly to those who are not good Judges, the new Wine with three Months *Estufa* imitates Wine of 4 or 5 Years old, & we dont think that the deception will be easily discovered – however the Secret will be soon known abroad & may perhaps prejudice the character of Madeira Wine.'[47]

The adoption of this new process appears to have quickly got out of hand. At first the wines seem to have been heated to extremely high temperatures, resulting in disagreeable tastes of toasting or baking quite uncharacteristic of wines slowly aged in cask or sent on a sea voyage. It appears that some merchants like John Leacock mistakenly thought that *estufas* might make poor wines more acceptable to the market. 'We shall endeavour by our new Process to improve the *cheap* Wines in such a manner that they will answer for almost any quality, after being mixed with other good Wines. We have no doubt by what we have heard and seen that the Porto do Cruz [*sic*] Wine of good quality made up with the best Wine of a good vintage & prepared in the *Estufa* may be shipped off for *particular* . . .'[48]

The impetus for making the greatest possible use of the new invention was quite simply the necessity of finding sufficient wine to satisfy the rapid upturn in trade as the century ended. England, which had remained a minor importer of madeira for most of the century, suddenly became an important market. This is partly explained by the return home of British nationals after the American War of Independence, and by the difficulty of trade with France after the 1789 Revolution and the outbreak of war in 1793, which led to tax discrimination against French wines.

It was also due, however, to the simple fact that over the second half of the century madeira had become increasingly fashionable as a drink. Christie's, the London auctioneers, began selling madeira at auction in 1766, and madeira figured largely in the trade-orientated wine sales that began to take place in the 1780s. Edmund Penning-Rowsell, who has made a special study of them, points out that 'in the late 18th century the most fashionable wine in Britain was certainly madeira, and to be "fine" the prerequisite was that it had been on a long sea voyage or kept in the Tropics'.[49] Indeed, *vinho da roda* began to occupy an increasingly important place in such sales, being known as East Indies and West Indies Madeira. Sometimes the wine remained abroad for a number of years, and this could more than double its price because connoisseurs of madeira were prepared to pay for the mellowness resulting from the voyage.

Viticulture

The reports of travellers and official documents tell us interesting things not only about the wine, but about vine cultivation too. A guidebook published anonymously by John Adam in 1801 explains that 'the vine is generally propagated from cuttings, as the preferable mode of culture, rather than from seed. In former times it was planted with the plough, to a depth pretty much the same as that which the vine is now planted in France, being a depth of 12 or 18 inches. But at this first period the soil must have been richer . . . The case however now is very different, from the poverty of the soil, and the frequent droughts. Hence it is found necessary to plant the vine to the depth of from 3 to 6 feet. It being protected from the hard ground at the bottom of the trench, by a quantity of loose earth placed underneath.'[50] James Cook, writing with the condescension typical of many English visitors, tells us that 'the inhabitants have made so little improvement in knowledge or art, that they have but very lately [1768] brought all the fruit of a vineyard to be of one sort, by engrafting their vines . . . Wherever there is ignorance there is prejudice [and] it was therefore with great difficulty that the people of Madeira were persuaded to engraft their vines, and some of them still obstinately refuse to adopt the practice, though a whole vintage is very often spoiled by the number of bad grapes which are mixed in the vat, and which they will not throw out, because they increase the quantity of the wine.'[51]

Cook's dim view of the islanders seems to have been shared by the authorities, who in 1783 told the natives of Porto Santo that the degeneration of their vineyards resulted from their 'inertia, the tenacity and obstinacy with which they clung to their old prejudices . . . and the hope which they had to a greater or lesser degree that nothing could throw them into the fatal abyss of hunger'.[52] Instructions were given to the Director and Inspector of Agriculture in Porto Santo about where to site vineyards and the proper grapes to plant. 'The varieties for everyone must be Verdelho, Boal or Tinta, and not Listrão, as is for the greater part planted; for its grapes, tasty though they are for eating, are not suited for wine.'[53] One visitor states that 'the island produces six kinds of grapes, viz. the Malmsey, two black, and three white kinds'.[54] Adam, on the other hand, lists twenty-six varieties (including Malvasia, Boal, Verdelho, Sercial, Bastardo and Terrantez) but agrees with the report on Porto Santo in saying that if the number were reduced 'to the Negro Mole, the Verdelha, and the Bual, the wines would certainly be of much better quality'.[55]

Here is a description of a typical vineyard: 'One or more walks, about a yard or two wide, intersect each vineyard, and are included by stone walls two feet high. Along these walks, which are arched over by lathes about seven feet high, they erect wooden pillars at regular distances, to support a lattice-work of bamboos, which slopes down from both sides of the walk, till it is only a foot and a half or two feet high, in which elevation it extends over the whole vineyard. The vines are in this manner supported from the ground, and the people have room to root out the weeds which spring up between them. In the season of the vintage they creep under this lattice-work, cut off the grapes, and lay them into baskets: some bunches of these grapes I saw, which weighed six pounds and upwards.'[56] A description of a vineyard today would be little different.

A contemporary description of the vintage would also have been quite up-to-date until about a quarter of a century ago. 'The vintage in Madeira begins early in September – the process of making wine is extremely simple. The grapes immediately when cut are put into the press, which is a machine of great simplicity in its construction, and not unlike the instrument used in England in the making of cyder. It consists of the *Paixa*, or reservoir [normally called the *lagar*], with the Fuzo, or spindle, and the *Vara*, or lever. The paixa is of a square or oblong square figure, made of the plank of chesnut [*sic*] tree, about two feet thick, and supported on three large beams. The vara, or lever, goes across the reservoir, which extending nine or ten feet beyond the paixa, is connected at its furthest extremity, where there is a female screw, with the fuzo, or spindle. The upper end of the fuzo is a male screw, while its lever end is fastened by means of an iron spindle to a large stone, the size of which is proportionate to that of the press. When the grapes intended to be prest are all cut and placed in the reservoir, three, four, or more labourers enter that part of the machine, and with their feet tread the grapes so long as any juice can be expressed from them. The juice is allowed to run into a vessel under this *paixa*, through a hole at its middle, or at one corner, over which is generally placed a small basket by way of a sieve, in order to prevent any of the husks, seeds, or stalks from escaping. After this first pressure, or treading, the mashed grapes are collected into one heap, which being surrounded by a cord in close circles, and having boards and pieces of wood laid about it, is then placed under the lever, which is forthwith sunk upon it, and allowed to remain in this position till the liquor ceases to flow. It is then raised, the boards and cords are taken off, and the mass being broken in pieces by tools something like hoes, is made to undergo a second treading or pressure, and again also subjected to the operation of the lever. This process is even repeated a third time, with a view to obtaining a further quantity of wine from the grape; and lastly, a fourth time, for the purpose of obtaining the *Aqua hé* [*sic*]. In this fourth or last time however the mass when broken up is as dry as a piece of chip, and therefore previous to treading it, it is necessary to add to it a quantity of water ... The mass for procuring *Aqua hé* is generally put under pressure in the evening and allowed to remain in this situation till next morning, when the *Aqua hé* is drawn off, and put into casks for immediate use.'[57] *Aqua Pé* is a weakly alcoholic drink made by adding water to the *bagaço*, or pressed grapes, and served to the labourers.

Towards the end of the century, the authorities did all in their power to improve the quality of the wines. A detailed regimen for the vintage was issued by the Governor on 12 August 1784 to combat the too-early and unselective picking of grapes.[58] This included the setting of dates in each parish before which the vintage might not begin (1 October in the case of Malvasia); the requirement to obtain permission from the Inspector General of Agriculture of each district before starting the vintage; the appointment of inspectors to ensure that only appropriate *lagars* were used; and the imposition of confiscations and prison sentences for infringements of the rules. These measures worked only imperfectly, and they were clarified and tightened up on 16 August 1786.[59] An order dated 18 October 1792 forbade the cultivation of corn, barley or potatoes as intercalated plants in vineyards.[60] Later, between November 1794 and March 1795, doubtless as a response to the recent growth in trade, more than 176,000 vines were planted in Câmara de Lobos alone.[61]

The wine

Malvazia remained a prestigious product, although available only in small quantities. In 1704 Bolton reports that 'all that was made in the Island does not exceed 80 to 100 p^s; they will be dearer by much than those the Last year, there being so few and every body's Eyes upon them'.[62] Croft-Cooke reports a shipper writing in 1757: 'As regards the Malmsey, the whole Island produces only about 50 pipes annually'.[63] Staunton, however, suggests that the average

annual production is 500 pipes.[64] This is probably a wild exaggeration, because Malvazia's rarity is attested by the fact that, according to merchants' ledgers of the time, it was generally shipped in
quarter-pipe or hogshead quantities.

Wines were made from other single grape varieties, as a few surviving bottles of Boal, Terrantez, Moscatel and Sercial attest, but
contemporary prices suggest that such wines were of a rarity equal
to, or even greater than, that of Malvazia. The so-called Rainwater
madeira also made its first appearance in the second half of the
eighteenth century. Designed for the American market, it was a
delicate Verdelho. Amongst various competing explanations of
the origin of the name, Cossart's account of the 'discovery' of
Rainwater by Francis Newton provides at least a certain cynical
amusement. If he is to be believed, some pipes of Verdelho awaiting
export were accidentally left unbunged on a rainy night, but were
nevertheless shipped and found favour in Virginia. Thereafter, a
special water-diluted blend was made up to satisfy the demand for
the new style.[65] The main emphasis in wine-making, however, was
on producing 'madeira', which was a generic wine into which a
wide assortment of grape varieties found their way, just as (until
comparatively recently, at any rate) was the case with port. That the
wines were a mixture is implied by a sentence from a letter by Jackie
Leacock in 1793, quoted by Croft-Cooke: '[Mr. Snell's wines] are
perfectly pale smooth and nutty flavoured as being mostly *Boyal*
and *Verdelho*, and have no Tinge from the red Grape'.[66]

During most of the eighteenth century this wine was sold according to its destination, though in the last quarter of the century categorization became much more elaborate than in the classification
of 1768. The names for generic madeiras, which survived into the
twentieth century, originated from the wine auctions held at the
London docks in the 1760s.[67] In the Invoices Book for 1794 of
Newton, Gordon & Murdoch (the firm which eventually became
Cossart Gordon), the following list of shipping prices is noted:

Malmsey	£63
Particular	£34
London Market	£30
India	£28
New York	£26
Cargo	£23[68]

The invoices refer to Fine Old Wine, London Particular Wine, Old Particular Wine, New York Wine, Particular Wine, India Market Wine, Cream Malmsey, Fine Old Malmsey and Fine Burgundy Coloured Wine. There is no mention of any grape variety other than Malvasia, but in the early nineteenth century Sercial and Tinta commanded the same prices as Malvazia.

On the other hand, the Purchase Book for the same period shows acquisitions of wine for each vintage as one of the following: Malvazia; wine from the north; wine from the south; or wine from a specifically named place (such as Campanário, São Martinho, etc.). The quantity of Malvazia purchased was minute, amounting to no more than some half-dozen entries amongst several hundred.

One market for madeira, singled out in the edict of 1768, deserves special mention before we leave the eighteenth century: ships' crews. Madeira was found to have health-giving properties for sailors deprived of fresh food for long periods afloat, and was carried for this purpose by Anson in 1740 and by Commodore Byron. Captain Cook loaded 'ten tuns of wine' for his first world voyage in 1768.[69] On the other hand, in 1785 Lapérouse, having had the intention of loading 30 pipes of madeira on to each of his ships, jibbed at the cost and wrote to his superiors from Madeira on 16 August 1785 that 'the information which I have had about the price of the madeira wine appropriate for crews makes me determined to set sail immediately for Tenerife where I will procure the same quality of wine'. Lapérouse himself, however, was happy to accept a gift of a hundred bottles of Malvazia from a Mr Johnston, an associate of Francis Newton.[70]

4

The Nineteenth Century I

The unpopular British

The new century saw an ever greater involvement of the British in the development of Madeira. During the Napoleonic wars there were two occupations of the island by the British army, largely to protect British interests by preventing a French invasion. The first, in 1801, lasted until the beginning of the following year. The second occupation was a much longer and more serious affair, lasting from Christmas Eve 1807 until October 1814. Both added to the growing anti-British sentiment on the island. Drunken soldiers involved in incidents such as church desecration did little to endear the British to the locals, and many suspected a devious British plan of out-and-out colonization. British merchants kept themselves apart, and they struck visitors to the island as aloof and petty. 'There is not that good feeling amongst the English which there should be; arising I apprehend, from all of them being dealers in the same article, wine.'[1]

During the War of the Two Brothers (1825–34), which determined the Portuguese succession, dissension amongst the British was extreme. 'Private society was completely destroyed; discord pervaded every family . . . the rancour and bitterness of party spirit evinced by these individuals surpast almost any thing of the description witnessed by me, even in England.'[2] In 1849 'factionalism became a way of island life'.[3] Only two philanthropic merchants, Robert Page and Joseph Phelps, appear to have enjoyed any popularity with the Portuguese. Page alone amongst the British opposed both occupations of the island; he was cordially disliked by his fellow British merchants.[4]

At the opening of the nineteenth century there were a score of important British merchants and about half that number of Portuguese. A slightly later but noteworthy addition to the British contingent was John Blandy. He served on the island as a soldier between 1807 and 1810, and returned from England with a wife to become a merchant in 1811. Only a few of these merchants – the oldest established and most powerful – actually belonged to the Factory House. In 1811, for example, despite the ever-growing number of British merchants, the British Factory consisted of only ten firms. An entry in the notebook of one of its members records under 5 November 1817: 'There was a Meeting today of the Members of the Old Establishment/or Factory; which keeps itself distinct, from the general Commercial Body.'[5] This division in the ranks of the British caused much resentment, and in 1812 the Factory House levy which had been imposed on all British merchants' exports was abolished under pressure from the junior merchants, and its property was administered by the British residents in general.[6] Of the firms then trading, only the names of Blandy, Leacock and Gordon have survived into the twentieth century. The firm of Condell, Innes & Co (later to become Duncan, Innes, Lewis & Co), however, is also noteworthy because one of its members – Mr Innes, perhaps – kept the notebook from which we have just quoted, into which he meticulously copied a great deal of information concerning his firm and the wine trade generally. It covers the period 1789 to 1820, and provides an unparalleled insight into the workings of a merchant's firm at the turn of the century.[7]

Boom and bust

In business terms – despite the continuing worries about fraudulent madeira and the misuse of *estufas* – the nineteenth century opened in an optimistic way with exports, according to Biddle, totalling 16,981 pipes in 1800 and not falling below 11,011 pipes a year during the first decade.[8] Biddle unfortunately gives us no information about the years 1812–19, but with the help of the Condell Innes Notebook we can fill in some of the blanks.[9] From the report of a British Factory meeting dated 15 January 1815, we learn that 'the General Shipments last year exceeded 18,500 pipes by the Custom House Books, a larger quantity than for Several years past: about 12,000 of which were by British Vessels'.[10] A further undated note tells us: 'NB. Shipped in 1815 – 13,500 Pipes in British Vessels – 2,500 Do in Portuguese Vessels –16,000 Pipes'.[11] It is evident, therefore, that exports remained very high until 1815.

This boom, which was due to the Napoleonic wars, was however short-lived. Whereas 1811, 1812 and 1813 had all been productive years, there followed a series of disastrously short vintages: 1814 was less than half of that for 1813 and 1815, at about 6,000 pipes, was again less than half the previous year. 'Exports of wine must for Some time be very limited, for a most Substantial Reason, it has not been produced: If one fourth is taken from the whole produce of last year [1815] as consumed on the Island & unfit for Shipping, there will remain only about 4,000 pipes of New Wine for Exportation. The Stock of Old wines was in General comparatively very Low.'[12] With poor vintages, booming exports, diminishing stocks and rising prices, and a post-war depression looming, disaster was inevitable.

As before, when considering wine production and export totals during this century, considerable caution is necessary. Competing figures abound, and it is difficult to know which to believe. Most are only guesstimates. For the five years after 1815 the Condell Innes Notebook provides us with the following figures.[13] 1816: production 'about 10,000 pipes'. 1817: production 'about Ten thousand pipes, with this advantage that mostly the whole will be fit for Shipping'. 1817: 'the general Shipments by the Commerce here, for 1817, was only about 8,000 Pipes'. 1818: 'the general shipments for the Year ... amounted to about 12,000 pipes. The produce of the last Vintage is estimated at from 18 to 21,000 pipes, but the First Quality very limited'. 1819: the vintage 'very productive' and 'very Superior' after a season 'the finest we remember for upwards of 30 years'. No figure is given for exports, but the comment for 1820 is relevant: 'The shipments of the Factory House last year [1820] were 6263 pipes, which is about 500 pipes more than the preceding [year]. The rest of the Commerce may be about one third more.'[14]

From these figures we can see that exports dropped significantly after 1815, and that even when better vintages came along they fell far short of the records established during the war years. The consequences to Madeira were grave: misery and near-starvation for the vast majority of the island's inhabitants. 'While the war lasted the ports of France and Spain were closed, good and bad wine found a ready market, the island of Madeira flourished, and

Madeira and Portugal alone exported their fortified wines . . . but once peace had been made the ports opened, and with this the export of Spanish and French wines increased while the number of consumers diminished enormously.'¹⁵ Things were not about to get any better, and thus began a slow decay of the fortunes of madeira wine which has not, even today, really been reversed.

Disaster looms

During the first half of the nineteenth century the use of *estufas* and the reputation of madeira abroad were continuing concerns. No sooner had *estufas* become established at the end of the previous century than their use was banned by an edict of the Governor dated 23 August 1802, on the grounds that the good reputation of madeira was already suffering from the misuse of *estufas*, that there was a fire risk in Funchal and that smoke and coal fumes were affecting the health of those living near the *estufas*. Protest led to the lifting of the ban on 7 May 1803, largely because of the following economic argument: 'The shippers are obliged to store superlative wines in quantities corresponding to the orders which they are accustomed to receive annually, and to assign them a period of time of at least 4 years, such that the shipper who exports 300 pipes of old wine each year, finds himself needing to have a reserve of not less than 1,000 to 1,500 pipes lying stagnant and dead in his lodges; and his commerce suffers from these tied-up funds, because with only part of them he could embark on new adventures and speculations, which would legally augment his fortune, put his establishment on a more solid base, and would certainly benefit the public and augment the Royal taxes so much more.'¹⁶

Relief was temporary, for the ban was reimposed on 6 November 1803, only to be rescinded yet again on 7 May 1804. The plain fact was that *estufas* were necessary to enable the trade to meet the growing demand for madeira. It seems clear that initially the wines were generally overheated for short periods, producing harsh results. Interestingly, Condell & Innes stood out against the trend. 'We are one of the few Houses on the Island, who have never made any use of the Stew fired Wine, or what has been in the Estufa; a mode of forcing it by fire, to have the appearance of being much Older than it realy is; & our opinion is, that it will, after undergoing that operation, rather go back than Improve, however it may deceive at first Sight.'[17] *Estufas*, however, provided new opportunities to impose taxes. By 1828 there was an annual tax of 1,920 réis per pipe on *estufas*.[18] A municipal commission on *estufas* was set up in 1834, and in the same year, by a decree of 23 July, a *monthly* tax was imposed on each pipe undergoing *estufagem* – a strong incentive to opt for short and sharp, instead of long and gentle, heating and a further burden on the over-taxed trade.

As far as fraudulent madeira was concerned, the efforts to stem this trade came much too late. The deceptions became increasingly sophisticated, with *estufas*, for example, being set up in the Azores, the Canaries and even in the Cape of Good Hope.[19] A law of 22 July 1801 yet again banned the importation of wine from the Azores. It was occasioned by the activities of a Madeiran merchant called Domingos d'Oliveira Junior, who had a base in Faial (in the Azores) from which he plied mock madeira. He had evaded the previously imposed anti-fraud regulations by such ruses as taking coopers from Funchal to Faial to make imitation madeira casks; and when he had attempted to import Faial wine into Madeira in 1800, and had been stopped by the authorities, he had even tried to get the royal court in Lisbon to override their decision. These 'sordid projects by a non-patriot' backfired, but advertisements had to be placed in English, American and Asian newspapers to counteract the bad publicity. Foreign authorities were urged to be vigilant in checking the papers of ships importing alleged madeira into their countries.[20] The next quarter century saw the council many times struggling to enforce anti-fraud measures and trying to persuade the Crown to support them, but without lasting success. By 1836 Cape Madeira, Sicily Madeira, Faial Madeira and Tenerife Madeira were being advertised daily in London.[21]

During this period, however, the emphasis quickly shifted from the importation of Azorean wine to the importation of brandy (from Brazil) and of gin. The authorities became alarmed over two matters: the general health of the population, which they believed suffered greatly from 'the immoderate and disgraceful use' of spirits, and the question that arose after 1820 of how to deal with over-production and how to dispose of excess wine. Thus we find an edict of 21 March 1814 restating the ban enacted in 1789 on the sale in taverns by any persons 'of whatever rank, quality or condition they may be' of 'ardent spirits or any other spirituous drink which is not produced in this island'.[22] The solution favoured by the authorities was, briefly, to exclude from the island all foreign spirits, except the French brandy needed to fortify the wine (whose entry had been permitted since 1760),[23] and to direct the surplus wines into local taverns.

Smuggling was rampant, and apparently connived at by the customs authorities themselves. Holman [1827] reports that during his visit 300 cases of gin were smuggled ashore and stored in a cave near Prior Bay, a little west of Funchal. The following day two lovers on an excursion to Câmara de Lobos took shelter in the cave and later reported what they had discovered there to the Customs, hoping for a reward. 'The Custom-house people, who were probably already aware of the circumstance, did not appear to be very anxious to interfere, and told the disappointed informers that they might take a few cases for themselves, and say nothing more about the matter.'[24]

The main villains, however, were perceived to be the British merchants, who took advantage of permission from the customs house (controlled from continental Portugal) to import foreign spirits in defiance of the town council's wishes. The taxes were punitive, and the Royal exchequer was glad to have them. In 1816, for example, the council complained that they had carried out 'a duplicitous importation of foreign spirits by paying the fines which were imposed on them by the edict of this Council of 21 March 1814 ... an abuse which can alone be avoided if the Junta of the Royal Estates allows only the importation of French brandy for the making of our wines and totally prohibits the clearance of all other drinks made outside the island, as is ordained in the royal proclamation 22 July 1801.'[25] The crown failed to respond to this appeal.

At the same time, while pleading that the council's attempted embargo on the importation of foreign spirits was an infringement of free trade, the British merchants further alienated the authorities by delaying their purchases of new wine for up to three years,[26] thereby putting producers, especially the tenant farmers, in an impossible position. 'Our commerce is absolutely inactive; the English take our wines prisoner, with the following effects: the money of the agrarian workers is completely in their power for long periods, because payment has to be dragged out of them; and to increase still further their domination and commercial ascendancy, they manage to leave a large excess of wine in our hands only so that it will later pass into their hands at the prices they desire.'[27]

The denunciations of the British merchants to the Crown by the town council became increasingly shrill as their conduct had graver and graver consequences for the island's economy, with references to 'the odious and intolerable projects of the [British] consul and other negotiants who only cherish goals of sordid self interest',[28] and 'the evils which stem from this system of egoism which predominates in the British community [which] will end in the total ruin of our agriculture (which is already so much run down), since the English wish for nothing more than to increase our poverty and keep us in eternal dependence on them'.[29]

Doubtless the merchants had their own problems. With trade stagnant and warehouses full, it was natural that they should stop buying and try to drive prices down. There was, as the town council suspected, something of a conspiracy on the part of the British merchants: 'There was a Meeting today [5 November 1817] of the Members of the Old Establishment/or Factory ... to endeavour to fall on some means, to bring down the prices which the planters, & others aspire at.'[30] But an anonymous commentator found their efforts inept: 'This high price is occasioned by the want of unanimity among the English merchants, or indeed a want of good faith towards each other, for they appear occasionally to rouse from their lethargy, meet at their consul's, and agree to give only certain prices for the wines at the press; but, immediately after, each outbids the other, and the wine jobber laughs in his sleeve, and profits by their folly.'[31]

However, there were other problems for which the British were not responsible. Post-war recession hit hard. Exports to the United States dropped dramatically. In 1827 an American wrote that 'we imported 355,837 gallons annually for more than 20 years, which amount has now sunk to 16,483'[32] – this despite a reduction in American duties on madeira in 1822. (355,837 gallons amounts to some 3,235 pipes and 16,483 gallons to about 150 pipes.) Nor did the post-Napoleonic fashion for madeira in England sustain itself for very long. By 1841, imports into England, which had been close to 6,000 pipes in 1815, had sunk to a derisory 800 pipes.[33] But most of all, there were the difficulties Portugal itself put in the way of the islanders. There was a prohibition on the import of madeira into Brazil (the natural destination for the inferior produce of the north), so surplus stocks of wine could not be disposed of there – something which affected the native Madeiran merchants more than it did the

British. Secondly, there were high taxes on exports and property, and taxes to maintain the state. There was still a 'temporary' tax first imposed in 1641 to defray wartime expenses. Worst of all, however, there was a tax, rising to 15 per cent by 1843, on the import of the island's staple, corn. The state arranged everything to help itself and nothing to help Madeira. A letter dated 18 May 1822 to the *Patriota Funchalese* put the point succinctly: 'Obliged to be consumers of certain goods produced by Portugal, with which we have no commercial relationship, whilst we can receive equivalent goods from other nations with whom we do do business with our wines (and cheaper), puts us, as Mr De Pradt has sagely remarked, in a state of war with the Metropolis, which forces us thus solely to its own advantage.'[34]

The supplications for help, like the denunciations of the British, became increasingly urgent but fell on deaf ears. 'The lessening of taxes is a matter your Majesty should consider. Without doubt they are overwhelmingly damaging to the island of Madeira in present circumstances, and almost impossible to pay, which people certainly could do when your Majesty deigns to privilege them by favouring the export of their wines ... How are the inhabitants to pay if there is nobody to buy what they produce? ... How are the proprietors and merchants to pay if their wines remain stuck in their stores without any outlet? ... Your Majesty would weep with sorrow if he could see with his own eyes the efforts and pains which the inhabitants of the south of Madeira suffer in making a pipe of wine ... Their prosperity is that pipe of wine; if they cannot sell it they die in misery.'[35]

This was in 1821; but by 1824 the picture was even grimmer. Although bulk imports of French brandy had been stopped by a regulation of 31 July 1822,[36] bottled French brandy was still permitted and some 3,000 pipes of ardent spirits from various foreign sources were being imported. There were some 40,000 pipes of old wine remaining in the hands of the growers.[37] The council even presumed to lecture the crown on its lack of wisdom and responsibility: 'The true interests of the royal exchequer are those which result in national happiness and prosperity, and those which oppose the general good are always disgraceful';[38] 'It is not impartial justice for your Majesty to promote the advantages of one part of the nation with the ruin and misery of the other part'.[39] The lack of help from the crown inevitably made the islanders feel that discrimination against Madeira was unfair. They were right: it was. Nor was it an exaggeration when the council advised that 'it might be necessary, in order that they should not die of hunger, that his Majesty should command the dispersal of two-thirds of the population to the interior of Brazil'.[40] Before many years had elapsed, emigration was indeed to become the only alternative to starvation.

It would be impossible to guess at the desperation of the social situation just from looking at export totals. Between 1820 and 1825 they averaged over 13,000 pipes a year, which compares quite favourably with the record average of 15,722 pipes a year for the first decade of the century.[41] Indeed, such figures were to become remarkable in retrospect, because after 1825 the figure of 10,000 pipes a year was never again equalled during the century. So, were the town council exaggerating from a desire to reduce taxes so that they could try to recapture the boom? Perhaps it would have been against human nature not to do so, but dire poverty there undoubtedly was. It cannot have been an entirely pleasant place for invalids and visitors to come to. 'Bands of sturdy beggars, almost in a state of nudity, greet the traveller on his arrival, exposing to view ghastly wounds, and thrusting themselves upon his notice with an eagerness and ferocity not only revolting but appalling.'[42]

Wine shippers had to apply themselves to commerce afresh. If trade would not come to the island, then it had to be sought out. Peter Cossart, a young member of Newton and Murdoch (later to become Cossart Gordon), was therefore sent on a visit to England and America to drum up business. He left Madeira on 14 July 1833, not to return until 15 May 1835. We gather his frame of mind from an entry in his journal for 23 July 1833: 'Letters from Madeira – all quiet there to 2nd inst, business very dull – fear our trade has seen its best days. Nor do I calculate on much if any improvement.' In under a year his sales campaign had taken him the length and breadth of America. 5 May 1834: 'I have now set foot in all the four & twenty States and in two out of the three territories (and very few, even Americans, can say as much) besides Upper & Lower Canada & New Brunswick'.[43] The only time he found any madeira worth mentioning was in Savannah, where at the Quoit Club 'the wine, which is furnished by said Members in turn, was excellent being N & M [Newton and Murdoch]' and at the Mayor's, where he was given 'good wine of our own Sending'.

During the quarter-century up to 1850 exports dropped to an

average of 7,649 pipes a year, or about 60 per cent of the average for the previous period. As the writers of petitions to the throne never ceased to point out – and as we too must always bear in mind – Madeira was virtually a wine monoculture, dependent on its exports to buy three-quarters of its food (and other) supplies; so that, during this period, the profits on the export of an average of fewer than 10,000 pipes had to support a population of considerably more than 100,000 – with the proprietors and merchants getting proportionately more of these profits than the peasants. So the situation of the vast majority of the islanders, already fairly desperate by 1825, grew steadily worse, and was not improved by the uncertainties of the War of the Two Brothers, which began in that year and lasted until 1834. The one positive and lasting achievement of this decade was the founding in 1836 of the Associação Commercial do Funchal, the outcome of the deliberations of a commission of five (which included John Shortridge and Joseph Phelps) which the Governor had set up the previous year. It immediately provided the trade with a single voice to represent its interests, and the Association has had a continuous existence (though somewhat transformed) to the present day.[44]

While the council continued to petition the crown for reduced taxes, denunciations of an increasingly revolutionary kind appeared in local papers. In 1841 a remarkable and lengthy liberal 'catechism' appeared in *O Defensor*, calling for wise constitutional laws on the British model. There was a perceived risk of a peasant uprising. Emigration had always taken place in times of misery,[45] and between 1835 and 1855 around 40,000 people emigrated from Madeira to Demerara and the British East Indies. The exodus really got going in the 1840s, with 4,045 in 1841, 4,945 in 1846 and 4,720 in 1847. In the autumn of 1846 the potato crop,[46] the staple of the peasant diet, failed. This coincided with another notable decrease in the price of wine. Relief supplies arrived from abroad, and public subscriptions in the United States, Britain, Ireland (astonishingly, in view of its own similar problem), Germany and Russia raised quite large sums. By 25 May 1847, merchants and farmers had themselves raised a 32,500 milréis food fund; but there was no food to buy, and some of the money financed public works. Taxes on corn were reduced to 25 réis, but not abolished. Of this sad country in 1849 Dean Peachcock of Ely wrote that he had 'nowhere seen, not even in the worst parts of Ireland, more intense misery than among the people of this island. A stranger is assaulted, whenever he appears near these destitute and overpeopled districts, with crowds of mendicants, whose emaciated and diseased appearance shows too plainly that their food is insufficient and unwholesome.'[47]

This is the background against which wine was being produced as the first half of the century came to an end. An article in the *Correio da Madeira* for 1 June 1850 catalogued the taxes then current on wine, and showed that wine from the north was taxed at between 70 and 80 per cent, and wine from the south at between 30 and 40 per cent, of its value as must.[48] How, the article asked, was it possible for wine so burdened to compete on the international market? How, indeed? Yet calamitous as the situation must then have seemed, its gravity paled into insignificance by comparison with what happened when the first of two vine plagues, *oïdium*, made its appearance in February 1851. Its impact is graphically illustrated by comparing two editions of Robert White's *Madeira, Its Climate and Scenery*. The first, published in 1851, portrays a flourishing culture of the vine; in the second, published in 1857, the section on wine has been entirely transcribed into the past tense! For the writer madeira wine was already a thing of the past, a fact of history.

The first crisis

Oïdium Tuckeri, known in Madeira as *mangra* but now better known as *uncinula necator* or as powdery mildew, was originally identified in the United States in 1834. In Europe, it was first detected in England in 1845, in Mr Tucker's garden in Margate. It is a fungal disease which first attacks the leaves – causing white patches which eventually rot and wither – and then covers the grapes with white powder and causes lesions, after which the vine itself succumbs. It is thought to have been brought to Madeira by a French plant salesman who sold vines brought from an *oïdium*-infected part of France. The disease spread quickly, and by the following year, 1852, it was evident in all parts of the island, though the west was comparatively unaffected. After that it seemed unstoppable. First to be attacked were vines grown in corridor formation, then those on trellises, and lastly *vinhas da pé*, where the vines had little or no support. Isabela, the American variety, proved to be most resistant by far to the disease; Verdelho and Tinta varieties such as Negra Mole were attacked with less ferocity than those, like Boal and Malvasia, with higher sugar levels. Just occasionally, for some inexplicable reason, a single vineyard would remain defiantly untouched. In the whole of the Funchal area the only example was the Quinta das Maravilhas, which belonged to Miss Norton, an English lady resident on the island. The 'Quinta of Marvels' must indeed have seemed well named.

There was then no known cure, and over the next three years the producers and merchants could only stand by and watch as their vineyards were systematically destroyed. The devastation was not just immense, it was complete. According to Silva and Meneses,[49] wine production, which had been averaging only 11,956 pipes a year up to 1851, plummeted to 1,913 pipes in 1852, 717 pipes in 1853 and a mere 143 pipes in 1854.[50] In 1855 production was only 36 pipes.[51] This represents a drop in production of 99.7 per cent over four years. A total wipe-out, and for the island virtually total economic ruin. The annual loss to the proprietors and growers was estimated at upwards of £230,000 sterling.[52] The cost to the island's economy was very slightly offset by the revenue from invalids and visitors, estimated at £30,000–£40,000 per year,[53] but this did not directly help the wine trade.

The impact on the already fragile economy of the island was cataclysmic. It was the culmination of years of decline and, as one commentator put it, 'the disease of the vines must not be accused of ruining the viticultors in Madeira; this ruin was imminent, the disease only hastening a crisis which was already very near'.[54] Mass emigration rocketed. It is estimated that in the twenty years up to 1855, 40,000 people left the island (only half of them with passports).[55] The least prosperous of the British wine merchants gave up and left the island.[56] On 22 November 1852 the Governor nominated a commission to solicit help from abroad, and subscriptions were opened in various countries. For the second time within a decade Madeira had to throw itself on the mercy of international aid. A shipload of food and clothing was sent from London, and a total of 37,000 milréis was collected. Schemes to employ the poor were also set in motion, but labour for 300 men for six months building (but not completing) the first major road on the island, the Estrada Monumental which connects Funchal with Câmara de Lobos, was a pitifully inadequate response to the magnitude of the disaster. Another response, however, though doubtless thought eccentric at the time, was later to develop into a significant ingredient of a more diversified island economy. Elizabeth Phelps, the daughter of Joseph Phelps, a partner of Phelps, Page & Co. and noted philanthropist, introduced embroidery as a cottage industry amongst the womenfolk of the unemployed workers on the company's vineyards. The project prospered. Within twenty years, more than a thousand women were employed on embroidery, and in 1862 a British firm was established on the island to handle exports. By 1923, more than 70,000 people were employed in the industry,[57] and now [1997] embroidery outperforms wine as an export industry.

The gravity of the wine crisis was not at first realized. Newspaper correspondence assumed that the disease would run its course and things would return to normal. Amid exhortations from the Governor to trust in God's bountifulness, the more thoughtful of the populace saw the *mangra* as a warning of the dangers of a monoculture, and they advocated more diversity in agriculture: more sugar cane, coffee, tropical fruit. On 29 July 1853 an agronomist named João de Andrade Côrvo arrived in Funchal. He had been sent to observe the situation by the Royal Academy of Sciences in Lisbon, to which he presented a long report on his findings in February 1854.[58] He had nothing to say, however, about what might be done to counter the disease. On 18 April 1854 the Governor issued a decree setting up a Commission, but it too seems to have been of little help.

In 1852, most of the grapes that had been attacked were jettisoned on the grounds that the value of the wine would not justify the expense of making it. By 1853, however, the shortage of wine for ordinary consumption on the island, coupled with the rising price of ever-scarcer *aguardente* – the importation of brandy was still prohibited – induced some proprietors to make a wine from grapes in such an advanced state of decomposition that even a person 'wretchedly consumed with hunger would hesitate to touch'.[59] The must was diluted, and had the colour of muddy water and the smell characteristic of *mangra*, 'which is easier to recognize than to describe: a repugnant and sick smell, somewhat akin to that of cleaning copper with a light acid'.[60] After a short, quiet fermentation and clarification it produced a liquid to which it would be difficult to give the name 'wine', with a detestable smell and an insupportable, bitter taste of the parasite fungus. It was considered, however, that drinking this 'wine' presented no risk to the health of the people!

Happily for the poor people there were alternatives. Wine was made from pears, oranges and sugar cane; there was some beer; but, most importantly, there was non-alcoholic ginger beer, first made by João Caetano about 1851. Nevertheless, when the fall in municipal income in 1854 led to new taxes on alcoholic drinks, ginger beer was also taxed – but only at half the rate of real beer, so it became the staple drink of the populace.[61]

After the all-time low of 1855, production figures for the rest of the decade slowly increased: 87 pipes in 1856; 101 pipes in 1857; 184 pipes in 1858; and 151 in 1859. Again, export figures give no clue to what was happening in the vineyards, for they remained surprisingly buoyant during the 1850s, never dropping below 1,000 pipes a year until 1862 (although not rising above 1,000 pipes a year again until 1870).[62] These figures were initially made possible by using reserve stocks, but over an eight-year period (1852–59), during which exports exceeded production by some 12,000 pipes, these became almost exhausted. Moreover, the current levels of production did not provide for internal consumption or for distillation into brandy. Other solutions had therefore to be found.

The obvious solution was to import wine from abroad and re-export it as madeira – precisely the same abuse which everyone had struggled to prevent at the start of the century. The pressure to do this started in March 1857, when a project to import wine from Lisbon was advanced by António Correia Herédia. This met with popular acclaim, but nothing happened. The idea was floated in parliament in 1860. A Ordem was the only newspaper in Funchal to oppose the idea, on the same grounds – that it would damage the future integrity of the wine – that had been argued sixty years earlier. This argument, supported by the town council and the Associação Commercial, carried the day and, despite later attempts to remove it, the ban remained in place.[63] So help was not forthcoming from this quarter.

The merchants remaining on the island – particularly Blandy, it seems – were astute enough to buy up the stocks of departing merchants at knock-down prices. As the stocks diminished the price rose, according to Vizetelly, from £25 to £75 a pipe for the lowest qualities.[64] Many of the shippers adopted the solera system, sometimes called fractional blending, as a means of eking out their stocks of old vintages. More recently, old soleras have been seen as a not-quite-fraudulent way of selling young wine under old dates, but it does seem that they answered the need of the moment to conserve stocks and maintain quality.

Mr Tucker became famous not just because he was the first person in Europe to be visited by *oïdium*; he was also responsible for finding the best means of combating it, and after 1854 sulphur dusting became the universally recognized means of controlling the fungus. However, it took a long time for the vineyards to recover. Large areas of vines were dead, and because of shortages of suitable cuttings, they often had to be replaced with stock imported from mainland Portugal. This brought new varieties such as Arinto to the island, and Isabela, being virtually immune to *oïdium*, had an understandable appeal to growers.

Many vineyards, however, were not replanted. Although sugar was again being cultivated in Madeira at the beginning of the nineteenth century, the quantities were insignificant until the *oïdium* disaster, which gave an impetus to the diversification of Madeiran agriculture and led to considerable replanting with canes instead of vines. A regenerated sugar industry in Madeira flourished for more than a century, making it once more an important element in the island's economy.[65]

Slowly, things got better for the wine trade, if not for the general population. In 1856, as if things were not bad enough, there was a serious outbreak of cholera. It is estimated that out of a population of 105,000 at least 10,000 died. It was once more a matter of subscriptions and shiploads of relief supplies. The efforts of the British community on this occasion earned the thanks not only of the Governor, but of the Portuguese king.[66]

An event of importance to Madeira occurred in 1861, when all the taxes which had so grievously afflicted the island throughout the century were abolished. It may sound as if the islanders' prayers had at last been answered. A law of 11 September stated that, as from 1 January 1863, Madeira would pay the same taxes as continental Portugal. It proved to be a mixed blessing, however, and soon the cry was that taxes devised for the mainland were often wholly inappropriate to the circumstances of the island. Another legal event of lasting significance to the wine trade, even if its effects took time to show themselves, occurred in 1863. The same António Correia Herédia mentioned above began to campaign in February

1849 for the abolition of *morgados* (the institution of property entail),[67] which had existed in Madeira since the fifteenth century. Many enlightened people felt that it inhibited agricultural progress. The opposition from the landowners was immense, and they managed to block this reform. However, a law was passed on 11 May 1863 which abolished entails throughout Portugal. Thereafter, these large properties were gradually broken up as from generation to generation they passed into wider ownership.

During the period of retrenchment in the 1860s, even if exports diminished, production stabilized and increased slightly. The quality of the vintages was consistent and on the whole encouraging. As the decade ended, although still rather small, production of about 16,000 pipes was again being achieved.[68] The outbreak of the American Civil War in 1861 brought exports to America to a virtual standstill, but the winding-up of the East India Company after the Indian Mutiny in 1857 was compensated for by an increase in exports to the subcontinent to supply military messes and clubs, and this built up steadily into the next century. Against this, however, the opening of the Suez Canal in 1869 meant that ships bound for the east no longer called at Madeira. Russia, to which exports had slowly started as far back as 1793, had from the 1830s become a major market, and exports to Britain competed in size with those to Russia to the end of the century.[69] Stocks began increasing once more, and by the end of the decade there was a collective sigh of relief that the worst was over and that the trade had managed to come through the crisis. Madeira wine was not to become, as had once been feared, a thing of the past.

5

The Nineteenth Century II

The second crisis

Phylloxera (*Phylloxera vastatrix*) was first identified in Madeira in 1872. It is a vine louse which attacks the roots of European vines and is endemic in America, where some varieties of vine are immune to it – no one yet fully understands why. Like *oïdium*, the first time it was detected in Europe was in England, this time at Hammersmith in 1863. During the 1860s phylloxera had devastated European vineyards, and there must have been a fear that it would sneak into Madeira, as *oïdium* had done. But no thought seems to have been given to taking precautions, and ironically the plague appears to have arrived with some sprigs of Isabela, imported because of the variety's *oïdium*-resistant properties. It took more than ten years to come to terms with phylloxera, and in Madeira as elsewhere, confusion, ignorance, misunderstanding and panic contributed almost as much to the length and ill-effects of the plague as the vine louse itself.

It was an international rather than a local problem, and required international co-operation to solve it. Many remedies were tried. Between 1872 and 1876 some 1,044 suggested treatments were assessed at the School of Agriculture at Montpellier in France. A few retarded the progress of the devastation, but the most effective measure in practice was the injection into the roots of a carbon bisulphide solution. The value of this treatment, although apparent to many vineyard proprietors, was unaccountably not recognized at Montpellier, though it was taken seriously by the International Phylloxera Congress which met at Bordeaux in 1881. The competing solution – grafting a vine shoot of a European variety on to the roots of a resistant American variety – eventually suggested itself when empirical observation made it clear that some American vines in European vineyards survived phylloxera while all native varieties succumbed. Grafting had been gaining support in France since 1880, and it eventually established itself as the best, and so far the only wholly effective, way of dealing with phylloxera.[1]

When a Comissão Anti-filoxérica was set up in December 1882 (ten years after the louse was first detected), it was not yet entirely clear that grafting was the proper solution to the problem, and the Commission simply endorsed and actively promoted the alternative, ultimately inadequate, solution of sulphide injections. Even after there was a consensus that the way forward was by grafting, it took considerable trial and error to discover the most suitable root stocks: not only because some American root stocks (such as *Labrusca*) are not particularly resistant to phylloxera, but because some which are do not suit all types of soil. The growers in Madeira, therefore, were in no worse a position than anyone else: everyone had to do what he could for himself.

The way in which phylloxera attacked the vines was not so immediately dramatic as the onslaught of *oïdium*, and nothing like as severe as it was in the Douro or in France. Henry Vizetelly, visiting the island in 1877, five years after the blight began, remarked on its slow spread, 'having confined its ravages . . . to a comparatively small area',[2] and he was able to find many vineyards which were apparently quite unaffected. The main damage was at Câmara de Lobos, where phylloxera destroyed nearly all the vines and reduced production from 3,000 to a mere 100 pipes. On the other hand, at Estreito de Câmara de Lobos, to the north, phylloxera had only attacked the lower vines. At Quinta Grande, to the west, the vines were but slightly affected and promised to give a very fair yield. Further west still, Campanário was 'untouched at present'. In Funchal and in surrounding villages there were symptoms of phylloxera: at São João many vines had been seriously affected; at Santo António there was some phylloxera side by side with healthy vineyards; whereas at São Martinho the attack had been slight. East of Funchal, Caniço and Machico were not seriously affected, while at Santa Cruz there were no signs of blight at all. Thus the worst problems seem at this time to have been confined to a relatively small area, albeit the most important in terms of quality. Phylloxera spread slowly in the north. For example, it took until 1883 to reach the Visconde de Val Pariso's vineyards at Porto

Moniz on the north-western tip of the island. By this time, however, the situation elsewhere had deteriorated to the point that only 20 per cent – about 500 hectares – of the vineyards in production at the outset of the attack were still yielding: their production of some 3,500 pipes, however, compares very favourably with the miserable totals of the mid-1850s. Vizetelly, the most knowledgeable of nineteenth-century commentators, gives us an interesting account of his visit. The overall impression he conveys is, contrary to what might be expected, not one of desperate crisis. Efforts were being made to defeat phylloxera, but life and trade were otherwise going on as usual.

Thomas Slapp Leacock, a grandson of the first member of the family to come to Madeira, appears to have been in the forefront of those experimenting with ways of curing the problem. He owned a vineyard at São João, and there, as early as 1873, he found that periodic painting of the roots of the vine with a solution of resin and turpentine in hot water, described by Vizetelly as 'a kind of varnish', effectively retarded the progress of decay. It was, however, thought by other proprietors to be too expensive a treatment for general use. Leacock's son John was a member of the Comissão Anti-filoxérica, which met between December 1882 and 7 November 1883. It decided to establish a treatment post and a nursery of American vines, and a property of about one hectare in São João was acquired for that purpose. A ban that had been imposed on the importation of American vines in the wake of oïdium was lifted. A team of three started carrying out anti-phylloxera treatment with sulphide injections in February 1883. The results were thought auspicious.[3] An official district inspector called Almeida e Brito was appointed in June and was put in charge of the operation.

Two nurseries were established in Funchal, one at Ribeirinho and the other at Torreão, and by 1883 some 60,000 vines had been distributed. At first Riparia, Jacquet, Herbemont, Rupestris, Solonis, Taylor, Clinton, Elsimbro and York Madeira were all cultivated. Later Cunningham, Viala, Elvira, Othelo, Cinerea, Black Pearl and Gaston Bazile were added. Experience showed that Riparia, Herbemont, Cunningham and particularly Jacquet were best suited to conditions on the island, and they became the preferred root stocks for grafting. Not all were grafted, however, and it is in this period that the predominance of American vines in Madeiran viticulture for more than a century began. Nor were all the former vineyards replanted. Vizetelly several times mentions that he found sugar cane had been planted in place of dead vines, especially in Câmara de Lobos. However, although some of these vineyards, like those of the Torre Bella estate, reverted to vines, there was a net loss of vineyards across the island.

Fortunately, the island had had relatively large stocks of wine when phylloxera arrived – Vizetelly estimated them at 30,000 pipes in 1877 – and exports, having managed to rise above 1,000 pipes a year in 1870, actually increased to over 2,000 a year for the rest of the decade. Thereafter they mounted steadily, from just over 3,000 pipes a year in 1880 to just over 5,000 pipes a year by the end of the 1880s.[4] Some markets were lost. According to the Conde de Canavial, the imports of madeira into the States in 1882 amounted to only 48 litres, or a little less than an eighth of a pipe – a figure which makes one blink.[5] There were few casualties amongst the shippers this time. Of the fifteen British merchants listed by Cossart for 1855, thirteen were still active in the 1870s and 1880s, and there were sixteen Portuguese firms (of which three – Henriques and Henriques, Justino Henriques, and Borges – are still in existence today).

The effect of phylloxera on the Madeira population at large was also less dramatic than that of *oïdium*. A certain amount of emigration continued, but the numbers leaving Madeira fell far short of those seen during the *oïdium* period. The Sandwich Islands became a favourite destination after 1878, and Portuguese colonies in Africa, such as Angola and Lourenço Marques, became popular after 1884. Another cottage industry, wickerwork, grew in importance. It had started in a small way at Camacha around 1812, but expanded greatly during the 1870s. Today it is still a significant source of foreign income for Madeira, although it earns only about 30 per cent as much as wine.

A period of consolidation followed the upheavals of the 1870s and 1880s. The Conde de Canavial, a prominent wine expert, began campaigning in 1879 for the foundation of a commercial society of growers to protect their interests, but it took more than twenty years for such an association to come into being, in 1900. However, a Commission to Assist Farming (Comissão de Auxílio á Lavoura) was set up in 1888, led by a crown commissioner named Manoel de Moraes who had been sent to study the state of the vineyards and to distribute free American vines. From this we must suppose that the number of American vines continued to grow. Production went up to about 8,000 pipes in 1895 and reached 9,200 pipes in 1900.[6] Exports remained buoyant, hovering between 5,077 and 6,346 pipes during the first part of the 1890s.[7] With returning prosperity the price of madeira again fell and island stocks rose again. During the vine plagues of the second half of the century, madeira had lost markets to sherry and malaga, which could be sold at a fraction of the cost. At the same time, however, Tarragona, the Midi in France and Hamburg all cashed in on the production of counterfeit madeira. This spectre, which had haunted Madeira for more than a century, was at last laid to rest when in June 1900 John E. Blandy finally won a protracted legal case in France against a Spanish firm which had shipped 500 pipes of imitation madeira to Le Havre. 'Madeira' thereafter established itself as a term which could only be properly applied to the produce of the island, and this was reflected in an Anglo-Portuguese treaty signed in 1914.[8]

Viticulture and the wine

Finally, we must review the development of viticulture, wine-making and the wine itself through the nineteenth century. The vines grown in the north, according to Holman [1827], were all of white varieties, whilst those in the south were chiefly red. Low trellises continued to be the predominant method of training vines, and were recognized as giving the best fruit. Only exceptionally, as at Leacock's São João vineyards, were vines trained in rows along horizontal wires.[9] After *oïdium*, the growing of vines on chestnut trees in the north was progressively replaced by the trellises of the south. Vineyards were situated as high as 700 metres in Estreito de Câmara de Lobos, 670 metres in Camacha and 520 metres at Monte, north-east of Funchal, but it was recognized that the best wine came from vineyards no higher than 150 metres.[10] Before phylloxera, propagation was either by the traditional method already described,[11] whereby cuttings or rooted vines were planted in trenches, or by grafting, which as we have seen[12] was also used in the eighteenth century. Bowdich [1823] says that when the latter method is used, 'they prefer the *verdelho* of the north, when forming a plantation in the southern part of the island, as it improves considerably from the better soil, climate and aspect: on this they engraft any other variety they may wish: the grapes yield no wine until the fourth year'.[13] Vineyards were watered three times, if possible, when the summer was dry or the vines were young, but growers were aware that although irrigation might improve the quantity, it would reduce the quality of their grapes. Animal manure, used by some, was shunned by others because they thought it affected the flavour of the grapes. Instead, they grew lupins in the January of every second year, cutting them down and turning them into the soil after the rains which are common at the end of April.

The best time to prune the vines was disputed – between January (unusual), February (normal) or the middle of March (late) – but depended on predicting from the weather when flowering would occur. The best method was also debated – long or short pruning – as was its effect on the life of the vine. Many vines were healthy and productive for only 10 to 15 years, and this was blamed on inappropriate pruning, which had not been adjusted to the variety and circumstances of the individual vines. Small vineyards generally had a mixture of varieties, white and red, and only in larger vineyards was it possible to harvest grapes of a single variety.[14] Yields varied. It was common to remove some leaves and expose the grapes to the sun to assist in their ripening. Bowdich calculated that four pipes of must an acre (almost ten per hectare) were possible in the most favourable conditions, but that one pipe was the average across the island. Growing vegetables under vine trellises was common, and grass abounded. All writers mention the depredations caused by lizards and rats, which never touched Sercial but fell upon Tinta Negra Mole with a vengeance. According to White [1851], 20 per cent of the harvest was generally lost in this way:[15] Harcourt [1851] puts the losses at 10 per cent.[16] Woe betide the farmer who harvested after his neighbours – which may be the explanation for the premature picking which so upset the authorities from time to time.

References to about forty named grape varieties abound, though some are synonyms of others.[17] Several writers, from Adam onwards, claimed that Verdelho, Tinta Negra Mole and Boal were the best varieties for making generic madeira, the latter two giving flavour to the former. Verdelho was, according to Holman [1827], the chief grape variety grown in the north. According to Vizetelly [1877], Verdelho constituted two-thirds of the vines on the island,[18] while Taylor [1882] put the proportion as high as three-quarters.[19]

As we have seen, however, the number of American vines increased progressively in the last quarter of the century, and new varieties were imported from mainland Portugal to replace dead vines. Most of the new varieties do not, as far as one can tell, appear to have had a lasting presence on the island.

To reinforce the legislation of 1784 preventing the harvesting of unripe grapes, three inspectors were in 1819 appointed for each parish,[20] and growers had to obtain their permission before starting the vintage. The distinction in quality between wines of the north and south remained important throughout the century. There were three categories of quality (reflecting the height above sea level of the vines) for grapes in each council area, and prices, which were set by local councils, varied widely. The following table, showing the average prices in 1851 at Câmara de Lobos in the south and Santana in the north, illustrates the extremities of this range:[21]

Average price of wine

	in Câmara de Lobos	in Santana
1st quality	4,320 réis	1,780 réis
2nd quality	3,440 réis	1,580 réis
3rd quality	2,500 réis	1,600 réis [sic]

The British Factory had continued to try to control prices by co-ordinated buying until its abolition in 1838, and as late as 1885 Johnson reports that many shippers still bought their must in advance of the harvest. Methods of vinification do not appear to have changed very much during the century. Descriptions of the vintage are all very similar, although White [1851] tells us that 'the grapes, when gathered, are "escolhido," or picked; those of an inferior quality being generally reserved by themselves'.[22] Vizetelly [1877] mentions that at Leacock's São João vineyard 'the grapes would be picked at no less than eight different times, only the per-fectly ripe bunches being gathered on each occasion'.[23] All varieties except Tinta Negra Mole were fermented off their skins, Tinta being macerated to increase the colour. Whereas it was common to press the grapes two or three times after treading, Negra Mole was pressed only once. Sometimes the pressings would be kept separate from the trodden wine, at other times added to it. Fermentation took place in open-topped vats (*bica aberta*) and lasted from six to eight weeks, sometimes longer for rich wines, unless checked. Until about the middle of the century, gypsum was added to the wine made from grapes grown in the south to clarify it, but apparently not to the wine from the north.[24] After the violent fermentation had subsided (10–12 days), gypsum would be added and the wine stirred twice a day until the carbonic acid gas stopped. It was then racked, usually in January. Subsequently, clarification was carried out using egg whites or blood.

Until the middle of the century it was usual to fortify the wine only when it was being prepared for shipping. However, Thudichum and Dupré [1872] report a more elaborate process: 'The must is mostly mixed with brandy at once, stated to be from half a gallon to a gallon to the Portuguese pipe. After the first fermentation is over, the wine is racked from the gross leas, and again mixed with a similar quantity of brandy. After about three weeks, it is racked a second time, fined, and a gallon of brandy is again added. When the wine has become bright, it is racked for the last time, and placed in large barrels for ripening. This process requires about six years. Before exportation each pipe receives another gallon of spirit.'[25] Fortification was with French brandy until 1822, when its importation other than in bottles was forbidden. Thereafter, distilled spirit from the north of the island and Porto Santo was used.

After the vintage the wine was transported to the shippers' lodges. When possible this was done in cask, drawn in ox carts from the suburbs of Funchal, or brought by sea from further afield, the half-filled casks often being floated out to boats propelled by men swimming behind them. Once safely on board they were then topped up. From the interior the wine was moved to the shippers' lodges in Funchal by processions of *borracheiros*, so named because they carried on their shoulders, steadied by a strap round their foreheads, containers of wine (*borrachos*) made from goat skins which still retained the rudimentary form of the animal. The weight of a full goat skin was about 50 kg. A file of *borracheiros* might contain forty or fifty men, and they would sing as they marched along. The almost complete lack of roads made this method of transport general. Wise shippers took precautions. 'One of the merchant's clerks attends at the *lagar* to see that the operation of crushing is properly carried out. He ascertains the specific gravity of the juice as it comes from the press, and the must is again tested on its arrival at the store, so as to prevent the carriers tampering with it on the way.'[26]

Vinho da roda, or *tornaviagem* madeira, continued to be produced until well into the twentieth century.[27] It became common in the United States to name the wine after the ship in which it had been carried or the country in which it had been matured, or even after the family which owned it.[28] Even today, some of these wines still surface from time to time.[29] *Estufas* remained contentious throughout the period, but their use was widespread – although Vizetelly [1877] notes that two firms, Welsh and Donaldson, did not use them.[30] At the beginning of the century, when fortification was done prior to shipping, the wine was heated without brandy; later, when fortification became part of the wine-making process, it was heated after the addition of brandy, and this was acknowledged to give a better final product.[31] It was also generally agreed that prolonged slow heating at low temperatures gave the best results. In 1847 there were 39 *estufas* in Funchal alone.[32] Some were run by shippers, who would rent space to other shippers who had no *estufas* of their own. There were also public *estufas*, where according to Bowdich [1823] the wine was all but boiled. Later *estufas* were elaborate and sophisticated. Vizetelly [1877] visited both *estufas do sol* and *estufas* with artificial heating. Some firms, such as Krohn Bros. and Henriques and Lawton, had both. Vizetelly gives a detailed description of one of the latter: 'The Estufa stores of Messrs. Cossart, Gordon, & Co. comprise a block of buildings of two stories, divided into four distinct compartments. In the first of these common wines are subjected to a temperature of 140 deg. Fahrenheit – derived from flues, heated with anthracite coal – for the space of three months. In the next compartment wines of an intermediate quality are heated up to 130 deg. for a period of four and a half months; while the third is set apart for superior wines, heated variously from 110 to 120 deg. for the term of six months. The fourth compartment, known as the "Calor," possesses no flues, but derives its heat, varying from 90 to 100 deg., exclusively from the compartments adjacent; and here only high-class wines are placed.'[33] This store could deal with 1,600 pipes at a time. Evaporation led to the loss of 10 to 15 per cent of the wine. Leakage of casks was an undesirable effect of the heating, and this had to be monitored night and day.

The main problem was that, owing to the expansion of the wine when heated, the casks which contained it could not be completely sealed, and the combination of extremely high temperatures and contact with the air caused a most disagreeable over-oxidization and the production of acetic properties. An improvement on this situation was advocated by the Conde de Canavial who, impressed by the work of Pasteur, invented a new method which he put into operation in 1889 and which briefly found favour. The idea was to raise the temperature of the wine rapidly to pasteurizing heat – as high as 80°C – by passing it through a sort of *bain marie*, and then to let it cool slowly in sealed containers, out of contact with the air. This killed off bacteria and any remaining ferments, and preserved the balsamic qualities of the wine without risk of the baked, over-oxidized characteristics imparted by conventional *estufas*.[34] The disadvantage of pasteurization is that it makes the wine into an inert substance, incapable of further development, and is therefore unsuitable for a wine intended for even a brief period of evolution. The enthusiasm for pasteurizing madeira soon passed. It was followed by the development of *cubas de calor*, vats at first made of wood, and then of concrete, that were heated by means of internal spiral tubes containing hot water. By varying the heat of the water the temperature of the wine could be controlled. Technically, the early *cubas de calor* were undoubtedly an improvement, though not all the problems associated with *estufagem* were removed. Such *cubas* are still used by many shippers, but those with the most modern technology have *estufas* made of stainless steel. These are well insulated and are heated by means of tubes of water around their exterior. Inside, they have an expansion space and they can be hermetically sealed.

I cannot leave the subject of *estufas* without repeating a delightfully zany story which first appears in White [1841], is later repeated by Wortley [1854], and casts a new light on the notion of fraudulent wines. Speaking of the wines which, after *estufagem*, take on a 'dry and smoky flavour, which can never be entirely eradicated', White tells us that 'this class of wines is shipped annually, in large quantities, to Hamburg, where it undergoes a process which changes its character to that of Hock, under which name a large portion of it finds its way into the English market'.[35] The mind boggles at the idea. Is it possible, perhaps, that Mr White got his story a little mixed up – or could the Germans really have been so fiendishly clever?

In the last century, as now, the vast majority of the production was of generic madeira, with a base of Verdelho and Tinta Negra

Mole, but according to several writers, frequently containing Boal, Bastardo and Terrantez. Whereas generic madeira had, at the start of the nineteenth century, been marketed as a wine of a particular vintage, after phylloxera it was 'nearly always a blended wine, and very seldom a vintage wine, the main object of the merchant being to keep up continuously, as far as possible, the same character and type in the different qualities'.[36] It was mostly fermented dry, and sweetening was added as required to cheaper blends after fermentation by using a variety of additives, as explained later in this book.[37] According to Thudichum and Dupré [1872], better wine had to be kept for ten years in wood, followed by ten years in bottle, to be at its best.

Malvazia continued to be made in minute quantities, and apparently in different types and qualities. The best quality remained that made from Malvasia Cândida, and the Fajã dos Padres is continually cited as its *locus classicus*. Inferior kinds were made from Malvasia Babosa and Malvasia Roxa, and a generic Malvazia 'requiring burnt sugar, &c. to give it a sweeter flavour' was also produced.[38] Even a Green Malmsey, 'bearing some resemblance to Frontignan', is mentioned.[39] In 1825 we hear for the first time of the fermentation of Malvazia being 'checked earlier than that of other wines, to increase its sweetness'.[40] At the start of the century, Sercial, with a production limited to less than 50 pipes a year,[41] emerged as the real connoisseur's wine. Boal was equally scarce and expensive, but seemed to some commentators not to merit the cost. Terrantez was 'held in some estimation when old'.[42] By the middle of the century there was a fairly large selection of single-variety wines.[43] Tinta, as a wine, seems to have remained a comparative (and costly) rarity. Although originally the name for a white wine tinted with the juice of red grapes, it subsequently became an unfortified beverage wine made from Tinta Negra Mole. It was said to be at its best from two to three years old; thereafter it lost colour, and after twenty years tasted like any other madeira. This kind of Tinta continued to be made long after it became standard practice to fortify other sorts of madeira, but eventually, after *oïdium*, it was treated like the others. Several writers say that not much was made because of the limited foreign demand for it.[44] It is quite difficult to imagine what unfortified Tinta was like. Universally described as astringent, it was suggested by some that, when young, it was like burgundy, and by others that it was like Hermitage; that it made an acceptable substitute for port (the importation of which was forbidden) for the British in Funchal; and that it was good for making sangria! Johnson [1885] warns the reader to distinguish Tinta, made from Negra Mole, from Tinto, the name for any common red wine – which, according to Thudichum and Dupré [1872], was deficient both in quality and quantity.

Vinho palhete is what the Portuguese call Rainwater; it was made from Verdelho clarified with charcoal, which 'destroys the rich colour, and in a great measure destroys the body and fine flavour of the wine'.[45] From time to time a number of curiosities were produced: Negrinha, a rich red wine or cordial made from Maroto grapes dried in the sun on the roofs of houses;[46] Nun's Wine, a commercialized *vinho surdo*;[47] Vizetelly mentions White Madeira, a Verdelho with 4 per cent added alcohol, shipped under that name to Russia.[48] Towards the end of the century *vinho quinado* was developed mainly for the Portuguese African colonies, and this remained in production until just after World War Two.[49] Finally, something called *vinho verde* (literally 'green wine'), also called 'refuse wine', was produced from unripe grapes and those of inferior varieties.[50] Most was doubtless distilled into brandy.

Inevitably, during the wine plagues the quality of madeira must have been even more variable than usual. In 1882 João da Camara Leme spoke openly of 'all the artificial wines made on this island in imitation of madeira wine'.[51] The making of madeira from ungrafted American vines, or 'direct producers' as they are called locally, must have become increasingly widespread. Desperate situations breed desperate solutions. And so a tradition of making madeira from direct producers, which lasted until the entry of Portugal into the EU, became established. It was, without doubt, the least desirable development in wine-making of the entire nineteenth century.

6

The Twentieth Century

Changing markets and the German 'threat'

The nineteenth century in Madeira was a period of drama and despair. By comparison, the history of the twentieth century has been prosaic but finally, in my view, gives grounds for optimism. Exports up to World War One rose to over 7,000 pipes a year, and at first remained buoyant, despite events: in 1916, with a striking 11,375 pipes, they exceeded 10,000 pipes for the first time since 1825.[1] During this period, however, the price of madeira slowly fell, and markets during the first two decades of the century changed radically. Although Britain had remained a principal market up until the end of the century, the popularity of madeira there began to decline. Imports, which had averaged 2,204 pipes between 1884 and 1893, dipped to 1,650 pipes between 1894 and 1903 and, at 810 pipes, reached less than half that figure between 1904 and 1913.[2] Russia's imports at the opening of the century were only marginally higher, and they were to cease abruptly in 1917 with the Revolution – as reflected in the total export figure for that year of 3,035 pipes, the lowest since the start of the century. The beginning of prohibition in 1920 meant that the American market was lost until 1934, by which time the era of cocktails had arrived and thoughts of madeira were a thing of the past. On the other hand, France and Germany became growing markets. From an annual average of 1,017 pipes during the period 1884–93, exports to France increased slightly to 1,472 pipes during the period 1904–13. But it was the German market which showed the most spectacular growth: from an annual average of 578 pipes in the first period, exports doubled to 1,161 pipes during the period 1894–1903, and almost doubled again to an average of 2,109 pipes in the period leading up to the war. This was more than two and a half times the quantity being taken by Britain, and was accompanied by a growing German interest in Madeira.

This interest had been growing throughout the 1880s and 1890s. Germans had effectively taken over the burgeoning embroidery industry, German shipping had taken an ever greater share of freight and the number of German tourists had also been rising. Considerable efforts were made to establish a commercial footing on the island, with hotels to rival Reid's and even a German wine company. Customs concessions and various monopolies threatening British interests (including the expropriation of British property such as Reid's Hotel) were agreed to in return for piping water from the mountains to the edge of Funchal. The Funchalese authorities supported the German initiative, and traditional anti-British feeling quickly turned into popular enthusiasm for all things German. What had threatened to escalate into a diplomatic incident ended in farce. The Portuguese withdrew the concessions when the scheme was revealed as cover for a fraudulent plan to open gambling casinos (then illegal in Madeira) and make Funchal into a sort of Monte Carlo. The joke was that although William Reid had protested loudly that competition from casinos would completely ruin his hotel business, he had himself hired out the Quinta Pavão, which he had purchased to test the expropriation threat, to a gambling syndicate.[3]

In spite of everything, a treaty between Germany and Portugal was signed in 1910, but those German business enterprises which remained in Madeira disappeared in 1916, when Portugal joined the allies in World War One and German property was confiscated. (The low exports of wine in 1917 and 1918 were largely due to the threat of German submarines.) The reputation of the British suffered further. Had not the defence of their commercial interests deprived Funchal of a free water supply? A leaflet referring to the 'Usurpers of Madeira', which was sent to all British firms in October 1911, threatened to blow up their buildings. It turned out to be a hoax, but is nonetheless indicative of popular sentiment.[4] During the war, when the poverty of the masses once more increased, many of the British were once more perceived as indifferent. For example, in 1916 – when wine exports were the highest for over ninety years – the British Foreign Secretary received the following report from a resident, himself British: 'It sounds queer for Mr Blandy to say that the mail and other boats not calling makes no difference to the prosperity of the island. The poor boatmen and coalmen are starving, there is no wickerwork being exported or embroidery . . . the poverty is terrible, soup kitchens cannot keep up with the needs of the hungry.'[5] The struggle against hunger remained a stark reality for many of the population during the first half of the century, and increases in the prices of flour and bread caused serious rioting in 1921 and 1931.[6]

Developing control of the trade

The twentieth century has seen considerable evolution in the way the production and marketing of Madeira were regulated. A law of 18 September 1908 – in parallel with Oporto, Carcavellos and Setúbal – revoked all previous legislation and introduced more stringent regulations to control the manufacture and sale of madeira. In 1909 a Comissão de Viticultura was set up with the following objectives: to control the entry of wines and spirits into the region; to make a register of the properties producing fortified wine; to compile production statistics for each council area, including where possible the name and address of the recipients of the wine; to issue certificates of origin to growers or shippers who required them. The Commission consisted of two growers from each of five councils in the south, and one from Porto Santo, Machico and three councils in the north. Although in Oporto a *Grémio* (Guild) of exporters was set up to regulate their activities, in Funchal customs officials were made responsible for keeping a register of exporters of madeira, and for listing the quantity and verifying the quality of all existing stocks of madeira in growers' and shippers' hands. The plantation of new vineyards was suspended for six months to allow another commission to investigate what future controls would be desirable. New experimental stations were authorized. A further thirty-six articles covered miscellaneous points. The regulations as applied to Madeira were promulgated on 11 March 1909. Although much transformed by the passage of time, these regulations have remained the basis for the control of the trade throughout the century.[7]

It must have been a heart-stopping moment when, in 1912, another vine plague made its appearance on the island: mildew (*Plasmopara viticola*). Although this caused damage enough, the remedy was at hand. Downy mildew (to distinguish it from *oïdium*, or powdery mildew) had wrought havoc throughout French vineyards as early as 1882, and a cure in the form of the copper sulphate-based spray called Bordeaux Mixture was already available.

A charter for the madeira wine industry was proposed in November 1913 but not approved; this was followed by another charter in 1915, which met with universal opposition but was nevertheless imposed. Finally, in January 1924 the Ministry of Agriculture set up a commission to advise on what alterations should be made to the 1913 charter to establish the most rigorous control of wine and avoidance of adulterations.[8] This had become necessary because, although the foreign competition from false madeiras had virtually ceased, the poor quality of madeiras made from ungrafted American stock was again undermining the wine's reputation. These vines, with their good colour, high productivity and comparatively easier maintenance, were continuing to replace traditional vines.[9] According to Noël Cossart, only 20 per cent of the vintage came from grafted European vines.[10]

In 1900 the Associação Vinícola da Madeira was founded, with an annual council subsidy of 100 milréis. It was the realization of a project first conceived in 1774, but sadly it did not last long. On 12 July 1909, prompted by the continuing drop in the price of madeira on the international market, there was a meeting to discuss the founding of another wine association or even of a commercial wine company. Despite the good will of many proprietors nothing came of this either.[11] In 1913, however, a different sort of wine association did come into being, and this profoundly influenced the subsequent history of the trade.

On 9 August 1913 Wm. Hinton & Sons joined with Welsh and Cunha – itself the amalgamation of two nineteenth-century companies – and Henriques, Camara & Cia. These were reconstituted as a new limited company called the Madeira Wine Association. This was the prelude to a complicated series of amalgamations which continued intermittently for the next twenty-seven years, during which all the British firms and many of the Portuguese firms joined forces – to a total of twenty-eight exporting companies – under the umbrella of the Madeira Wine Association, which was eventually to become the dominant commercial force in the wine trade. No further changes took place, however, during the next twelve years.

The inter-war years

Immediately after World War One, in 1919, a new export record of just short of 20,000 pipes was established, but this heady total was not to be maintained or ever again matched. It may have reflected the general lack of wine resulting from the war, but it is worth noting that Sweden alone imported 7,734 pipes – 38.7 per cent of the total. After a couple of lean years, reminiscent of the latter stages of the war, export levels climbed to over 11,000 pipes a year in 1923 and apart from dipping in 1926 and 1927, oscillated between this figure and 9,500 pipes a year until 1931.[12] Prices also increased sharply during the decade. It is perhaps remarkable that exports performed so well, given the loss of the Russian and American markets and the depletion of the important German market. However, Sweden and Denmark, which had imported only a little madeira just before the war, became the nucleus of the emerging Scandinavian market, which continued to grow steadily up until the outbreak of World War Two. The French and British markets remained steady, with small oscillations.[13]

On 17 June 1925 a new company was founded, the Madeira Wine Association (1925) Limitada. Its shareholders were the original Madeira Wine Association (with its three founding member companies), Blandy Bros & Co, Leacock & Co, and Thomas Mullins. Mullins was not himself a shipper, but became the efficient and highly respected manager of the new company, of which he was a shareholder. No further changes took place until 1934, when on 9 May a third company, simply called (like the original company) the Madeira Wine Association Limitada, came into being. This third company, which had a capital of £85,000, resulted from the amalgamation of the companies which made up the second company with Power Drury & Co and a proportion of the shares of T. T. da Câmara Lomelino Lda. Each company joining the Madeira Wine Association maintained a separate legal identity, but became a shareholder in the Association. As each shipping company joined, then and later, it brought with it its business premises, its stocks of wines, etc., which then became the property of the Madeira Wine Association. The companies ceased, however, to have a separate trading identity. Their brands were produced in conformity with established styles, but were blended from the common stocks of the Association by its chief blender. The Association continued to trade under the companies' names through their existing agents, but in organizational terms it was just one big company which maintained the image, for commercial reasons, of being a collection of several separately functioning smaller companies. Only stocks of old wines (vintage and solera), while they lasted, maintained their identity as the wines of the shipper who had brought them into the Association. Subsequently other firms joined the Association, and there were seventeen associates by the end of the decade.[14]

In common with other wine markets, exports of madeira suffered from the slump of the early 1930s, but gradually recovered to their late 1920s level by 1939, only to be struck again rather badly by the outbreak of World War Two.[15] In general terms, the best wines went to Scandinavia and the worst to France.[16]

The period immediately before World War Two saw important changes in the way madeira was marketed. The names by which it had been known – such as 'London Particular' and 'Old East India' – which often reflected the market for which it had been destined, were largely, if not completely, abandoned. They survived longest on the American and Scandinavian markets. Elsewhere they were replaced by branded blends such as Blandy's Duke of Clarence Malmsey,[17] Cossart Gordon's Good Companion Bual and Lomelino's Henry the Navigator Sercial. The use of varietal names for these brands did not, however, mean that the contents of the bottle had been vintaged from them: it simply indicated a wine in the style associated with that variety. Thus Sercial indicated a dry wine, Verdelho a medium dry wine, Boal a medium sweet wine[18] and Malmsey (Malvazia) a sweet wine. This misuse of varietal names, which had started in the late nineteenth century in the wake of phylloxera and the proliferation of ungrafted American vines, now became general. A decrease in the production of the four classic varieties between the wars acted as a catalyst. As Noël Cossart explains: 'At first my company did not agree with the practice of using the names of special growths (grape names) on blends, but in the end we had to go along with the rest. My father's cousin, Sidney Cossart, who was in the London house at the time, would spit with fury when he saw a comparatively modestly-priced madeira labelled Malmsey.'[19] While vintage wines and soleras continued to be what they purported to be, commercial blends for current drinking were almost exclusively made from hybrid vines (for the cheapest end of the market) and from Tinta Negra Mole (for the better blends). By present-day standards of authenticity it was a fraudulent system, but it survived until 1990. It should also be noted that at this time almost all madeira was still exported in cask and bottled at its destination.

In 1933, the year after Salazar became Prime Minister, the Federação dos Viticultores do Centro e Sul de Portugal (Federation of Viticultors of the Centre and South of Portugal) was formed, and in 1937 this was reorganized and renamed the Junta Nacional do Vinho (abbreviated to JNV). It became the official government body controlling the production of wine throughout Portugal, taking over responsibility for the direction of the Grémio of port producers. More revised regulations were published in a law dated 12 October 1939, and in August 1940 the Junta installed a Delegation in Funchal to control wine production in Madeira.

The way in which shippers purchased wine from the growers had been changing throughout the century. After 1922 it had become common to offer different prices for must according to the variety of grape from which it had been made, the traditional varieties quite naturally commanding the highest prices. This was a natural outcome of the preponderance of musts from American varieties, and it effectively marked the end of the north-south division which had governed the purchase of wines for several centuries. Moreover, the system by which the shippers agreed the prices of musts and wines before the vintage (taking account of the size of the vintage, their export requirements and so on) survived until 1938. After this date an effort was made to stabilize prices and the free market came to an end. Tables of minimum prices were fixed by the JNV.

Climbing out of the doldrums

World War Two had a devastating effect on madeira sales, not just during the hostilities but after they had ended. Social habits changed and have continued to change, and fortified wines, although they have had periodic revivals in fashion, have declined sharply in popularity all over the world. Along with port and sherry, madeira has been the relatively helpless victim of this trend. The subsequent history of madeira, one might therefore say, can be expressed either as a fight for survival, or less bleakly as a gradual contraction and rationalization of the trade. During World War Two there were around sixty export firms registered with the

Funchal customs. By 1973, when I first visited the island, that number had shrunk to twenty-three, and in 1997 it was down to nine. What will the total be as the millennium is passed?

At this point it will be useful – and I hope not too confusing – to make the transition, in conformity with current practice, to talking about the volume of exports in hectolitres rather than in pipes. The reader who wishes to translate into equivalents is reminded that there are 218 litres to a pipe. Thus, 2.18 hectolitres equals 1 pipe.

Exports, which had dropped to under 10,000 hectolitres in the first three years of World War Two, began to increase again in 1943, reaching 31,871 hectolitres in 1947. Thereafter they dropped back to former levels until 1951, when they reached 34,471 hectolitres, and then fell below 30,000 hectolitres only three times before climbing to 44,145 hectolitres in 1960.[20] During this period – and indeed until the 1970s – Sweden and Denmark remained the foremost importers of better quality madeira, with Finland an increasingly important market, but France began to increase its imports of bulk wine for cooking to become, in volume terms, the largest foreign market for madeira. Great Britain came after Germany, the fifth market in order of volume, though still a prime customer for fine wines. British imports of madeira, although they grew steadily throughout the 1950s, were only a fraction of what they had been 150 years earlier. By comparison, the United States at this period seldom exceeded half the volume imported by England.

Annual production in the mid-1950s was around 12,000 hectolitres. During the first five years of the decade only 26.1 per cent of the crop, on average, consisted of traditional grape varieties, and by far the greatest part of that would have been Tinta Negra Mole. On 25 June 1957 a new law (No. 41 166) was promulgated to 'provide a more efficacious functioning [of the export of madeira] within the framework of the national economy'. Its aim was to regulate the activities of the shippers, allied to measures designed to improve the quality (and defend the genuineness) of madeira, and to stimulate a return to the growth of the grape varieties on which the excellence of madeira was based. It confirmed or revised many of the regulations which had been established in 1909 and superseded some of those imposed in 1939. Many of its provisions are still in force and are discussed later in this book.[21]

The 1957 law makes reference to wine co-operatives. These, which provided smaller growers with some independence from the landowners and the shippers, now began to make an appearance. There had always been (and still is) co-operation of a good neighbourly kind where the use of *lagars* was concerned, but this now began to take on a commercial aspect. The first regional co-operative was established in Porto Santo in 1955 and started production the following year. Another was built in Câmara de Lobos in 1959 and a third, the Adega Cooperativa do Norte, was started at São Vicente in 1980. Their main function, like that of the *partidistas*, was to keep wine made during productive periods for sale when vintages were small, maintaining the price to their members and a supply to the shippers. But they were not a success. As Eduardo Pereira puts it, 'notwithstanding the convincing advantages from the agrarian, economic and social point of view, these have not yet entered into the minds and experience of viticultors'.[22] None of these co-operatives any longer exists.

During the 1960s exports rose to more than 40,000 hectolitres and remained above this level, usually quite substantially, until 1980, once even breaking through the 50,000 hectolitres barrier with 52,128 hectolitres in 1972.[23] Comparing decade with decade, trade was therefore, in volume terms, at its best since the start of the century. Yet it has to be said that most of these exports were of bulk wine, mainly destined for cooking and of a very poor quality. The proportion of fine wine sales was lamentably small. Standards of viticulture and vinification were still quite primitive, having changed little during the century. Living standards for the vast majority were very low. Oddly, as exports increased production went down. This was because some growers, mainly the smaller tenants, were being increasing attracted to bananas as an alternative crop. The advantages of bananas were that they offered a year-round income, needed little maintenance and were less subject to the vagaries of the weather. For many these remain persuasive advantages. Many of the conversions of vineyards to bananas took place in the south, particularly in the Câmara de Lobos area, where the best varieties were grown. By 1970 it was clear that this trend could produce a long-term shortage of wine, and in 1972 the government introduced subsidies to encourage growers to regraft their vineyards with the so-called classical varieties. The scheme was a modest success, and between 1973 and 1983 more than 1,125,500 vines were regrafted free of charge. As a result the production of the classical varieties had increased by almost 150 per cent by 1980.[24]

Modern times

The most significant event of the 1970s for Madeira was of course the Revolution in 1974, which brought the old fascist dictatorship to an end and re-established democracy. Not only did the Revolution lead to constitutional and social change, it hastened the modernization of the island. It also brought about change in wine terms, not all of it wholly desirable.

Shortly after the Revolution the government approved a system of land enfranchisement whereby tenants under the *contrato de colonia* system could purchase the freehold of their land. Many were of course in no position to do so, but those who did soon discovered that they could make a fast profit by reselling the land for non-agricultural purposes. Anyone who knew the island before the Revolution and who visited the south now would be astonished at the housing development, partly due to returning emigrants, that has taken place in the last quarter-century. This, coupled with the rapid development of an infrastructure, the road-building, and the light industrialization which has come about as a result of Portugal's entry into the EU, has particularly affected classic vineyard areas such as São Martinho, to the west of Funchal, Câmara de Lobos, and large tracts of land on the south of the island where, it used to be considered, the best wine was produced. Over the years, land enfranchisement and the effects of joining the EU, whatever their social benefits, have resulted in a grievous loss of prime vineyard land.

On 6 April 1979 the Delegation of the Junta Nacional do Vinho was abolished. In its place was put a new controlling body called the Instituto do Vinho da Madeira (Madeira Wine Institute), with wide-ranging responsibilities for the production on the island of wines and other alcoholic products, their marketing and export, and the import into Madeira of similar products. Since then, the Institute has directly regulated all aspects of the madeira industry except the vineyards, which are the responsibility of a collateral branch of government, the Direcção Regional da Agricultura (Regional Directorate of Agriculture). The latter discharges its responsibilities through a sub-department of its Direcção de Serviços de Produção Agrícola (Directorate of Agricultural Production Services) called the Divisão de Viticultura (Viticultural Division).[25] The regulations currently imposed by the IVM (the common abbreviated form of the Instituto's name) will be dealt with later in the book.[26] The IVM, of course, played a major part in the tricky discussions on wine matters that preceded Portugal's entry into the EU in 1986. In some cases it has voluntarily embraced or even extended EU norms – such as the rule that when a label mentions a varietal name, the wine must contain at least 85 per cent wine from that variety,[27] which was implemented on 1 January 1993 after a seven-year transition period. In 1988 the IVM, as a mark of the industry's increasing self-respect, inaugurated a trade guild, the Confraria do Vinho da Madeira.

In the 1980s exports suffered a sharp drop. This was mainly due to the fact that in 1980, under pressure from the EU, the IVM banned the use of direct producers in the making of madeira. The immediate result was a 30.5 per cent fall in the volume of exports. However, figures for the period up to the present have at least levelled off, never having dropped below 30,000 hectolitres, and averaging an annual 33,371 hectolitres during the 1980s and 32,009 hectolitres for the first six years of the present decade – not spectacular, but healthily steady. Table 2 of Appendix 4 shows the structure of the export market between 1980 and 1995, and it is evident that although volumes have remained constant, the make-up of the market has changed quite significantly. At the beginning of the period 88.74 per cent of exports were in bulk, whereas fifteen years later that figure has dropped to 68.35 per cent. This is a clear indication of efforts to raise quality standards, but progress has been lamentably slow. France has remained the most important market in volume terms, but mainly for bulk wine of rather poor quality. Germany has maintained second place, and Britain has mostly been in third place, with an ever-increasing proportion of higher quality bottled wine. Denmark and Sweden, still important customers, have moved down the league a little, but Japan has become the second most important customer for bottled wine. The USA, another big market for bottled wine, slipped in the early 1990s but is now back where it was in the early 1980s. Switzerland is now a much smaller customer, but still a significant one. Spain's 1990 imports are an unrepresentative rogue figure, which caused Switzerland to drop out of the top ten. In 1995 Spain imported a derisory 9 hectolitres.

Totals of must production are also revealing. The following figures include the (virtually negligible) production from Porto Santo.

Of the twenty-five harvests up to 1995, the largest vintage was in 1986, with 137,819 hectolitres, and the smallest was in 1994, with 52,866 hectolitres. Eleven harvests had yields in excess of 100,000 hectolitres, of which seven were in excess of 110,000 hectolitres. Only six yielded less than 70,000 hectolitres. Table 1 of Appendix 4 shows production figures at five-yearly intervals from 1980 (a particularly abundant vintage) to 1995. It will be seen that, while in 1980 32.8 per cent of total production was of European varieties and 67.2 per cent was from direct producers, by 1995 the balance had turned round, with 54 per cent from European varieties and 46 per cent from direct producers. There has therefore been some increase in the proportion of European varieties. Although in 1992 a wine writer recorded the fond hope that the direct producers might be eliminated by 1997,[28] at the present rate of progress this could take another thirty years. It is also interesting to note that during the same period the number of farmers diminished from 3,916 in 1980 to 2,284 in 1995.

The statistics provided by the IVM from 1990 onwards give a further breakdown of the totals for the production of the European varieties, with sub-totals for the classical varieties. In 1990 there were only 2,791 hectolitres of classical varieties (6.9 per cent of all European varieties and 3.6 per cent of total production); and in 1995 there were only 2,817 hectolitres of classic varieties (8.6 per cent of all European varieties and 4.6 per cent of total production). The balance of the European varieties production would have been almost entirely of Tinta Negra Mole. Although these figures also show a welcome increase, it is a pitifully small one.

Portugal's entry into the EU has brought substantial benefits to the madeira industry in the form of subsidies, and the larger shippers have not been slow to take advantage of them. Details of what they have brought about will be given later in the book. Increasing modernization of the madeira industry is very much in the air. It is possible that in time to come – as everyone who enjoys the wine must fervently hope – the 1990s will be seen not just as the end of a rather static century in the history of madeira, but as a turning point in the revival of its fortunes.

PART II
Viticulture and the Wine

7

The Soil and the Grapes

The soil

The soil in Madeira is of volcanic origin, consisting mainly of basalt, trachytes and trachydolerites, tufa, scoria (clinker) and conglomerates. Over time, the volcanic rock disintegrates under the erosion of sun and rain and produces a variety of soils. In general terms, these soils are clayey, acid, rich in organic material, magnesium and iron, poor in potassium and adequate in phosphorus.

Basalt predominates at lower altitudes, and is the origin of more or less clayey dark or reddish-brown soils. Trachytes are grey or dark-grey rocks found above 300 metres. Trachydolerites are lighter coloured and are found at very high altitudes. Tufa is solidified volcanic mud and occurs in two forms: *pedra mole*, which is yellow, and *cantaria de forno*, which is red. They have a variable composition. Scoria is solidified cellular lava, dark (sometimes purple) in colour, and porous in texture. Conglomerates are formed from basalt and tufa detritus.

From these basic geological types are derived various mixtures of soil, which have been classified into sub-types using regional names:

Massapez	heavy clayey earth that does not drain water and cracks when dry
Salã	a reddish clay similar to *Massapez*
Terra Grossa	a heavy mixture of clay and grit
Pedra Mole	a mixture of yellow clay and grit
Meia Terra	a red and yellow medium soil.
Poeira	a fine, dusty red and yellow soil found in the highest, coldest areas
Delgada	a very gritty soil, rich in organic material

Solta	a mixture of white clay and grit, rich in organic matter
Areão	sandy soil

The best soils are gravelly (*saibro*) or positively stony (*cascalho*). Those derived from red tufa (*cantaria de forno*) are preferred, especially when they have a stony admixture of basaltic rock. *Pedra Mole* and *Massapez* are the least suitable for growing vines. As in the Douro, vines do best in what seem to the layman to be the least propitious circumstances, and in these soils they are too prolific, producing grapes with inferior sugar levels, and they age prematurely. On the other hand, when such soils contain an appreciable quantity of organic matter and small stones to facilitate drainage, their disadvantages are considerably lessened.

In general, vines are grown in *Salão* and *Terra Grossa* in the north and *Terra Grossa*, *Delgada* and *Solta* in the south. However, the widespread use of man-made terraces, which after construction had to be furnished with soil brought from various other locations, has frequently resulted in random mixtures of soil types. It is therefore not uncommon to find several types of soil within relatively small areas and within a single vineyard. This said, very large areas of the island provide soils which are suitable for viticulture. There is no particular soil type which is more suitable for one variety of vine than another.

The grapes of Madeira

It would give a rather misleading picture of Madeiran viticulture to concentrate solely on those varieties used in the production of fortified wine: that is, the traditional varieties and the all-purpose workhorse grape, the Tinta Negra Mole. Astonishingly, just under half the grape production on the island – around 46 per cent – is of varieties which do not find their way into fortified wine at all.

Those which do go to make fortified wine all belong to the genus *Vitis vinifera*; that is to say, the traditional European vine varieties whose roots are vulnerable to attack by the louse *phylloxera vastatrix*. To counter this problem, it has been normal since the widespread phylloxera devastation of European vineyards in the second half of the nineteenth century to graft *Vitis vinifera* on to phylloxera-resistant American root stock. Various vines, consisting of *Vitis labrusca*, *Vitis riparia* and certain hybrids derived from them, were used in Madeira for this purpose in the nineteenth century. However, as also happened in other countries, these vines were used not just to provide root stock for grafting purposes but were themselves extensively planted. They are slowly being eliminated.[1] In Madeira these American vines and hybrids are known as 'direct producers', which terminology I shall also use.

Direct producers, although preponderant, are not now permitted to be used for the production of the fortified wine, although they were extensively employed for this purpose from the end of the nineteenth century until relatively recently. From the point of view of madeira production, they are therefore no longer directly relevant. They are used in fact to make a rustic table wine called *vinho seco* for local consumption.[2] After 1998, however, it will be illegal to sell this wine, and it will be available only for domestic consumption. From the point of view of the island's viticulture and economy, therefore, direct producers occupy an embarrassingly large amount of the available vineyard space.

Having made this point, there is no need to dwell on it. Although I shall briefly include direct producers in my survey of the grape varieties to be found in Madeira, it is those which are currently used in the production of fortified madeira that are of more immediate concern.

Vitis vinifera

The four classical and best-known types of madeira (Rainwater and East India apart) are named after the grape varieties from which they are made: Sercial, Verdelho, Boal and Malvazia, all in current production. A further three types, relatively uncommon and therefore not so well known, have also been used traditionally to make single-variety madeira. Terrantez, always very scarce, is still seen from time to time, whilst Bastardo and Moscatel, known mainly from old vintages, are hardly ever made nowadays and are to be considered almost as curiosities.

Tinta (made from one or other of the *tinto* varieties) used to be produced, and old bottles of it surface occasionally; but although Tinta Negra Mole is the variety from which by far the greatest amount of madeira is produced today, it cannot at present be sold legally under its own name. Tinta can therefore only be considered as a type of madeira in a strictly historical sense. However, a number of small producers continue to make Tinta for their private use.

The official classification of grape varieties recognized as suitable for making madeira used to be divided into three categories: 'Noble', 'Good' and 'Authorized'.[3] The use of the term 'noble varieties' is officially discouraged nowadays, however, and the phrase 'traditional varieties' to refer to Sercial, Verdelho, Boal, Malvazia, Terrantez and Bastardo has been substituted. Even so, this phrase is not used in the present official classification, which is divided into two categories – 'Recommended' and 'Authorized' – each of which is further sub-divided into white and black grapes.

RECOMMENDED VARIETIES

White Boal, *Malvasia Cândida, Sercial, Terrantez, Verdelho Branco*
Black *Bastardo, Malvasia Roxa, Tinta da Madeira, Tinta Negra Mole*
   and *Verdelho Tinto*

AUTHORIZED VARIETIES

White *Caracol, Carão de Moça, Listrão, Malvasia Babosa, Malvasia Fina,*
   Moscatel de Málaga, Rio Grande, Valveirinha
Black *Complexa, Deliciosa, Tinto Negro* and *Triunfo*

Several rather surprising things must be noted about these lists. In the first place, since there is no *cadastro* – that is, no register of island vineyards and the varieties which they contain – it is impossible, once you go beyond the six mentioned at the beginning of this chapter and Tinta Negra Mole, to be sure whether several of the other varieties are still being grown in Madeira and, if so, where. Of the recommended varieties one, Verdelho Tinto, appears to be completely extinct on the island; another, Tinta da Madeira, is not represented in the government's experimental vineyards, but may still exist somewhere on the island; and a third, Malvasia Roxa, although represented in the experimental vineyards, is certainly not commonly found.

When we turn to the authorized varieties, the situation is no less extraordinary: apart from Complexa they are virtually insignificant, and the total amount of authorized grapes used for making wine is probably less than 0.5 per cent of the total production. One of them, Valveirinha, appears to be totally extinct. Caracol, Listrão and several types of Moscatel exist in small quantities on the island, but are almost exclusively used for the table. Of the others, Carão de Moça, Malvasia Babosa and Malvasia Fina are known to exist for certain only in the government's own experimental vineyards! Doubtless some exist elsewhere on the island, but I have found no one able to say for certain where, let alone how extensively. Deliciosa and Rio Grande are said by the Serviços de Produção Agrícola to 'occupy areas of some significance'[4] which nevertheless remain unquantified. Portalegre is placed in the same category, but is not an authorized variety. Conversely, there appear to be small quantities of Tinto Negro and Triunfo on the island, but not in the government's experimental vineyards. It is odd that the official list of varieties should appear, in these cases, so out of touch with the situation on the ground.

Secondly, of the many varieties now neither recommended nor authorized whose cultivation has been reported in the past, very few can still be found. In most if not all cases, mention of these names nowadays mostly produces a shrug of the shoulders and a blank look. Very few seem to have survived.[5] The following is a list (in alphabetical order) of the grape varieties – excluding those on the current officially authorized or recommended lists mentioned above – which are mentioned in writings up until the 1920s. Those marked with an asterisk are to be found in Viala and Vermorel's vast seven-volume *Ampélographie*, published in Paris between 1901 and 1910. This was certainly the most authoritative world-wide survey of grape varieties of its day, and in certain respects has never been surpassed. Comments opposite each variety indicate what little I have been able to discover about its identity, and the likelihood, according to the Serviços de Produção Agrícola and other Madeiran viticultors whom I consulted, of its still existing in Madeira. Judging from information in the *Elucidário Madeirense*, some now-extinct varieties appear to have survived longer in Porto Santo than in Madeira.[6]

Alicante Branco[*]	Table grape; probably extinct in Madeira
Alicante Preto[*]	Table grape. Synonym: Ferral
Arinto	Introduced after *oïdium*; now only in government experimental fields
Bagonal[*]	Probable synonym: Boal
Barrete de Clerigo	Synonym: Barrete de Padre
Barrete de Padre[*]	Probably extinct in Madeira
Barrete de Frade	Porto Santo synonym of above
Bastardo Preto	Still exists; very limited

Boal de Cheiro	Possible synonym: Maroto
Boalerdo Branco	A form of Boal?
Branquinho	Unrecognized
Bringo	Unrecognized
Cachudo*	An inferior form of Boal; probably extinct in Madeira. Synonym: Babosa
Cadel	Synonym: Malvasia Cândida
Carão de Dama	Synonym: Bastardo Branco
Castelão*	A Tinto variety; probably extinct in Madeira
Casuda*	Synonym: Casculho. Extinct in Madeira
Chasselas*	Probably extinct in Madeira
Corintho*	Extinct in Madeira
Dedo de Dama*	Possible synonym: Ferral
Fernão Pires*	Probably extinct in Madeira
Ferral*	Still exists; very limited
Gancheira	Unrecognized
Great Muscadine	Probably a synonym for Malvasia Cândida
Lestrong Galija	An anglicized form of Listrão?
Malvasião	Synonym: Malvasia Babosa
Maroto	A poor Tinto variety. Synonym: Negro. See also under Boal de Cheiro
Maroto Branco*	Extinct in Madeira
Moscatel Tinto	Synonyms: Ferral, Alicante Preto
Negrete	A Tinto variety; probably extinct in Madeira
Negrinha / Negrinho*	A Tinto variety. Possible synonym for Maroto or perhaps Castelão
Negrinho de Água de Mel	A form of Negrinho?
Negro	Synonym: Maroto
Palomino	Extinct in Madeira
Pergola	Unrecognized
Peringó*	Extinct in Madeira
Sabba	Unrecognized
Serilha	Unrecognized
Simão	Unrecognized white variety
Terrantez Tinto	Extinct in Madeira; mainly a table grape
Tinta de Bago Pequeno	Synonym: Negrinha
Tinta de Lisboa*	A little still exists on the island
Tinta do Padre António	Introduced after *oïdium*; probably extinct in Madeira
Tinta do Porto Santo	May still exist in Madeira
Tinta Molar	May still exist in Porto Santo
Vermejolho	A type of Malvazia with thick-skinned grapes; probably extinct in Madeira

This list must of course be subject to revision when a *cadastro* is eventually compiled.

There is one significant variety, however, which appears on neither the recommended nor authorized list but which is at present tolerated (though the IVM insists only provisionally) for sweet madeira. This is the so-called *Malvasia de São Jorge*, a white variety with a large production at Santana on the north coast and so baptized by the local farmers. It is not to be confused with Malvasia Cândida. Although not officially recognized, it is the most extensively used variety for making Malvazia. The official position of the IVM is that it has referred this variety to the Serviços de Produção Agrícola for analysis and comment, and will not rule on its status before receiving the official report. Were the report to result in a negative ruling, however, Malvazia would come close to disappearing altogether – so my guess is that for political reasons, even if for no others, it will have to become a recommended variety.

Thirdly, there appear to be inconsistencies in the official policy of limiting the production of single-variety madeiras to the grapes on the authorized list, even accepting that Tinta Negra Mole is an exception. A number of vintage Moscatels are currently obtainable on the island, and have *selos de garantia*. When I drew this to the attention of the IVM, I was given a non-committal answer: the question has not arisen recently because no Moscatels have recently been submitted for approval. Apart from this, a fortified Listrão is currently on sale by one of the shippers although the variety is merely authorized.

The recommended varieties

Before engaging in a detailed consideration of each variety, we must say something about the average sugar content of Madeiran grapes, which is notoriously low. This is the consequence of several factors, amongst which two may be singled out. As we have repeatedly seen in the historical part of this book, the north of the island is climatically unsuited to producing grapes with the same maturity as the south of the island, the difference between them being as much as 1.5° Baumé. And secondly, anticipating slightly, the tradition has been for most firms to pay a flat rate when purchasing grapes, thereby reducing the incentive for farmers to achieve maximum ripening. The figures given below for the range of potential alcohol of each variety have been supplied by the MWC. They differ markedly, however, from the official figures for *average* potential alcohol supplied by the Divisão de Viticultura of the Serviços de Produção Agrícola, which must also be considered an authoritative source.[7] I have chosen to rely on the former, but for completeness and comparison have shown the official average figures in square brackets after the MWC's figures.

Malvasia Cândida is, for historical reasons, *the* classical grape variety on Madeira, having been cultivated there since the fifteenth century. Of Greek origin, this variety, though it makes the most famous madeira of all, has never been as extensively cultivated as its celebrity might suggest. Like Terrantez, it almost became extinct. An official report in 1944 states that Malvasia Cândida 'has almost completely disappeared, one or another farmer keeping only a few as a relic of a past era'.[8] According to Cossart, the 1920 Malvazia was the last vintage to be made from the Cândida variety. Malvasia Cândida is particularly sensitive to situation and climate. It thrives only at very low altitudes (not more than 150–200 metres above sea level) and in microclimates which provide sunny, sheltered locations to protect it from dampness and mildew, to which it is particularly prone. Given a good habitat, it is reasonably prolific. The grapes are picked when they are beginning to shrivel, and have a sugar content in the range 10° to 13° [giving an average potential alcohol of 10.5°]. The best Malvasia, grown almost exclusively on the south of the island, currently comes from Jardim do Mar. The Fajã dos Padres, the *locus classicus* of Malvasia on the island, has a tiny private production. At one time, according to Cossart, Malvasia was fermented on the skins with some of its leaves,[9] but not only is this apparently no longer done, I could not find a wine-maker who had ever heard of such a thing.

Boal, a relatively uncommon variety, grows at fairly low altitudes (100 to 300 metres) on the south of the island, and at present the best seems to come from Campanário and Calheta. It is a sturdier vine than Malvasia and is relatively low-yielding. It produces dense and compact fist-sized bunches of rather small, sweet grapes with a sugar content in the range 11° to 13° [but an average potential alcohol which is, perplexingly, officially rated as low as 9°]. It also makes a good table grape.

Verdelho in Madeira is different from Verdelho Branco or

Gouveio, the variety of Verdelho found in mainland Portugal, but is the same variety as that found in the Azores. Verdelho was the commonest variety until phylloxera, at which time it is estimated that two-thirds of the island's vines were Verdelho, but now has the smallest production amongst the classical varieties. It was not regarded as anything more than a good variety until early this century, when it was elevated to classical status. Verdelho now grows mainly on the north of the island, where it is suited to the harsher climatic conditions. It responds better to being grown in vineyards whose vines are close to the ground than to being trained over trellises, and prefers well-drained soils. It thrives at up to 400 metres, close to the sea. The best Verdelho is currently said to come from Ponta Delgada and São Vicente. Picked during the middle of the harvest and highly acid, Verdelho gives musts with a sugar content in the range 10° to 12° [giving an average potential alcohol of 10.5°].

Sercial, as it is known in Madeira – very occasionally spelt *cerceal* – is the same variety as the Portuguese mainland's *Esganocão* or 'dog strangler', so called because of its mouth-puckering, astringent acidity. For a long time it was said to be related to the German Riesling, with which it actually has no connection at all. It can grow at the highest altitudes (from 600 to 700 metres) – which makes it, with Malvasia (but for different reasons), one of the last varieties to be harvested – but on the north it grows along the coast at 150–200 metres. Sercial has the reputation of being difficult to grow and thrives in only a limited number of island sites on both the north and south coasts – Porto Moniz and Seixal are reputed the best – and Jardim da Serra at Estreito de Câmara de Lobos is its *locus classicus*. Prolific in the right habitat, it is resistant to mildew and *oïdium*. Sercial provides extremely acidic musts which, in general, never exceed 11° sugar [and have an officially rated average 10.5° potential alcohol].

Terrantez, which has a black variant *Terrantez Tinto*, is first recorded in Madeira in the eighteenth century.[10] We know, however, that it was widely cultivated at Lamego in the Douro region of mainland Portugal as early as 1531,[11] so it may well have arrived in Madeira earlier. The grapes are sweet and the sugar content fairly high. Terrantez all but died out during the phylloxera blight. In 1921 Silva and Meneses report that it is 'cultivated on Porto Santo, but appears to be extinct or almost extinct on Madeira'.[12] Happily it is still with us and appears, if the increasing number of more recent vintages to be found is any guide, to be gaining ground.

Bastardo is the same variety that is used in the Douro to make port. It appears never to have had any definite preferred growing locale in Madeira, and like Terrantez was almost wiped out by phylloxera. It is now so scarce that very few makers can get a viable amount to vinify. Whenever it does, the MWC vinifies Bastardo with its Tinta Negra Mole. Artur de Barros e Sousa, on the other hand, are perfectionist enough, and small enough, to make it in small quantities. Although its grapes are sweet, the wine is occasionally made in a dry style, and shares to some extent the bitterness characteristic of Terrantez.

Tinta Negra Mole, it is sometimes claimed, was derived originally from crossing Burgundian Pinot Noir with Grenache,[13] but I am informed by the Serviços de Produção Agrícola that this is not so. 'Tinto' wine, as we have seen, is mentioned as far back as 1687, although I have not come across a specific mention of Negra Mole prior to 1801,[14] when we also encounter other Tinto varieties such as Castelão, Maroto and Negrinho. Negra Mole currently provides over 90 per cent of the grapes used in the manufacture of madeira; which means that all the previously discussed varieties *combined* account for less than 10 per cent of total production. Until 1993 it was one of Madeira's best-kept secrets that, amongst the better qualities, most of what was sold under the names of Sercial, Verdelho, Boal and Malvazia was made from Tinta Negra Mole. Nothing has changed since then as far as the wine itself is concerned: it is just that it is now labelled in a more honest way.

One of the reasons for Tinta Negra Mole's dominance is its remarkable versatility – sometimes called chameleon-like – which enables a skilful wine-maker to use it to make madeiras which to some degree mimic the characters of the four classic varieties. Cossart states that Tinta Negra Mole 'is unique in its ability to acquire the characteristics of the different *castas nobres* according to the height at which it is grown'.[15] This appears to imply that a wine-maker wishing to make a Sercial lookalike would have to choose Tinta Negra Mole grown at about 600 metres, whilst if he were aiming for a Malvazia lookalike, he would be looking for Tinta Negra Mole grown at about 200 metres.

There is one element of truth in Cossart's assertion, which is that the sugar content of Tinta Negra Mole will vary somewhat with the altitude at which it is grown, which will govern the amount of sunshine and other climatic factors affecting the ripening of the grapes. So, if such a choice were to be made, it might be quite an apt one – but in practice this choice is never made. Life is too short. The wine-maker is constrained to accept the grapes as they arrive, and there is no question of sorting them into batches according to altitude of growth. Whether the Tinta Negra Mole ends up making a dry Sercial-like style or a rich Malvazia-like style depends wholly upon the skill of the wine-maker. The chameleon-like quality of the variety is, in prosaic fact, a certain neutrality in the kind of wine it produces which accepts, fairly gracefully, the interpretation the wine-maker gives it.

Tinta Negra Mole is grown on the south of the island and at São Vicente. Its leaves turn an intense scarlet with russet patches in autumn, making the vineyards with Tinta Negra Mole easy to identify. Its grapes have thin skins and their softness yields to the touch – hence the name *mole,* meaning 'soft'. Although a red variety, its pulp is always clear. Tinta Negra Mole gives musts which, in general, are not very concentrated, with a potential sugar content in the range 9° to 12°, depending on where they are grown [but an officially rated average potential alcohol of only 9°]. They make good table grapes.

Of the remaining recommended varieties, *Verdelho Tinto* appears to be extinct[16] and *Malvasia Roxa* is at best extremely uncommon, leaving *Tinta da Madeira*, of which a very little appears to be produced for wine. It is very like Tinta Negra Mole. Its grapes are very sweet and have a clear or lightly coloured pulp.

The authorized varieties

With Valveirinha extinct and Carão de Moça, Malvasia Babosa, Malvasia Fina, Rio Grande and Deliciosa known to exist for certain only in the government's experimental vineyards, we are left with just Caracol, Listrão, Complexa, Moscatel (of which there are several varieties), Tinto Negro and Triunfo to account for. Of these, Caracol may perhaps be disregarded because it is now solely produced as a table grape.

Listrão is also a table grape, and in Madeira exclusively so. However, it is extensively grown in Porto Santo where, apart from the table, it is used to make a rather ordinary table wine and, by one shipper, a fortified madeira. It achieves (for Madeira) a remarkably high (over 13°) alcoholic potential.[17]

Moscatel, being familiar as the muscat table grape, probably needs little comment. Its grapes are large, pale green in colour and have a distinctive sweet flavour. Therein lies the main reason why it is virtually no longer made into madeira: it fetches about three times the price of the most expensive wine varieties when sold for the table, and is therefore beyond the wine-maker's economic grasp. It is high in sugar and low in acidity. Most wine-makers think it makes an atypical wine. When old, it has a heavy, rather treacly character – very akin to the style of old Moscatel de Setúbal.

Tinto Negro was reported in 1921 to be found on Porto Santo but no longer in Madeira.[18] I am told by the Serviços de Produção Agrícola, however, that a little is still thought to exist. Its grapes are sweet and have clear or pale violet pulp. Its must yield is high, but of indifferent quality.[19]

Triunfo in Madeira is not the same as the hybrid of Chasselas Musqué and Concord produced in America in 1880, but is a cross between João Santarém and Moscatel de Hamburgo. It produces musts with a potential alcohol of up to 12.8° but low acidity. It is still rather an experimental variety.

Complexa, like Triunfo, was developed by Engineer de Almeida at Oeiras. It is a tetrahybrid of João Santarém with Tintinha and Tintinha with Moscatel de Hamburgo. Neither the Estação Agronómica Nacional nor the Madeira Serviços de Produção Agrícola, however, has been able to provide any ampelographical details of this variety, which apparently has not been studied by the former establishment 'because it is a variety without importance in Portugal'! Complexa produces musts similar to Tinta Negra Mole. It is recommended by the Serviços de Produção Agrícola with moderate enthusiasm, and preferred by one wine-maker to Tinta Negra Mole. About one-fifth the amount of Verdelho – the least grown of the classical varieties – is produced, mainly in Calheta and São Jorge.

Portalegre was introduced from the mainland about thirty years ago, but it is not authorized and little appears to exist. Of the three other non-authorized varieties known still to exist on the island – Bastardo Preto, Ferral and Tinta de Lisboa – not much need be said. In 1921 Bastardo Preto was said to be plentiful on Porto Santo but cultivated in Madeira only at Estreito and Jardim da Serra; Ferral was found in Funchal, Seixal and Ponta Delgada; and Tinta de Lisboa was confined to the surroundings of Funchal and reputed to be poorly esteemed as a wine grape. All three produce good table grapes and are probably currently used exclusively for that purpose.

The direct producers

Most, but not all, of the direct producers were introduced to Madeira following the onset of phylloxera in 1872. In that panic-filled moment any possible remedies had to be tried, and the importation of American varieties was widespread. Some have now more or less disappeared: Black Pearl, Gaston Bazile, Clinton and many others. The most common direct producers remaining are: Isabela (*Vitis labrusca*), the first to be imported and commonly known in Madeira simply as *Americano*; Jacquet, Herbemont and Cunningham, which were introduced much later and are hybrids of the American genus *Vitis aestivalis* with *Vitis vinifera*. There is also some Seibel. Direct producers, although they are no longer used in making fortified wine, account for some 46 per cent of the island's vines, and if for no other reason, demand some attention here.

Isabela – so named (around 1816) after Isabella Gibbs of Brooklyn, New York, in whose garden it was cultivated – is a vine notable for its resistance to *oïdium*, which made it extremely popular in Europe during the first half of the nineteenth century. It was introduced to the island from Africa, probably Algeria, in 1843,[20] eight years before *oïdium* appeared in Madeira. It is prone to mildew and black rot, however, and, not being resistant to phylloxera, was often grafted at the end of the nineteenth century. Despite this, it is planted, and survives, ungrafted in Madeira.

Isabela is the original 'mile-a-minute' vine, with a vigorous growth and rampant habit. Its tendrils can easily smother a living tree, climbing to the top, descending and remounting the same or a neighbouring tree. It requires a lot of water, hence its suitability to the north of the island. Its grapes (and hence the wine) are characterized by what is called a 'foxy' character – which distinguishes all wine made from *Vitis labrusca* grapes – and have a smell very reminiscent of *fraises de bois*. Isabela makes a light, often rather acid, deep *rosé* table wine which is known locally as *vinho americano*. It is not often bottled, but is drawn from cask when required or stored in demijohns, and it is generally used up within the year. Some people find it refreshing; I find it usually has the disagreeable over-acidity which characterizes cheap Beaujolais *nouveau*, although I find the wine's foxiness rather invigorating.

Jacquet (alternatively spelled *Jacquez*) is practically immune to phylloxera and was brought to Madeira for that reason. Its musts are low in quantity, low in acid, fairly high in sugar but lacking in flavour. If well made, and if the low acidity is corrected, Jacquet produces a tolerable, quite alcoholic, if somewhat rustic red wine. It does not age well, however, and although more often bottled than *vinho americano*, tends to be drunk within a year or two. Wine produced from Jacquet and other *Vitis aestivalis* hybrids is known in Madeira as *vinho seco*. There is a white variety of Jacquet, said to be similar in appearance to Terrantez, but I have never had the opportunity of tasting the wine made from it.

Herbemont and *Cunningham* are the two other main red direct producers to be found in Madeira, and they make wine which is similar to, but not as good as, Jacquet. It has been claimed of Herbemont, as of Jacquet, that it had a Madeiran origin. This is not impossible. According to Cossart, a variety known as York Madeira was taken from Madeira to Georgia in 1732,[21] and given the amount of trade between Madeira and the American colonies for two hundred years, the mutual exchange of vine cuttings is by no means impossible, or even improbable.

No statistics exist for the amount of each variety, but red Jacquet appears to be the most extensively planted direct producer, closely followed by Isabela, then by Cunningham and lastly by Herbemont. They proliferate along the north of the island, to which they are suited by reason of their robustness and general resistance to disease. This, which reduces their need for constant nurture, coupled with their productivity, endears them to lazy or absentee farmers.

The grapes from direct producers – indeed, from all American hybrids – have the common identifying feature of containing a substance called malvina (anthocyanin diglucoside), the presence of which can of course be detected by analysis. Such tests are routinely used by the IVM to ensure that wine from direct producers is not used in the making of madeira.[22] The medical effects of malvina have been, and still are, disputed. At one time it was (wrongly) thought that prolonged exposure to malvina could lead to liver disease, and it is sometimes asserted today by Madeirans that it causes mental problems. Whatever the truth of this, under EU regulations musts from direct producers are not permitted in the manufacture of fortified madeira.

Those who remember the trade just after World War Two are not shy about admitting the use of direct producers. While the musts were quite certainly poor compared with those of *Vitis vinifera*, they could give cheaper wines a reasonable structure. Some makers, such as Peter Cossart of Henriques & Henriques, liked them for this reason. Younger members of the trade say that they do not age well; older members tend to disagree. Noël Cossart says of a 1907 Jacquet, bottled in 1926 and tasted in 1967, that 'it was a typical old madeira, although rather a heavy peasant wine'.[23] But, in any case, keeping qualities are irrelevant when it comes to making cheaper wines.

8

The Vineyards

Where are the vineyards?

'The vineyards do not appear so numerous as the stranger would expect.'[1] This is as true today as it was in 1824 when Cyrus Redding visited Madeira. The visitor expecting to see fields of vines like those in continental Europe will be very disappointed. Nothing could be further from the reality. This tiny island has an estimated fourteen thousand[2] plots of ground-growing vines. Although the average area is 1,292 square metres, 94.8 per cent are of less than one hectare and many, which are even smaller than the average British urban back garden, are located in residential areas on the south of the island. The commonest situation is for the family's house to be built on the plot of land which it farms.

Climbing the road from Câmara de Lobos towards Estreito de Câmara de Lobos in the autumn, when the leaves of the Tinta Negra Mole (the predominant variety here) have turned to scarlet and copper brown, gives one a good idea of the disposition of the vines, because at this time of year they can be more easily distinguished from the other major crop, bananas. This is a densely populated area, and the vines seem to jostle with the houses for space. Thus, although vines represent 49 per cent of all the land in Madeira under permanent cultivation, they are scattered around the island in mostly small plots; especially during the summer, because of the all-pervasive greenness of the bananas, they are quite easy to overlook unless you are being particularly observant.

It is often helpful in wine areas to look at the past in order to understand the present. I am therefore going to examine two 'case histories' – both rather sad – which will, I think, illuminate the current vineyard situation.

The Torre Bella estate

The original distribution of land in Madeira, shortly after the discovery of the island in 1420, is described in detail in Chapter 1. The three captains granted land to influential aristocrats and most of these subsequently founded *morgados*, or strict entails, to maintain their wealth. The Torre Bella estate was one such case. Not only is it interesting in relation to the study of the vineyards, it also offers a sidelight on the relationship between British and Portuguese families in the nineteenth century.

The family is descended from João Afonso Correa, a companion of Zarco, who was Prince Henry's treasurer and who acquired a great deal of land. Fernando José Correa Brandão Bettencourt de Noronha Henriques, seventh in line of succession from João Correa, was born in 1768. A diplomat, he was successively Portuguese ambassador to Vienna, Berlin and Naples, where he died in 1821. He was certainly the largest landowner in Madeira in the eighteenth century. Diplomatic life being expensive, however, he decided to sell some of his estates – despite the family motto: 'We never sell, we only buy properties'! He managed to break the entail, and there was a scramble to buy what was being sold off. One property was the Quinta da Achada with its great vineyards at São Martinho, which now belongs to the Blandy family. Another was the Fajã dos Padres. However, as a consequence of his success as a diplomat, he was created Visconde de Torre Bella in 1812.

His son, the second Visconde (1794–1875), died without a male heir, so the estates and title were inherited by his daughter Filomena Gabriela, born in 1839. In 1857 she married Russell Manners Gordon, the grandson of the Thomas Gordon who had arrived in Madeira to become a wine merchant in 1758.[3] He was offered, and accepted, the title of Conde de Torre Bella by the Portuguese king, on condition that he changed from English to Portuguese nationality. This he did, but in consequence had to resign from Newton, Gordon, Cossart & Co, whose constitution did not permit foreign members.

The remainder of the family history can be briefly told. Russell Manners Gordon and his wife also failed to produce a male heir, and their only daughter Isabel married an Irishman called Joseph Bolger. Their only son Dermot married Phyllis Alexander, who was Scottish, and they had two daughters, Ann and Susan, both of whom married but neither of whom had children. Thus the original Portuguese family effectively became transmuted into an Irish-Scottish one, the only Portuguese blood of the present generation being that of their great-grandmother. Susan, Viscondessa and Condessa de Torre Bella, is now a widow living in the south of England, the last of the family; there are no immediate cousins.

According to one estimate, the Torre Bella estates at the time when Russell Manner Gordon married into the family comprised almost 60 per cent of the entire island. Even if this is an exaggeration, we may be sure that the Torre Bella land holdings were very large indeed. More accurately, the family estates at the time of Dermot Bolger's death in 1974 were assessed at 10.5 per cent of the island – much less than two generations previously, but still considerable. Although officially abolished, the *morgado* remained *de facto* intact because until the present generation there was only ever a single heir.

The Torre Bella estates, as one would expect, have always been diversified, and until now included a huge number of vineyards. Indeed, from the eighteenth century up to 1974 (and quite probably during the two previous centuries as well), the Correas were by far the largest wine producers on the island. In 1974, at the death of Dermot Bolger, there were vineyards at São Roque, Câmara de Lobos – where the Torre Bella (the 'beautiful tower'), traditionally said to be the site of the first vineyards on the island, used to stand – Campanário, Ribeira Brava, Arco da Calheta and Estreito da Calheta. These vineyards were, of course, farmed by tenants under the *contrato de colonia* system described in Chapter 1,[4] the wine being divided between the family and the tenants. There were *lagars* at São Roque, Torre, Campanário and Arco da Calheta. Formerly these were used to make the wine which was sold to the wine merchants – most recently to the MWA and Henriques & Henriques – though latterly, with the coming of adequate roads, the crop was sold as grapes. A certain amount of wine was also made and kept for the use of the family and its tenants, though this was but a fraction of the main crop.

Quite coincidentally, the Revolution of 1974 occurred within three months of Dermot Bolger's death, and this added considerably to the problems of sorting out his estate, especially as one of the first measures taken by the new government was a provision to enable tenants to buy out their landlord's interest.[5] Not all tenants could afford to do this, but most did, with the consequence that today the Torre Bella estate has only three or four tiny vineyards, none of any significance. The Torre hill itself, a tourist vantage point above Câmara de Lobos, has rather ugly housing on its eastern side and plenty of bananas. There are a few vineyards with Tinta Negra Mole on its western side. Within less than a quarter of a century, therefore, the vineyards of the most significant wine-producing family on the island have been entirely dispersed.

Fajã dos Padres

The Fajã dos Padres[6] is without doubt the most celebrated of all the vineyards in Madeira. It is first mentioned at the end of the sixteenth century by Fructuoso[7] and has been constantly praised for the quality of its Malvazia – the finest on the island – by all commentators from the seventeenth century to the nineteenth. It is not only the most famous of Madeira's vineyards, it is the *only* famous one, equivalent in Madeira terms to Château d'Yquem in Sauternes.

Not the least remarkable thing about the Fajã dos Padres is its situation on the south coast of the island, at the foot of a 300 metre-high cliff to the west of the Cabo Girão. It was for centuries only accessible by sea. Only in 1984, when the present owner installed a small and precarious lift down the cliff face, did it become possible to gain direct access to the Fajã without coming by sea. Even now, however, its air of remoteness has not been compromised.

We first hear of Malvazia being a monopoly of the Society of Jesus from Ovington in 1689. The Jesuits, he says, have 'secured the Monopoly of *Malmsey*, of which there is but one good vineyard in the whole island, which is entirely in their possession'. This was the Fajã dos Padres. It strikes one as odd that Malvasia, which seems originally to have been the principal grape variety on the island, should have so quickly dwindled to this extent, though it perhaps explains how it came to be in such short supply.

Edward Bowdich, the first English writer to mention the Fajã by name, visited it in 1825: 'A fall of water, of one shallow, and two deep stages, descends the whole depth of the western end of the cliff, which adjoins the Fazenda dos Padres, perhaps the finest malmsey plantation in the island, and created entirely by an *avalanche* of tufa, which, falling from a height of upwards of 1,200 feet, has lodged and spread at the bottom of the cliff. The house and vineyards are only accessible by water, to those who shudder, as most persons do, at the daring route of the labourers, who ascend and descend the cliff by a succession of simple stakes driven into, and projecting from it.'[8] Nobody who sees the cliff face today can really believe it possible that anyone could go up and down in the way described by Bowdich. The usual mode of access is confirmed by John Driver in 1834: 'The best Malmsey is from the vineyards of *Fazenda dos Padres*, adjoining the western end of Cape Giram – only accessible by water, and this attended with danger'.[9] Other nineteenth-century writers who refer to the Fajã are Dillon, Isabella de França, Wortley and Vizetelly.

The Fajã became the property of the Jesuits in 1595, shortly after they had established themselves in Madeira.[10] It was part of Quinta Grande in the parish of Campanário, the most important of the Jesuits' agricultural enterprises on the island. Apart from being maintained by a permanent settlement, we also know that the Fajã was used as a retreat, and a chapel dedicated to Nossa Senhora da Conceição was already in existence there by 1626, when the Fajã was sacked by pirates. This chapel was later converted into an *adega* (which it still is), the original use of which is apparent from a holy water stoup let into one of its walls.

The Jesuit order was expelled from Portugal in 1759 and its properties auctioned off.[11] Thereafter the Fajã's history becomes somewhat confused, as much in wine terms as in a general sense. It appears to have been owned for a brief period by the Torre Bella family, but was sold again when some of the family land was sold off by the first Visconde. Subsequently it became, according to Vizetelly, the property of a family called Netto, by which time, he says, it was 'planted principally with vines of the verdelho variety'.[12] Later still it became the property of Colonel Manuel de França Dória, who 'after having grown sugar cane on his land, but without much result, went back to growing vines, which seem to be more suited to the soil of the area'.[13] Doubtless the sugar cane was planted, as elsewhere, when phylloxera – which at the time of Vizetelly's visit had not yet reached so far west – took its toll. We also learn from the *Elucidário Madeirense* that 'besides the best Malvazia wine produced on the island, Sercial and other excellent quality varieties are grown there'. It appears, therefore, that the Fajã stopped being a wholly Malvasia vineyard after about 1870, virtually stopped being a vineyard at all after phylloxera, and then became a mixed vineyard once more. The Fajã was sold in 1919 by a Captain Dória to Joaquim Carlos de Mendonça, the paternal grandfather of the wife of the present owner, Mário Eugénio Jardim Fernandes. At this time there were still vestiges of sugar cane, vines (but no Malvasia) and vegetables. Cossart's statement[14] that 1920 Malvazia was the last vintage to come from the Fajã does not therefore accord with either the information in the *Elucidário Madeirense* [1921] or what I have been told by the present proprietor.

With a seaboard of about 1,020 metres and a depth towards the cliff face of about 200 metres at its greatest, the Fajã has a total area of about 9 hectares. Although relatively flat, the ground rises quite steeply towards the cliff, where at one time there were stone-walled terraces. Around 1930 bananas were planted, and somewhat later the Fajã was developed as a tropical fruit farm. At the moment there are two hectares of mangoes, 1.5 hectares of bananas, one hectare of avocado pears and smaller quantities of other tropical fruits. In all, about six hectares are under cultivation. The effect is of a park planted with fruit trees. A new and larger elevator designed to carry tourists is in course of being installed, a small restaurant and bar have been built, and the first of about seven derelict cottages has been charmingly restored for self-catering holiday accommodation. In no time the Fajã dos Padres will again be celebrated amongst visitors – as a theme park.

So, is the Fajã now of purely historical interest? Not quite. In 1940 a single Malvasia Cândida vine had survived in a rocky situation, and from it clones were generated and planted at Torre by Dermot Bolger.[15] It seems unlikely that they have survived. In 1979 the present proprietor Mário Fernandes, conscious of the history of the Fajã, repeated this operation from the same single vine (now gone), sending materials from it to the Gulbenkian Institute in Lisbon. The resulting clones have been planted at the Fajã, but sadly they have been mixed with Jacquet and are mainly grown on pergolas. At the moment Mário Fernandes is able to make about five hectolitres of wine a year, without any *estufagem*, which is exclusively for domestic use and for visitors to sample. There is already a delicious 1986 Malvazia in cask.

I asked Mário Fernandes if, in view of its former glory, he had ever thought of converting the Fajã back to an exclusively Malvasia vineyard. 'Yes, I've thought of it, but I do not think the conditions are any longer suitable. Besides, the profits from tropical fruit are quicker and more secure.' However, he has set aside a plot of about 0.2 hectares at the west end of the Fajã, and in 1997 he intends to plant it exclusively with Malvasia Cândida. Approached through two banana plantations by a wide pergola-covered avenue, over which new Malvasia vines have been trained, this little vineyard will be the culmination of the tourists' visit. Will it one day revive the reputation of the Fajã for Malvazia Cândida? Sadly, it has no real competition.

The present situation

Whatever the advantages of the redistribution of land from the point of view of social justice, the transformations of land use in cases like the Torre Bella estate – which happens to be a particularly striking example of a general trend – have been rather disastrous from the point of view of wine. As has already been said, the period after 1974 was one of decline for wine production and export. Many of the farmers who enfranchised their land therefore decided to convert from vines to bananas, which were beginning to become more important to the island's economy and which provided an all-year-round income independent of the vagaries of bad vintages. This period also saw the start of the development boom, which accelerated with Portugal's entry into the EU, and is still continuing. The increase in house construction meant that much of the land close to Funchal (particularly in São Martinho) and in Câmara de Lobos, where the best vineyards of the island are to be found, became more valuable for building development, and many of those who had enfranchised their holdings decided to cash in on their investment. The result has been a sad and virtually irreversible loss of vineyards, either to bananas or to building. Although there is a government-assisted scheme for the conversion of banana plantations back to vineyards (and other forms of exploitation), disappointingly few farmers are being tempted by it.

All this has exacerbated the effects of inheritance laws based on the Napoleonic model which have operated for almost two centuries, whereby all children have an equal right to inherit property. This has resulted either in the multiple ownership of land or in its division into ever-smaller lots; hence the mosaic configuration of extremely small vineyards in Madeira. Despite this, some traditional, though relatively small, quintas remain – particularly at Estreito de Câmara de Lobos. The Quinta do Jardim da Serra, owned by the Araújo family, still provides the island's best Sercial. The Quinta do Estreito, owned by the Veiga França family, remains a traditional property, as does the Quinta de São João, with its chapel dating from 1693. This property extends to six hectares, of which half is planted with bananas and half with vines (mainly Tinta Negra Mole, which is sold to Barbeito). It is owned by João César, whose father and grandfather were once the largest wine producers in Estreito de Câmara de Lobos, with a total of thirty hectares yielding some 500 hectolitres of must. These vineyards remain in the family, having been divided between three brothers and their children. In general, however, the vineyards at Câmara de Lobos and Estreito de Câmara de Lobos have become much more divided than on the north of the island, and it is in São Vicente that one now finds the largest producers.

In the absence of a *cadastro* it is almost impossible to establish precisely the disposition of larger vineyards. It is possible to get some idea from production figures, but it has to be remembered that large producers will have many parcels of land and these figures do not represent the production of a single vineyard. Thus, for example, in 1996 the largest amount of grapes bought by the MWC from a single grower was 40,000 kg. Of the 700–800 producers with which the company deals, just over thirty produce more than 10,000 kg of fruit. The average for a farmer is about 400 kg. By comparison, the largest amount bought by Barbeito from a single producer (at São Vicente) was 15,000 kg, consisting of Verdelho, Boal and Tinta Negra Mole. This was half his total production, and he is regarded as one of the biggest producers on the island. Barbeito also have a very few producers supplying more than 6,000 kg each year. To demonstrate how dramatically the volume of production can vary, the smallest amount Barbeito received in 1996 was 140 kg. About six or seven of the largest producers live in Venezuela, and return to the island only for the vintage. For the majority of producers, big and small, growing grapes is secondary to their main livelihood. One of the two largest producers in the north makes his living by running a taxi firm. The largest producer on the south of the island – who was once pointed out to me walking up the Estreito de Câmara de Lobos road with a load of grass on his back to feed cattle – sells about 30,000 kg a year. When I asked a spokesman for the Direcção Regional da Agricultura how many producers own ten or more hectares, the reply was 'One or two'. That is the extent of precise information available.

One can, however, put the vineyards into a fairly accurate perspective in relation both to the general agricultural situation on the island and to other forms of cultivation, although the figures are not quite up to date. According to the 1989 agricultural census, the total agricultural area of Madeira was 9,674 hectares, which is 68.2 per cent of the island's total surface area. Of this, 1,803 hectares were utilized for vines. With restructuring, however, that figure had by 1993 already risen to 1,912 hectares, or just under 20 per cent of the total agricultural area. Vines are the largest form of permanent cultivation, followed by potatoes (1,636 hectares); then come subtropical fruit (1,636 hectares), cereals (377 hectares), other fruit (285 hectares) and wicker (184 hectares).[16]

The Douro comes to Madeira

Vizetelly makes it clear that at the end of last century it was common for shippers also to own vineyards, rather as port shippers do today. Thus we learn of vineyards belonging to Krohn, Leacock (the São João vineyard), Donaldson and Davies. The São João vineyard, mentioned by Cossart as late as 1984, is now a thing of the past, and the Quinta do Furão, which he mentions as a new acquisition of the MWC, was relinquished by them in 1993. Among the shippers only Henriques & Henriques (always the owner of family vineyards) has bucked the trend with its new bulldozed vineyard on the sides of a re-entrant at Quinta Grande. It occupies ten hectares of a seventeen-hectare site, extends from about 600 metres to 750 metres (which is rather high for Madeira) and is claimed by the owners to be the largest single vineyard on the island today.

This was the first of as yet only two vineyards with bulldozed *patamars* in Madeira.[17] It was planned and constructed under the supervision of Miguel Corte Real of Cockburn's, the port shippers. The Douro technicians who built it had to adapt their techniques both to the lie of the land and to the changes in the soil types, which are visible evidence of the diversity of soils encountered in a single vineyard. The terraces are 2.5 metres wide and the planting distance is about 0.75 metres. An elaborate double cordon pruning regime has been established. The posts and wires are placed towards the front of the terraces, and a small tractor is able to move behind the vines, weeding and carrying out spray treatments.

Within the vineyard there are four (possibly five) different micro-climates, either because of the undulations of the contours or because of the differences of altitude. 18,542 vines have been planted: 54 per cent Verdelho; 28 per cent Sercial; 8 per cent Boal; 6 per cent Malvasia; and 4 per cent Terrantez. Early results have been encouraging.

Porto Santo

Grapes from Porto Santo, the little island to the north-east where vines were planted before those in Madeira, can be used to make madeira – but nowadays they seldom are. The island is climatically quite different from Madeira. It suffers from a chronic shortage of water and over the years this has had an adverse effect on all its crops, to which the deserted terraces covering the island bear eloquent testimony. Quite recent photographs show vineyards along the shore in front of Vila Baleira, the capital, and stretching towards the south-west point of the island. The centre of the island, north of Vila Baleira, was once also covered with vineyards, but the new airport was driven through them in 1960, was further extended in 1973, and is due to be extended once more in the near future. Consequently the production of grapes has decreased enormously, and most of what is now produced is Caracol and Listrão destined for the table. The remaining vineyards, apart from some front gardens in Camacha, border the airport runway to the north and south. They are small, bounded by low freestone walls (called *muros de croché*), which are also found in the Azores, and the vines are trained over the ground without supports (*vinhas da pé*).

The vines in Porto Santo grow in sand, which made them immune to phylloxera. Consequently only a few direct producers were planted. However, neither they nor any classical varieties have been registered in vintage declarations in recent years, so they seem to have largely died out. Some Listrão is used for local table wine, and some Triunfo is also grown. Formerly, however, Porto Santo musts were popular with madeira wine-makers because of their high alcoholic potential of 13° or more. Listrão ages well and quickly, maturing in one year as much as Tinta Negra Mole will in three. Henriques & Henriques used to buy a Listrão in the 1950s and

1960s until the high cost of transport in casks made it prohibitive. As late as 1991 Barbeito were buying up to 3,000 litres of Listrão a year. Being fermented completely dry before shipment to Madeira, it was particularly suitable for addition to their 10 year old blends of Sercial and Verdelho. The high cost of transport again brought this to an end. Only Barros e Sousa still produce a Listrão madeira.

Vineyards round the island

Most maps of the vine growing areas of the island are if not plain inaccurate, at the very least misleading. They usually purport to show where the varieties of *Vitis vinifera* are grown, but make no reference to the hybrid direct producers, which account for some 46 per cent of the total grape production. However, most areas in the north have only minuscule plantings of either recommended or authorized varieties. In the vineyard map on pp. 230–31 I have attempted to remedy this by indicating the proportions of varieties to be found in each *concelho*, based on the 1995 vintage. However, the reader must understand that, with replanting and restructuring, more classical varieties appear every year, and a map based on one vintage alone can be at best only indicative of current vineyard dispositions. To supplement the map, therefore, I shall provide the reader with a wine tour of the island, similar to that of Fructuoso at the end of the sixteenth century. We start from Funchal and work our way clockwise around the island.

Funchal, despite being a city, is the fifth largest grape-producing area on the island, even though the vineyards of São Martinho, which used to be so notable, have almost completely succumbed to urban development. Notable amongst those surviving are the vineyards belonging to Pereira d'Oliveira, the shipping family. Câmara de Lobos and Estreito de Câmara de Lobos, though also depleted, remain the best and largest of the grape-growing areas. Production here is mainly of Tinta Negra Mole (averaging 66 per cent of the total crop), but all the classical varieties are grown here. Having dropped over the last twenty years, production is now levelling off. Further west we come to Campanário, of which Quinta Grande forms a part. Still famous for its Boal, Campanário is not however as important as it used to be. More than 60 per cent of the crop at Ribeira Brava is also Tinta Negra Mole, with some Boal, tiny amounts of Verdelho and Malvasia, but no Sercial. There is very little vine cultivation westwards until we get to Arco de Calheta, where Boal is the main crop (60 per cent). Ponta do Pargo, further west still, was once famous for its Sercial (now vanished) but is no longer a significant wine area, the predominant crop being vegetables.

At Porto Moniz, on the north-western tip of the island, we enter the kingdom of direct producers (over 70 per cent). Here, as we descend to the village, the eye is met by a multitude of little plots, each protected against the prevailing wind by *bardos*, the little fences made from shrubs. In winter everything is green, meaning that there is no Tinta Negra Mole in sight. The predominant variety is Jacquet, but all the classical varieties can be found, Sercial (18 per cent) and Verdelho (6.5 per cent) predominating. Eastwards towards Ribeira da Janela we see small plots of vines precipitately placed on the cliffs and wonder how anyone can ever reach them. Ribeira da Janela stands at a river mouth, and looking up the river valley one can see terraced vineyards, protected by their *bardos*, stacked on either side. Here it is mainly Verdelho that is grown. Passing through a long tunnel on the way to Seixal, we reach an area known as Contreiros, with a few vineyards, mainly of Sercial, perched on the hillside. The Serviços de Produção Agrícola have taken specimens of Sercial from these vineyards for use in their own experimental stations. The next notable vineyard site is at Seixal, where there is about three times as much Jacquet as Sercial. More extensive vineyards are found to the east of Seixal, again mainly Jacquet, with some Sercial and a tiny bit of Verdelho. Here one can see some of the steepest vineyards on the island, with slopes of up to 65 per cent. Vintagers require the agility of mountain goats.

At the centre of the north coast we come to São Vicente. From here there is a very wide valley running south and inland as far as the pass of Encumeada and along which runs the road to Ribeira Brava. This is now the second largest vineyard area on the island and getting bigger, with the smallest proportion (27 per cent) of direct producers. Of the tiny amount of classical grapes, over 65 per cent is Tinta Negra Mole. There are plenty of vineyards to the west of the Ribeira Brava road in Feiteiras and Ginjas. There is also a little Verdelho, with a single five-hectare Verdelho vineyard at Feiteiras. However, the majority of São Vicente vineyards are hidden from the view of the traveller on the main road south, and to see them one must turn east off the road near Rosário towards Achada do Til. This takes one back through the east of the valley via Lameiros to São Vicente. Here most of the vineyards are around one hectare in size, and there is a little Boal. Although we also encounter a great deal of Jacquet here, the production of *Vitis vinifera* from São Vicente is increasing. This is largely due to the restructuring of direct producer vineyards under various government schemes.

Going eastwards again, we find some vineyards which are mostly Jacquet, with a little Sercial. There are sporadic terraces along the coast, and at Ponta Delgada a large number of terraces close to the sea on the north of the road as well as inland. Here there are some extensive and impressive vineyards – again mainly of Jacquet, but with a certain amount of Verdelho and Sercial. Ricardo França's five-hectare vineyard, with three hectares of bulldozed terraces, is south of the road. It consists almost wholly of Verdelho, but with (surprisingly) some Cabernet Sauvignon and Merlot. Several of the other vineyards here have post and wire trained vines – evidence of restructuring – but some rows are so close together that it appears to be impossible to work them with a tractor.

From Ponta Delgada one rattles along the old stone-block road towards Boaventura and sees quite a number of vineyards as one approaches the town, this time mainly of Herbemont. Boaventura is built on a little shoulder of land and there are re-entrants to east and west, both covered with vines. Further along one reaches the junction with the road to Fajã Grande and Lombo do Urzal. To the south, looking up the re-entrant, there are more vineyards, as also at Fajã do Caneiro. A tunnel then leads to the area of Arco de São Jorge, part of the *concelho* of Santana, the third largest wine area on the island. The vineyards are best seen by passing through the town and climbing to a vantage point on the east beyond Arco de São Jorge. Looking down, one realizes that the vineyard area is effectively a small plateau set in a cupped recession of the sea cliffs. Unlike the other main wine areas of the north, there is no river, no valley and no slopes. This is another area mainly of direct producers (60 per cent), but several post and wire vineyards indicate restructuring. Some Tinta Negra Mole (8.5 per cent) and Sercial (1 per cent) are grown.

The road continues round an outcrop of cliffs, then descends to the mouth of the Ribeira de São Jorge. Vineyards abound on both river banks, and in the upper part of the valley there are new *Vitis vinifera* plantings, including a restructured two-hectare vineyard of

Verdelho. This is also where much of the so-called Malvasia de São Jorge (27 per cent for the *concelho*) comes from. One farmer wants to build a small winery to make table wine from Verdelho. From here we proceed to Santana, also a source of Malvasia de São Jorge. Undoubtedly the most eye-catching vineyard here belongs to the Quinta do Furão, which occupies an almost level site on a headland commanding a magnificent view along the coast to the most easterly point of the island. A country restaurant has since 1997 been complemented by a comfortable country hotel standing in the middle of the vineyard.

This vineyard stands in five hectares, already planted when it was acquired in 1980 by the MWC, which (possibly now to its regret) sold it off in 1992 after reversing its recent policy of having its own vineyards. The site now has 2.5 hectares under vines: one of Verdelho, one of Sercial and half a hectare of Tinta Negra Mole. This is an atmospheric place for the wine-orientated visitor to stay. There is even a traditional *lagar* beside the restaurant where visitors looking for a hands-on experience can tread grapes during the vintage, which ends with the customary music and dancing. Having been selling to the MWC, the Quinta do Furão in 1996 produced 50 hectolitres of its own wine instead. A two year old Verdelho in cask is already delicious. More interestingly, it makes a *vin nouveau* table wine from Tinta Negra Mole for its clients to sample. 'Madeira burgundy' lives again!

Further along the road at Ribeira do Faial the vines are mainly Herbemont, while at Porto da Cruz they are mainly Isabela. This is part of the *concelho* of Machico, the second smallest wine area (80 per cent direct producers). There are Sercial (13 per cent) and some new plantations of Verdelho here. Further east there are no vineyards, and between Santa Cruz and Funchal the vines one sees in gardens produce table grapes which are not commercialized.

Back on the south coast, a little Jacquet is grown at Machico for *vinho seco*, but at Ribeira de Machico and Santo António da Serra the most favoured drink is local cider, which can be found in bars. This has never been an important vine-growing area. Even Fructuoso considered the local wine the worst on the island, and over the centuries the island's wine producers seem to have shared his view. Santa Cruz, where the airport is, is the smallest wine area and has no classical varieties, being 100 per cent direct producers.

This effectively ends the wine tour, for the area along the south coast from the airport to Funchal has never been important for wine growing, but has traditionally produced other crops such as onions and tropical fruit. The observant visitor will see evidence of abandoned terraces to the west of this area, but these were on the whole never used for vines. Indeed, abandoned terraces are not hard to find in many parts of the island, and some of them undoubtedly date from the era of phylloxera. They give the lie to the guidebook cliché that cultivable land is so scarce in Madeira that not a square metre of it is wasted. Nevertheless, these terraces are often in the most inaccessible places, and not much easily cultivable land lies fallow.

9

Viticulture and the Vintage

Old vineyards

In viticultural terms, it is only recently that very much has changed from the way in which things were done for hundreds of years. To an observer used to the standards of viticulture in France, or even in mainland Portugal, Madeira is still living in a sort of viticultural Middle Ages.

Many of the old vineyards on the steepest slopes are on stone-walled terraces, or *poios*, laboriously constructed centuries ago. Inclines of 45 per cent are by no means unusual in Madeiran vine-yards, and on the north of the island they can be as steep as 65 per cent. In places where the slope is less severe, the terraces are broader and may hold more than one row of vines. The visual effect of these terraces, however, is vastly different from the orderly, stepped-up terracing which is such a familiar sight in the Douro. Here the terraces are adapted to outcrops of rock and other irregularities of the terrain, and being covered with *latadas*, or trellises, which themselves bear the continuous canopy of the vines, they are generally not clearly visible while the vines are in leaf.

Apart from a score or so of vineyards which have adopted the *espaldeira*, or post and wire, system of training (mainly as part of restructuring, and under pressure from the Direcção Regional da Agricultura), the description of a *latada* vineyard of the eighteenth century[1] might have been written yesterday, except that metal frames have in most cases replaced wood and bamboo for supports. The height of *latadas* is variable. Over paths and around houses they are high enough to walk under without trouble. Elsewhere, they tend to be remarkably close to the ground (1–1.5 metres), making it really very difficult to get underneath to weed, carry out treatments and finally to pick the grapes. The theory is that the reflected heat from the ground assists in ripening the grapes.

The growing of crops under trellises is officially frowned on,[2] but for the poorest producers, making the fullest use of the available ground to grow vegetables for the family is still an economic necessity. Many vineyards, especially in the north, are chaotic. In Seixal I once saw a small one which, apart from vines, had tomatoes, cabbages, oranges, avocados, papaya, custard apples, bananas, sugar cane, a peach tree and tangerines within its boundaries. Such diversity is admittedly rare, and potatoes, cabbages, onions and beans are the more usual crops. When potatoes are grown in the winter, while the vine is dormant, they do little harm. Summer crops are the worst, especially as watering them cannot be effected without also watering the vines (which is technically illegal, but practically speaking uncontrollable). Another disadvantage is that fertilizers for crops strengthen the vines and the quality of the grapes diminishes. Where there are no vegetables, it is a common enough sight to see weeds. Vineyard tidiness is not one of Madeira's strong points.

Farmers can obtain both root stock and bench grafts from the Direcção Regional da Agricultura, but generally prefer to use the latter. The two root stocks most used are R99 and 1103-P, though in the north some small farmers still use Jacquet and Herbemont. 5DV and SO4, which were in use until recently, are no longer recommended. For planned *latadas* the approved density of vines is 3,300 per hectare, planted with 2 metres between rows and 1.5 metres between vines. The training of the vine over the *latada* is effected by means of the following pruning regime. In the first year a cut is made above the first bud, which sends the cane to the level of the *latada*. In the second year, cuts are made at the level of the *latada* to leave three canes, which are trained in different directions over it. The canopy is thereafter developed by choosing a number of canes for training each year, the number depending on the strength of the vine and on the pruner's judgement. The aim is to have as uniform a canopy as possible. In old plantations, weak vines tend not to be replaced and their stronger neighbours are allowed to roam.

The productivity of vines trained on *latadas* varies with the variety. By law the maximum production of a hectare of vines must not exceed 80 hectolitres of must (which must have at least 9° of natural alcohol). Tinta Negra Mole will produce an average of 12 tonnes per hectare; Sercial and Boal 10 tonnes per hectare; Verdelho 9 tonnes per hectare; and Malvazia Cândida 8 tonnes per hectare.[3] These are the figures supplied by the Serviços de Producção Agrícola, and they make one blink when one reads in Cossart that 'one hectare of well-cultivated land with the best soil should, in an average year, produce from 15 to 20 tons of grapes, whereas in well-cultivated medium-quality soil only 10 to 15 tons may be expected'.[4] Cossart is talking of almost double the quantities now regarded as normal. Unless he is entirely wide of the mark, we can only conclude that the general quality of grapes must have improved with the reduction in quantity.

The advantage of *latadas* is that closeness to the ground helps in ripening the grapes, especially in the north, where the sweeter varieties can be grown quite well but not always satisfactorily ripened: the difference in sugar between the same varieties from the north and the south can be as much as 1.5°. The disadvantages are that it is difficult to gain access to the vines to carry out treatments and harvest the grapes, and dense foliage has to be lightened to allow sunshine through to the grapes underneath.

Some varieties, including Sercial, Malvasia Cândida and Tinta Negra Mole, seem to do consistently better when trained on *latadas*. The Divisão de Viticultura of the Serviços de Produção Agrícola say that they do not have enough data to say why this is so. In the case of Malvazia Cândida, however, this method of training is an advantage because the flowering is always at the end, rather than in the middle, of the cane. Consequently, yields of Malvasia Cândida on *latadas* tend to be greater.

Farmers use both organic material and chemical products for fertilization, and advice on the most suitable commercial fertilizers, based on the analysis of soils, is available from the Divisão de Viticultura. The general consideration is to balance the level of fertilization against the quality of the wine.

Short of the ban on the irrigation of vineyards – and even this is officially relaxed in very dry years – there is virtually no official control over the way in which a farmer chooses to grow his grapes unless, as in the case of restructuring, the farmer is to receive a subsidy towards the cost of replanting or of making a new vineyard. The role of the Serviços de Produção Agrícola, where established vineyards are concerned, is purely advisory.

New vineyards

In order to plant a new vineyard a farmer requires a licence, without which he has no legal entitlement to sell his grapes for wine. On receipt of an application, the site is examined by a government technician with a view to its suitability, its altitude, aspect towards the sun and other climatic characteristics, its soil and its general quality potential. If the assessment is affirmative, the technician will advise on which varieties are likely to do well on the site, on the density of the vines and the most suitable form of training.

Currently there are schemes, largely funded by the EU, for restructuring existing vineyards (with *Vitis vinifera* varieties) and for converting agricultural sites to different agricultural use, including vineyards. The first programme applies only to vineyards, specifically those with a minimum area of one hectare. The second programme, which applies to all forms of plantation, requires a minimum area of 500 square metres.

When an application is received under the first (restructuring) scheme, the site is assessed and whatever recommendations are made have to be followed in order to qualify for the subsidy. The progress of the project is monitored, and staged payments are made as it progresses. Subsidies are available for 75 per cent of the costs, up to a limit of 600 contos. Under the second scheme, only 55 per cent of the costs are subsidized. The take-up of both schemes is disappointingly low.

Present policy is to recommend the use of post and wire training wherever the nature of the site permits. This allows a greater density of planting: 4,500 plants per hectare. Production levels are generally the same as with *latadas*, but benefits include greater exposure of the grapes to sunlight, ease in spraying and applying treatments, and better plant hygiene.

The health of the vines in Madeira is greatly influenced by the generally high temperatures and humidity. *Oïdium* and mildew therefore remain major problems; 1995, for example, was a particularly bad year for *oïdium*. However, the worst vine ailment is in many ways *botrytis*. As with the other ailments, spraying is the answer – in this case with *iprodiona* when the grapes have reached full size.

Two main pruning systems – single cordon and Guyot[5] – are recommended, depending on the grape variety. Research is continuing into which system is best suited to each variety. Preliminary findings suggest that Guyot should be used for Sercial and Malvasia, whereas single cordon may be better for Verdelho.

The Serviços de Produção Agrícola

This government department, as mentioned in Chapter 6, is a division of the Direcção Regional da Agricultura, and one of its sub-departments, the Divisão de Viticultura, is responsible for the oversight of vineyards. Based at the Quinta do Bom Sucesso – which is situated behind Funchal's spectacular Botanic Garden – the Divisão de Viticultura consists of a director, two engineers (one in charge of vineyards and the other in charge of the experimental winery at Bom Sucesso), two technical engineers, five technical assistants and a staff of almost fifty.

Agricultural policy is made at the level of the Direcção Regional, but the Divisão de Viticultura has the responsibility of analysing proposals passed down to it, and of advising the government on all aspects of vineyard management. In addition, it has a number of specific tasks. Its main activity and largest responsibility is giving technical advice and assistance to farmers. A technical assistant at São Vicente looks after the north of the island. Operating an 'on request' service, the Divisão de Viticultura also organizes periodic meetings with farmers to offer advice on vine treatments, commercial products, pruning, etc., and it explains the advantages of (and tries to encourage participation in) the government's vineyard restructuring schemes.

The Divisão de Agricultura also runs various experimental stations throughout the island. At Caniçal there is a bench-graft station which supplies ready-grafted stock. This has the advantage of reducing by a year the time taken by the farmer to establish his vineyard, and of minimizing losses from grafts which fail to take. In addition, there are experimental stations at Estreito de Câmara de Lobos, Arco da Calheta, Ponto do Pargo, São Vicente and Arco de São Jorge. There is also an experimental station in Porto Santo, but it is wholly concerned with table grapes. Each station undertakes research. Apart from the investigation into pruning already mentioned, there are studies in progress into which are the best clones of each variety and which of the two approved root stocks is best for each variety.

The main research priority, however, is to find vines which can replace direct producers and enable the island to produce its own table wine. Varieties from France, Italy, Germany and mainland Portugal have been planted in the experimental stations, and include the following: Chenin Blanc, Sauvignon Blanc, Chardonnay, Ugni Blanc, Malvasia Bianco, Malvasia Fina (both Italian, and different from the island's Malvasias), Arnsburger and Arinto amongst the whites; and Cabernet Sauvignon, Merlot, Maria Feld, Touriga Nacional, Touriga Francesa and Tinta Barroca amongst the reds. In addition, research is being done into table wines produced from Tinta Negra Mole, Sercial, Verdelho, Complexa, and Deliciosa (for rosé wine).

Micro-vinifications have been made from all these varieties in the winery at Bom Sucesso, and in some cases mini-vinifications (500–1,000 litres) are now being made. The department receives technical advice on making the red wine from the Universities of Lisbon and Évora. Results are too tentative for publication, beyond saying that Verdelho can make a good white wine,[6] Sercial is less satisfactory, and the results from Tinta Negra Mole are very disappointing. It is fascinating, in view of the long history of Tinta in Madeira, to see this wine being re-invented. A satisfactory wine made from Tinta Negra Mole would naturally be of special interest – particularly as surplus production is purchased by the government at the minimum price – and experiments on length of maceration, amount of wood treatment, etc., are in progress. The basic problem, however, is that Tinta Negra Mole does not normally have a high enough sugar content to make a good red table wine. Indeed, shippers are ecstatic if they can get it with 10° potential alcohol (although stopping the watering of vines in April has been known to give Tinta Negra Mole with up to 13° Baumé). Whether putting concentrated must in with the fermentation will overcome this problem remains to be seen. I suspect that, in the end, Tinta Negra Mole will only prove satisfactory as part of a blend.

The vintage

Sadly, the colourfulness of the traditional vintage has all but disappeared. The only grapes trodden in *lagars* nowadays are to make *vinho seco*, though the procedures remain almost identical to the vintage as it was in the eighteenth century[7] – and indeed, as it was well within living memory. The vintage is the end of a cycle of very hard work. It is a time for co-operation between neighbours, for there are no *rogas*, or roving bands of pickers, as in the Douro. The younger people do the most strenuous jobs, picking the grapes on vertiginous slopes and carrying vintage baskets which can weigh up to 60 kg. In the evenings it is time to relax, and there is some serious eating and drinking. Music often accompanies the work in the *lagars*. Processions of *borracheiros* carrying the wine to Funchal were a common sight until the early 1980s. Sometimes *borrachos* are still used to carry *vinho seco*, and the odd *borracheiro* can occasionally be seen in the north, especially at Porto da Cruz.

For the fortified wine, however, the vintage is now a somewhat charmless industrial process, with a street party organized to please the visitors in front of the Turismo office in the Avenida Arriaga in Funchal. The larger shippers employ one or two agents who will provide technical advice throughout the year, and will negotiate purchases of grapes well before the vintage begins. Until 1992 the IVM, in conjunction with growers and shippers, would fix minimum prices. Now it merely suggests a minimum price, which is paid for grapes which remain unpurchased by the shippers, but which are bought by the Fundo Regional de Intervenção e Gerência Agrícola (FRIGA), an intervention agency set up in 1992 after Portugal's entry into the EU. These grapes are made into wine by the IVM and are periodically sold by auction to the shippers.

Some growers have been selling to the same firms for three or more generations. Two or three months before the harvest the wine-makers will go round the island to visit their farmers. They will inspect the vineyards and give advice, after which the larger firms will control the maturation of the vines. This is done by the oenologist or wine-maker and his assistant (if he is lucky enough to have one). The agent(s) will continue to deal with the growers and give advice. If a particularly difficult problem arises, they will refer it to the wine-maker. In place of the capacious vintaging baskets which were once used, each shipper issues his agent with distinctively coloured plastic containers holding about 15 kg to pass on to the farmers from whom he is buying. The rate at which these containers are issued can be used to control the rate at which the grapes arrive for vinification. When filled, they are delivered by lorry to the shipper's winery.

The harvesting and selling of grapes is now subject to tight controls by the IVM, although until about four or five years ago the system, I have been told by some shippers, was sufficiently 'leaky' for some direct producers to slip through. However, almost everyone now seems to be satisfied that this no longer happens, and that the controls, such as they are, work reasonably well. What happens is this. At the time of the vintage the IVM has nine teams each consisting of a representative of the IVM, a representative of the Department of Agriculture and a representative of another governmental body called the Actividades Económicas. They visit the sites where grapes are being received and fermentation is taking place, and they take random samples of the different varieties to see if there is any evidence of malvina. If any fraud is detected, the representative of the Actividades Económicas is empowered to seize the grapes and make direct application to a magistrate to institute criminal proceedings (which are not wholly unknown). At the time of the vintage the grape producers make a declaration, called a *manifesto*, of the amount of grapes of each variety which they have sold, and to whom. At the same time, those making the wine – in most cases the shippers – also make declarations of the quantities of grapes they have purchased, and from whom. The IVM receives both sets of declarations and collates them in order to detect any discrepancies. After the vintage the shippers make a declaration of the amount of wine they have made from each variety and, provided it tallies with their previous declarations of what they have purchased, this amount of wine is entered on to a current account (*conta corrente*).[8] The wine is now officially recognized and its commercial life, whether it gets sold as *granel* or is kept in cask for decades to become a venerable vintage wine, can thereafter be charted by the IVM.

The subsequent movement of this wine from vinification through each stage of its development – fortification, entry into *estufagem*, exit from *estufagem* and into second *estágio*, then after at least 180 days, into its final stage of being potentially saleable wine – right up until its eventual sale have to be reported to the IVM once a week on a declaration form called a *ficha*. At the IVM details from the *fichas* are then laboriously entered by hand into an enormous ledger (nearly a metre wide) inherited from the JNV and still bearing the Junta name and imprint. In February 1997, computerization was said to be in the final phase of implementation. This history of the wine, even making allowance for evaporation, is maintained until the moment when the disposal of all the wine has been accounted for and the current account is closed. No wine which has not been registered with the IVM in this way and which does not have a current account can be legally offered for sale – although, of course, private sales by individuals of old bottles of wine made before this system began are tolerated.

As far as I can see, the manifesto system works well enough, or has done for the last five years. Until recently, several shippers (who ought, one supposes, to know) told me that they thought a lot of fiddling of the manifestos took place and that the manifestos could not be entirely relied on. Naturally, this view is hotly denied by the IVM and the Directorate of Agriculture. However, on the grounds of arithmetic alone, one shipper was not prepared to rule out the possibility that illegal mixtures of direct producer and authorized madeira still occur in bulk wines. In 1996 a litre of Tinta Negra Mole must with alcohol cost around 222 escudos to prepare. *Estufagem*, *estágio* and evaporation before blending would have brought the cost up to 250 escudos, and the total pre-bottling cost would have been between 290 and 300 escudos. The export price of bulk wine was between 280 and 310 escudos. My source of information went on: 'Who is going to make wine just to give it away? The manifestos may be very well controlled, but that does not prevent me from mixing good and bad wine afterwards. I can have someone press Jacquet in a remote part of the island after verification. The control of the crop is no real prevention of this – especially when you remember that a litre of Jacquet costs only 15 escudos.'

I do not wish to make gratuitous accusations which I am in no position to prove; I simply report what I was told. However, I cannot believe that, if it happens at all, this sort of fraud can be on a large scale. The risk of being found out is high, as are the penalties, so the risk can hardly be worth taking. As the reader will discover later, all bottled wine is stringently tested by the IVM and the chances of adulteration are minimal.[9] However, the fact that a shipper is prepared to make such a statement argues rather strongly in favour of the establishment of a *cadastro*.

The date on which the vintage can begin used to be set by the IVM, but is no longer. It does not really get going much before 20 August and is generally over by 10 October, but sometimes picking can start as early as 5 August and can last into early November. Traditionally, some grapes are left on the vines in São Martinho until 11 November, because he is the patron saint of wine growers and this is his name day. A street fair is held just below the church.

The oenologist at the MWC monitors the maturation of the grapes in a Tinta Negra Mole vineyard on the west side of the famous Torre overlooking Câmara de Lobos, in conjunction with another a little further north at Covão, to decide when picking should begin. There are varying dates of maturation around the island, usually depending on altitude and exposure to the sun, and there are various micro-climates. Normally the vintage starts with grapes grown at sea level and on the lower altitudes (Verdelho and Tinta Negra Mole) and ends with late-maturing or high-growing varieties (Malvasia and Sercial). The grapes in the south are ready before those in the north.

IO

Making and Maturing the Wine

Vinification

Only in the 1980s did it become standard practice for the shippers to make their own wine from the grapes they purchased.[1] Before that the wine was made where the grapes had been grown and was then transported, as previously explained, to Funchal by processions of *borracheiros*. At this time the wine was fermented right out and therefore dry. It was then up to the shipper to sweeten the wine to suit his commercial requirements, and this he did in a variety of ways. For the best quality wines he would add *vinho surdo*, which was unfermented grape juice to which 20 per cent spirit had been added to stop it fermenting, or *vinho abafado*, which is similar to *vinho surdo* except that a small amount of fermentation is allowed to take place before it is smothered by the addition of alcohol (thereby preserving some of its natural sugar). Lesser quality wines were sweetened with *arrobo*, which was grape juice to which sugar and tartaric acid had been added. This mixture was then boiled down to a syrup one third of its original volume, the tartaric acid converting the sugar into equal amounts of glucose and fructose. The lowest qualities were produced by doctoring the dry wine with *calda*, which was simply boiled-down sugar, or caramel. Under EU regulations none of these is now legal,[2] and sweetening is effected, when necessary, by adding rectified concentrated must. It is interesting to note, however, that as late as 1984, when the now current method of making the sweeter wines was beginning to replace the traditional ways just described, Cossart speculates about whether, with ageing, wine made by the new method would 'loose [*sic*] vinosity and richness sooner than that sweetened with *surdo*'.[3] I fear I shall not live long enough to find out.

'Does anyone know how to make madeira?' was the name of an article written in 1991,[4] but the shippers had had to ask themselves the same question in the 1980s when a delegation had gone to Brussels to negotiate the status of madeira after Portugal's entry into the EU. 'We must defend our traditional way of making madeira' was the cry, but when it came to defining what the negotiators had to defend, the diversity of practices gave rise to problems. Thanks partly to pressure from the OIV (Office International de la Vigne et du Vin) – effectively the guardians of the EU's wine-making standards – and partly to the arrival on the island of modern wine-making equipment, there is now a measure of uniformity in vinification practice. The method now universally used is a large-scale application of the principle of *vinho abafado*, and it is employed in making both the generic madeira from Tinta Negra Mole and in making the traditional single variety wines. Needless to say, there are small variations between shippers, but none of radical importance.

In the account which follows I shall deal first with the making of the generic wine, almost exclusively from Tinta Negra Mole, and then with the traditional varieties. I shall indicate where appropriate the practice of individual shippers in relation to what generally happens.

Generic madeira

Grapes are received at the winery and weighed. Two companies currently pay for every potential degree of alcohol, and in their case the grapes are also tested for sugar content. The idea is to give growers an incentive to produce better grapes. The normal potential alcohol for white varieties is 10.5–11°, and for Tinta Negra Mole 9–10°. Although a minimum price is declared by the IVM, in practice prices are determined between the companies and the farmers. In 1996 the average price for Tinta Negra Mole was 16 escudos per degree per kilogram, averaging 160 escudos per kilogram, while white varieties averaged about 200 escudos per kilogram. Prices reflect inflation, and in 1995 the average price for Tinta Negra Mole had been 155 escudos per kilogram. The other shippers, who accepted the sugar levels as they came, paid a flat rate of 170 escudos per kilogram in 1996. However, several shippers are considering adopting the sugar-based system in the future.

After having been weighed and tested for sugar, the grapes are poured into hoppers. The next part of the operation is the destalking of the grapes, which is total, except in the case of smaller producers without up-to-date equipment who crush the grapes (pips and stalks included). Borges make an effort to restrict considerably the amount of stalks getting into the press. At this point the wine-maker has a choice between pumping the crushed grapes direct to the fermentation tanks or into a wine press. Henriques & Henriques have an automatic facility to enable them to do either; in other cases, it is a matter of connecting up the requisite pumps and piping. When the must is pumped into the fermentation tanks it is normal to add 15 milligrams per litre of sulphur dioxide to control the bacteria. Sometimes grapes from the north which have spent three or four hours in their containers become a little oxidized, and sulphur dioxide acts as an anti-oxidant. Silva Vinhos prefer to use potassium bisulphite. Barbeito also add a sulphite (10 to 12 milligrams per litre) and 1.5 grams per hectolitre of pectolitic enzymes to help clarify the wine a little before *estufagem*. It is also permissible by law to add some concentrated must, which boosts sugar levels, either during or after fermentation. The permitted amount is limited to the equivalent of 2° Baumé, and only 8 per cent of the harvest may be so treated.[5] If the must is deficient in acidity – normally never a problem in Madeira – gypsum, in conjunction with tartaric acid, can be added. This helps to balance the wine. Not more than 1.5 grams per litre are used (the legal limit being 2 grams per litre).

Fermentation on the skins (maceration) is becoming common for the vinification of Tinta Negra Mole, and is practised to differing degrees by different shippers. Henriques & Henriques have full maceration; Borges has partial maceration; Silva Vinhos give their sweet and medium-sweet wines full maceration, but the dry and medium-dry are macerated for only a day; the MWC gives its sweet and medium-sweet wines full maceration, but none at all to the dry and medium-dry. Barbeito uses a continuous press, so although pips and stalks are removed, the skins are incorporated into the must and, as already mentioned, the smaller producers have equipment which crushes everything. Justino Henriques believe that maceration is contrary to traditional Madeiran wine-making and will have nothing to do with it, so all their wine is put through an Italian press which removes skins and pips. When one considers that the traditional way of pressing grapes was to tread them entire

in *lagars*, and that maceration was common for Tinta in the nineteenth century, it is difficult to understand this opinion. The object
of maceration is mainly to extract as much colour as possible from
the skins because the polyphenol concentration is normally largest
in the wines with most colour. Thus, if a 3 year old wine has good
colour, this reduces the amount of caramel which needs to be added.

Vinification takes place in a variety of tanks: concrete lined with
epoxy resin, plain stainless steel containers, and autovinifiers of the
most modern design. Normally the natural yeasts are sufficient to
get the fermentation under way, and no commercial yeasts have to
be used. Some shippers control the temperature of the ferment,
either by means of thermostatically controlled cooling incorporated
into their fermentation tanks (Henriques & Henriques, Silva
Vinhos, Justino Henriques) or by pumping the must through
external chilling units (Borges, the MWC). Shippers' views of ideal
fermentation temperatures vary. For example, the MWC ferments
Tinta Negra Mole at a maximum of 26°C for sweet and medium-
sweet, and 22°C for medium-dry and dry wines; Silva Vinhos keep
temperatures between 25° and 27°C; Henriques & Henriques ferment in the range between 25° and 30°C. Barbeito vinify at a
normal maximum of 28°, but at 30°C for very dry wine – and they
believe that temperature-control systems are only for 'showing off',
on the grounds that *estufagem* is a leveller of wine which irons out
any advantages gained from low-temperature vinification. In the
past, temperatures were not controlled at all and this could result
in wines with very high volatile acidity – high enough, indeed, to
constitute vinegar. Most wine-makers believe, however, that the
oxidizing effects on the alcohol in the wine are reduced at low temperatures, and that when the volatile acidity is kept low the wines in
general mature better. This can be of particular importance for
wines destined to be sold at 3 years old. High acidity reduces the
potential of oxidation, and during two or three years of maturation
you do not get much characterization of the wine.

Practice varies with regard to monitoring the progress of fermentation. At the MWC each tank is checked every hour for its temperature, degree of sugar content, density and alcohol level. In other
cases the temperature is kept constant automatically. What is most
crucial, however, is the sugar level. During vinification the amount
of sugar decreases as it is turned into alcohol, at the rate of 18 grams
per litre of reducing sugars to produce one degree of alcohol. The

wine-maker has to stop the fermentation completely by adding more alcohol (in the form of spirit) when the sugar level gets down to the degree of natural sweetness appropriate to the type of wine he is producing.[6] Fermentation times vary for each type, and the use of autovinifiers can reduce these times by almost two-thirds. For a sweet wine, (with autovinification) fermentation can take anything from eight to twenty-four hours, depending on temperature, etc.; for a medium-sweet wine, it can take up to three days; for a medium-dry wine, fermentation can take from three to four days; and for a dry wine which is fermented right out, five or even six days.

After fermentation is completed, the *bagaço* (lees) left in the fermentation tanks is pressed. Silva Vinhos, for example, use a three-phase pneumatic press, and the resulting pressings are added to the wine. The MWC uses a horizontal press twice, the second pressings being kept separate for *granel*, the cheapest type of wine. Pressings can account for as much as 8 per cent of the total volume of wine.

Cane-sugar spirit (*aguardente*) was used for fortification until its use was banned in favour of wine alcohol in 1967. In 1973 it was made compulsory for producers to purchase alcohol from the Junta delegation. This monopoly was inherited by the IVM and lasted until 1992. Now 96 per cent rectified spirit (mainly from France and Spain) is used, and shippers can purchase it for themselves, though its quality has to be checked by the IVM. The process of fortification is simplicity itself. The IVM publishes a set of tables called *O Adegueiro* ('The Cellarman') which show how much alcohol needs to be added to the partially fermented must, based on density and temperature measurements, to arrive at the desired degree of sweetness. Generally speaking, by adding about 21 per cent spirit for sweet wine, between 13 and 16 per cent for medium-sweet wine, 12 to 13 per cent for medium-dry wine, and 9 per cent for dry wine, the wine-maker ends up with wine with the sweetness he wants at 17° alcohol, which is the level at which madeira is generally kept within the lodges.[7] The simplest way to fortify is to pump the wine into tanks containing the requisite amount of spirit.

This wine, called *vinho claro*, is now allowed to rest for several months during a period called the first *estágio*; it is common to store it in concrete or stainless steel tanks rather than in wood. This period provides an opportunity to assess the wines and prepare them for the next stage of the process, *estufagem*, which is the heating of the wines in *estufas*. Each tank is analysed to determine its quality, and the wines are divided into *lotes* (lots). Most firms (MWC, Henriques & Henriques, Borges, Silva Vinhos) clarify and filter the wine before *estufagem*. Barbeito and Justino Henriques prefer to leave these until after *estufagem*. Gelatine is the most usual clarifying agent, though bentonite, which helps to stabilize the proteins in the wine, is also used. Clarification of a tank takes about thirteen days. Filtering techniques are more varied, and include diatomaceous earth filters ('Spanish earth') and filtering pads. Centrifuges were in use by some shippers during the 1980s, but they were expensive and have fallen out of favour. The shippers who fine the wine before *estufagem* believe that this removes undesirable components of the *vinho claro*, such as thermo-resistant yeasts which can develop after *estufagem*; it can also lessen the risk of faults such as mercaptan developing, and help the wines to retain their primary characteristics – particularly their aromas – and a low volatile acidity.

At this point some shippers will select a small amount of the Tinta Negra Mole for ageing in cask like the traditional varieties, but the main part will go for *estufagem*, which generally starts in January or February. It is in their handling of this process, which has aroused controversy since it was invented, that we begin to see more note-worthy differences between the shippers. Formerly (until the early 1990s), when wine was fermented completely dry, it was not uncommon for wine destined for the cheaper blends – and in the case of some shippers, all their blends – to be put into the *estufas* before the alcohol level had been corrected to 17°.[8] This possibly had an advantage insofar as there was a marginal saving in alcohol, some of which is lost during *estufagem*. The disadvantage was that, with a relatively low alcohol level, the lactic and malic acids in the wine (there being no malolactic fermentation in madeira) meant it was more apt to develop excess acidity and disagreeable smells and tastes. At the moment, however, fortification before *estufagem* appears to be general.

All *estufa* tanks, whether made of stainless steel, concrete or wood, are essentially the same, and all have a facility for heating the wine by means of hot water piping. Because the legal limit to which the wine may be heated is 55° C, the tanks are also equipped with a maximum-minimum type thermometer gauge to record the upper limit of the heating. There is no lower limit. The tanks often have a small tap through which a sample of the contents can be drawn off. When the shipper decides to start *estufagem* he writes to the IVM, who will send a representative on the appointed day to oversee the filling of the *estufa* and to seal it with tapes and wax once it is full. The wine now has to remain in the *estufa* for a minimum of 90 days, and at the end of this period the representative from the IVM will return to check that the seals are intact and that the maximum temperature has not been exceeded. Some shippers may give the wine a little extra heating after this if they consider it would benefit – for example, if it has not lost enough of its red colour, or the levels of total acidity and sulphur dioxide are too high. The degree of sweetness of the wine makes no difference to the amount of *estufagem* it receives.

The simplest form of heating is to raise the wine to a preset temperature, keep it there for most of the three months, and then let it cool down. Although the chosen temperatures vary a good deal, this is what most shippers do. Thus, Barbeito have the highest temperature, heating the wines to a maximum of 51°C for three months. Justino Henriques come next with three months at 50°C, while Silva Vinhos heat the wine to a maximum of 47°C for three months and then allow it to cool to about 36°C during a further month. Henriques & Henriques heat the wine at 45°C for a minimum of three months, and Borges are further down the scale with temperatures of between 40° and 45°C. The MWC, however, subjects its wines to a more complex cyclic regime of heating and cooling four times over the three-month period. During the first week the wines are heated to 40°C, then allowed to cool slowly to 35°C over the next two weeks. The cycle begins again in the fourth week, during which the wine is brought up to 40°C, and is allowed to cool again over the next two weeks. The cycle is repeated a third and fourth time during the final six weeks. But whatever temperature a shipper chooses, and whatever individual variations he makes to the basic procedure, in all cases the wine has to be cooled to ambient, or near-ambient, temperature before being removed from the *estufa*, otherwise excessive oxidation occurs.

Estufagem, as has always been known, has a considerable effect on the wine. The aim is to give it a more mature character simulating wood ageing – it being reckoned that three months of *estufagem* is equivalent to about two years of *canteiro* ageing. The wine develops the characteristic slightly toasted smell of madeira.

Handled badly, *estufagem* can 'rip the guts out of the wine', as one shipper expressed it, and cause it to develop disagreeable stewed tastes and baked smells. In general there is some evaporation during the process, and the wine gains in sweetness as the sugars are caramelized, loses colour and increases in volatility. If any bad tastes and smells are present after *estufagem*, they can generally be remedied by the use of charcoal (*carvão*), but this tends to destroy the desirable characteristics of the wine (by reducing colour, flavour and smell) as much as it corrects the faults.

Modern stainless steel tanks, with their superior insulation, lose heat very slowly and trap the smell of the cooking wine. When concrete tanks are used, however, the area in which they are kept becomes something like a sauna, and a rich smell, somewhere between that of a gingerbread bakery and a blackcurrant jam factory, pervades the atmosphere. Pipes of *canteiro* wine which are showing difficulties after a year may be 'assisted' by being kept here for a short while. There used to be *armazems de calor*, stores which were heated to about 35°C by means of hot water pipes round their walls, in which casks would be kept for six months. This method does not appear to be used any more.

After *estufagem* has been completed, the wine-maker then has to re-examine the wine, deal with any faults, and decide on its quality. Some wine will be earmarked for *granel* and may be stored in stainless steel tanks; the rest will be put into large wooden vats, some destined to provide 3 year old wine, some 5 year old wine, and in some cases 10 year old wine.

Varietal madeiras

The making of Sercial, Verdelho, Boal and Malvazia is not greatly different from that of Tinta Negra Mole, except that *estufagem*, which is against the law for vintage wines, is never used.[9] This is principally because, if you use *estufagem* or artificial heat, you get a dry extract (what would be left if the water and alcohol were taken away) of about 20 grams per litre, which is too low for a vintage. All vintage wines are consequently *canteiro* wines. This description of the vinification of traditional varieties will therefore concentrate mainly on the significant differences from that of Tinta Negra Mole and on other matters of note.

Shippers vary in the degree to which they make special arrangements for the traditional varieties. As the quantity of grapes is so small, they either set aside special days for their reception, or receive them only 'by appointment'. The MWC has a hopper dedicated to white varieties and reserves two fermentation tanks solely for them. Barbeito use a separate continuous press, and for quantities of white grapes under 16,000 kg Justino Henriques use a smaller press brought from their former winery. Some shippers, like Henriques & Henriques, have smaller vinification tanks especially for the traditional varieties. Until some time in the 1980s it was usual to ferment these in lodge casks (*bica aberta*). The larger firms no longer do this, but Borges, Barros e Sousa and the IVM continue to do so. In most cases traditional varieties are vinified without any maceration, but here again there are exceptions. Henriques & Henriques give Malvasia full maceration, whilst the MWC destalks all white varieties and, after a little crushing in the machine, pumps the must to the tanks to have eight hours of maceration. The MWC also ferments the white varieties at 20°C, the lowest vinification temperature used by any company.

The traditional varieties are fortified on the same lines as the Tinta Negra Mole, and then rested for a while. They are then racked and fined, put into cask and allocated to a warm but not artificially heated store. This is also when they are analysed and classified according to their organoleptic qualities. For example, the best Verdelho, with vintage wine potential, may be designated 'Verdelho A', while 'Verdelho B' will appear more suitable for an eventual 5 or 10 year old wine. As he does with all his stocks, the wine-maker or oenologist will monitor the progress of these wines year by year. It will become increasingly clear which wines have the potential to age to become a vintage, and which are falling short. The latter are progressively designated as suitable for 5, 10 or 15 year old blends. Most wine-makers, however, develop a feel for wines of vintage quality, and say that after ten years they have a good idea which they are.

Maturing the wine

Madeira is essentially a wood-aged wine. In this respect it is like tawny port; but whereas tawny port has a bottled-aged brother known as vintage port, madeira has nothing corresponding. All madeira is wood-aged. Whether it is stored in casks or in large wooden vats, the aim is the same: to allow it a slow, controlled reaction with oxygen while its volume reduces and its components become increasingly concentrated. During the ageing process, therefore, the proportions by volume of sugar, acidity, alcohol and dry extract increase, and the wine develops in complexity and flavour. That is why, generally speaking, old wood-matured madeira has more character than young wine, and why it is worth storing, even at the cost of evaporation and diminishing quantities. It is most important that the wine can breathe through the wood. Without this – when, for example, it is stored in stainless steel tanks or glass demijohns – the wine will stay virtually (although not completely) inert.

The process of ageing in wood constitutes the maderization of the wine. When we talk of a maderized table wine, we mean that it has a nasty taste and smell because the air has got to it too rapidly (generally because of a faulty or dried-out cork) and the oxygen has reacted with the wine adversely. It has become oxidized. But when the oxygen gets to the wine very slowly through the wood, which acts in a way as a filter, *and there is a lot of alcohol present*, far from reacting adversely, the wine is stabilized by it. The chemical analysis of this process is extremely complicated, and not entirely understood.[10] Briefly, the high levels of acidity and alcohol in fortified madeira and the relatively small amount of oxygen to which it is subjected inhibit the formation of acetic acid, while the oxygen reacts with amino acids and proteins in the wine to change them slowly into other chemicals such as aldehydes, which give the wine the smells and flavours associated with wood ageing. As it ages, therefore, madeira is gradually stabilized by oxygen, which removes by chemical reaction those elements of the wine which tend to destabilize it. In time (after about 10 years) the wine reaches a stage at which it becomes relatively immune to damage from exposure to the air. That is why, after a bottle of old madeira has been opened, it does not 'go off', but remains drinkable for at least several months.

The most suitable wood for ageing madeira is American oak, which is mild and does not impart a taste to the wine, though it is an important component in the development of certain flavours. Most casks are made from American oak, but Baltic oak and Brazilian satinwood are much used for large vats. Because wooden casks are practically no longer used for shipping wine, many firms have a large supply of them and at present have no need to purchase new ones. With careful cooperage casks can be used almost indefinitely. When they are new they have to be seasoned carefully – formerly achieved by using them to ferment the wine – to avoid strong wood tastes in the wine.

As the wine matures in cask it changes, and how it does so depends largely upon the conditions in which it is kept. Evaporation, for example, is less from large vats than from casks because the surface area of the wood exposed to the air is smaller in relation to the volume of wine. In lodge pipes, for example, evaporation averages almost 4 per cent a year, or 18.5 per cent every five years, in ordinary atmospheric conditions. There is less evaporation of water and more of alcohol in conditions of high humidity, and this is inimical to the evolution of the wine. Dry, warm conditions are most conducive to a good evolution. For this reason, the MWC finds its São Francisco lodge in the centre of town better for maturing and concentrating the wines than its Mercês lodge, which being at a higher altitude is cooler. Conversely, evaporation can be excessive in very hot, dry conditions, such as occur when each August Madeira is subjected to arid winds (the *leste*) from the Sahara. Putting unusual conditions to one side and taking the 4 per cent average annual figure, this means that over seventeen years the shipper will lose half of his wine in lodge pipes through evaporation. It is consequently very easy to understand why old vintages which have been kept in wood, their rarity apart, become so very expensive. In fact, after a certain point (around ten years), when the wine's evolution is considerable, the shipper may decide to store the wine in larger wooden containers to reduce the evaporation.

Policies vary with regard to the topping up of casks. Some shippers will leave the wine undisturbed for a few years, but others check every cask during the course of the year (to test for faults) and take this opportunity to top up. Invariably this is now done with wine of the same variety and of the same vintage,[11] but a small 'breathing' space is always left in each cask. In the case of very old vintage wines, when the quantity is so diminished that topping up the cask becomes impossible and evaporation losses too expensive to bear, the wine will be transferred to glass demijohns, usually with a capacity of 20 or more litres. Once this happens the evolution of the wine is halted.

There is another tricky problem, however, which shippers are reluctant to talk about. Wine, as it ages in cask and reduces in volume, increases in viscosity. If one were simply to leave the wine to reduce in this way, in about sixty years or thereabouts it would have become as black as treacle and of much the same consistency. Leave it longer and it starts to solidify. (In Rutherglen, Australia, I was offered a taste of a 100 year old muscat, looking like meat extract, on a teaspoon.) Not only this, but the concentration of flavour becomes so overpowering that tasting the wine ceases to be pleasurable, while the concentration of alcohol burns the throat. It follows, therefore, that in order to keep the wine in condition it has to be refreshed from time to time. This does not need to be much or often, but it does have to happen. One port producer in the Douro, who let me taste wines which had been in cask for from sixty to over a hundred years, told me that they had been *minimally* refreshed by 5 per cent every thirty years. This had stopped them from getting like the Rutherglen muscat, but they were still treacly and very unpleasant to drink. It follows, therefore, that to be fit for marketing, old vintage wines which have been in cask for over sixty years will have had to be refreshed at some stage. Cossart cites vintages which have been in cask for over 140 years.[12] Indeed, when vintage wines lack the concentration which should be expected of such old wines, they may have been over-refreshed.

Why then is there such secrecy and evasion over this issue? One reason is that the refreshing of vintage wines is strictly speaking illegal – although a spokesman for the IVM agreed that it has to be done. Another reason may be that, if the wines are refreshed with different wine, this compromises their genuineness as a single vintage. The public likes to think it is getting a product which has not been 'tampered with'. Some shippers may escape this problem by removing the wines from cask before they start to reach the unpleasurable drinking stage, but I suspect that judicious refreshing is the normal response. It is nothing to be ashamed of, and anyone who understands the way in which fortified wine ages in cask will expect it to happen. There is in fact a way to solve the problem *and* maintain the integrity of the vintage, which is to store a little of the wine in demijohns once it is twenty years old. As it will not develop viscosity while stored in glass, this wine is ideal for refreshing the wine in cask at a later stage. I believe that this may occur in Oporto, but it does not happen, so far as I am aware, in Madeira.

The characteristic development of the components of the wine is that at first they drop and then, as the wine concentrates, they increase. Thus, when you start with a cask of wine at 17 per cent alcohol by volume, after one year it comes down to 16.8 per cent; after three years it will have increased to about 17.1 or 17.2 per cent; and after five years it will have increased to 17.5 per cent. The alcohol level will then increase steadily, so that wines which have been in cask for thirty or forty years sometimes reach 22 or 23 per cent – by which time they are a liquorous wine. It is the same with acidity. Normally you start with a wine which has 9 or 10 grams per litre of total acidity.[13] After fortification this comes down to 8 grams per litre, and after *estufagem* or three years in cask it comes down further to 6 grams per litre. After that, acidity is like alcohol and increases with age, and after thirty or forty years can rise to 14 grams per litre total acidity. Volatile acidity, which after twenty years will be about one gram per litre, can rise to as much as 2.2 grams per litre in old wines – though without imparting the flavour of vinegar, because most of this volatile acidity comes with concentration in the cask and so is in balance with the other flavours that develop. When you taste such wines, however, they are so round that nobody guesses that the total acidity is so high. A Verdelho which had been in cask for seventy-five years was recently found to have 24° alcohol and 17 grams per litre of total acidity. The sugar also concentrates, but this may not be so noticeable because it tends to be masked by the acidity and the two maintain a sort of balance. However, in very old wines – particularly ones made before there were strict guidelines on sweetness – this can blur the borderline between the different styles of wine, making it for example quite possible to mistake a Verdelho for a Boal. Finally, cask ageing affects the colour of the wine. Those which are dark to start with tend to lose colour during the first two years and then steadily gain in intensity. Light wines gain colour right from the start.

How a wine develops depends, at the end of the day, not just on how it is kept but on what it was like to start with. Only the very best wines, probably no more than about 5 per cent of the traditional varieties, will show themselves capable of the development necessary to become a vintage wine. The others fall in between the lowest grades and that summit, and are therefore suited for blending into the various qualities of wine between *granel* and vintage. It is therefore the work of the blender which we must next consider.

From Cask to Customer

Official classification of wines

Madeira is a V(L)QPRD wine: Vinho (Licoroso) de Qualidade Produzido em Região Determinada, 'a (liquorous) quality wine made in a specific region'. Within this category it is a DOC wine; that is, one with a controlled appellation.

There are restrictions on what madeiras, and what sorts of blends of madeira, can be put on the market. The lowest category is *granel*, which is wine exported in bulk. Much, but not all, is destined for use in the kitchen, but it is largely up to the discretion of the importer how it is bottled and sold. The wine can be sold after the 31 October following the vintage – that is, when it is one year old – and its degree of sweetness is determined by the customer's requirements.

The remaining categories were established in 1982 by legislation which defined a series of descriptive terms that may be used on labels. However, during the late 1980s the IVM issued a proposal to alter certain of these provisions and to add others.[1] This proposal has never been made into a regulation with the force of law, but is nevertheless adhered to by the trade. In the list of descriptive terms which follows, the modifications resulting from the IVM proposals are given the qualification 'unofficially'.

Rainwater. This designation is reserved for wine which has a colour between 'golden' and 'semi-golden', is between 1° and 2.5° Baumé, and is of good quality.

Seleccionado (Selected, Choice, Finest). This is wine of requisite quality which has been aged for a minimum of three years, is invariably made from authorized varieties (mainly Tinta Negra Mole) and can be dry, medium-dry, medium-sweet or sweet.

Reserva (Reserve, Old). This is wine of requisite quality which has been aged for a minimum of 5 years. It can be made either from authorized varieties (such as Tinta Negra Mole) and can be dry, medium-dry, medium-sweet or sweet, or from traditional varieties (Verdelho, Boal, Malvasia or Terrantez), in which case its sweetness will correspond with the levels laid down for each variety. Sercial, in order to comply with another regulation mentioned at the end of this list, should be a minimum of 7 years old, but its sale after 5 years is unofficially permitted.

Reserva Velha (Old Reserve, Very Old). This is wine of requisite quality which has been aged for a minimum of 10 years. It can be made from either authorized or traditional varieties. If from the former, it can be dry, medium-dry, medium-sweet or sweet; and if from the latter, its sweetness will correspond with the level appropriate for each variety.

Extra Reserva (Extra Reserve). This category does not exist in the 1982 legislation, but is unofficially permitted when the wine is of requisite quality and has been aged for a minimum of fifteen years. Like the *Reserva Velha* wines, it can be made from either authorized or traditional varieties, but in practice has so far been confined to the latter.

Superior. This designation is used 'when the product has requisite (outstanding) quality and is obtained from traditional noble varieties' and 'can be associated with the name of the variety (i.e. Bual Superior, Superior Malmsey)'.

Garrafeira (or *Frasqueira*). 'When this designation is associated with a vintage year, the product must be made from traditional noble varieties, having had the ageing referred to below, and must present requisite (outstanding) quality . . . Minimum of ageing: twenty years before being bottled, and two years in bottle'. Unofficially, the two years in bottle stipulation has been dropped. No English translation of *garrafeira* is offered. In practice, the shippers speak of these as vintage wines, and I doubt if anyone who has written in English about madeira during the last fifteen years has not done so too. However, in the view of the IVM, *garrafeira* does *not* mean 'vintage' in the sense of simply indicating a wine made in a certain year. It indicates that it was made in a certain year *and* has been matured for twenty years (in contrast to wine made in a certain year but matured for less than twenty years). This matter will be discussed further below.

Canteiro. To qualify for this description, wine must be fortified soon after fermentation and be aged in cask for a minimum period of 3 years.

Solera. The definition currently in use applies to new soleras, and not to those established last century or earlier this century. Soleras may or may not specify a date, but must be wines of a particular harvest, of requisite quality, which can only be bottled after 5 years of ageing in cask. After this time, only 10 per cent of the wine can be drawn off for bottling from each of the solera casks each year, the casks being topped up with younger wine of identical quality. This can be repeated nine times, after which all remaining wine has to be bottled. If a date is used in conjunction with the solera, it must be the date of the base wine.

There is a further regulation which in effect authorizes a category of *canteiro* wines which can be sold bearing the date of a harvest year, but which, unlike *garrafeira* wines, need not have been in cask or bottle for as long. It reads as follows: 'An indication of age or of a vintage year is reserved for wines of noble varieties and can only be used when the product has a minimum age of 7 years for wines made from the Sercial variety and of 5 years for wines of the remaining varieties'.[2]

This regulation has been unofficially modified by dropping the words 'age or of', making it apply only when the date of a vintage is mentioned. Had this not been done, it would have ruled out a 5 year old *Reserva* Sercial, as noted above. What has not been modified is its authorization of the use of a vintage year on a bottle of wine which does not contain a *garrafeira* wine as defined above – or in other words, what is customarily referred to as 'vintage madeira' – but a wine from a single harvest, made from a traditional variety, where that harvest was at least five (not twenty) years ago (or seven years ago in the case of Sercial).

If that leaves you confused, you are in good company. Until I drew their attention to it, a number of shippers themselves appeared to be unaware of the possibility of putting a vintage year on bottles of wine which are not of *garrafeira* quality. Two shippers, however, are aware of it and are selling such wines (less than twenty years old) with vintage dates on them, bearing the IVM's guarantee of authenticity. It was in response to my asking how this could be so that a spokesman for the IVM insisted that *garrafeira* does not mean 'vintage, in the sense of simply bearing the date of the harvest'. The implications of this are discussed elsewhere.[3]

There are other anomalies, some of which are mentioned elsewhere in this book,[4] but the patient reader who has followed me thus far through the labyrinth will now get his reward. The preamble to these regulations states that 'the dispositions of the present decree seek ... to protect consumers against the confusions to which labelling so often gives rise'.

Blending

The role of the blender is one of the most important in any shipping company. He starts with the stocks of wine that have accumulated in store after every vintage, and has to produce blends of these to suit the shipper's commercial requirements and to comply with the legally recognized types of blends. Not all companies work in exactly the same way, but the following account, modelled on practice at the MWC, is typical. Most shippers, unless they are starting up, have already-established brands. The blender's job is therefore two-fold: to continue to produce these brands with as much consistency of style as possible and, when required, to create new ones. The procedures are the same in each case. Most shippers maintain minimum stocks of each brand. As these are sold it becomes necessary to replace them and, on the basis of actual sales and forecast sales, the blender will work out a production timetable. He will also have to bear in mind large volume sales periods such as Christmas, and the necessity of emptying as many tanks as possible immediately prior to the next vintage. Let us, for the sake of argument, suppose that he needs to produce another batch of 3 year old Dry. This is how he will set about it.

He will have a stock book (or more likely a computer record nowadays) in which all the company's wines are recorded. For each commercial brand he will have details of the amount previously blended, how much was bottled, stock movements to indicate the present position, and how much (if any) is still in store waiting to be bottled. For each of the stock lots – the blending materials – in store, his stock book will record the lot number, the identification number of the storage vat, the number of litres, its age and maturity, and the history of problems (if any) the wine has suffered.

The blender knows his stock lots like he knows his children, and he will therefore have a good idea about which of them are likely to be suitable components for continuing a blend. In the case of the 3 year old Dry, he will send instructions to the cellarman to draw small quantities from those lots he is going to work with and send them to the laboratory. Here he will make up one or two trial blends, usually of about two litres and incorporating six or seven different wines, which will be submitted to a small company jury (who of course will have a sample of the existing version of the brand with which to compare them). If they approve one of the trial blends, the blender will then issue orders to the cellarman to make up a large quantity to the same recipe, using up the existing stocks of the component wines as far as is possible. This becomes what is known as the 'base wine' for the blend. A sample of this is sent to the laboratory for analysis – a process described in the next section of this chapter – and the blender will adjust and refine the sample. He may decide that he has to add another wine to impart a certain characteristic of the brand which is missing, or he may subtract something. He may have to adjust its colour, for example, either by adding caramel or (only in dire necessity) by using a charcoal filter to reduce it. He may have to adjust the sweetness so that it falls within the legal limits; this is done by adding rectified concentrated must or, less commonly, by blending with drier wine. He may have to adjust the level of alcohol. When he is satisfied, this new sample is then submitted to the jury and, if it is approved, the cellarman is instructed to make up a commercial quantity, using the base lot as the foundation, but incorporating the changes made to the second laboratory sample. Finally, to help maintain the style of the brand, the remaining stocks of the last batch (say about 5 per cent) will be added to the new batch.

There may be enough of the base wine to make more than one commercial batch, in which case what remains is stored for future use. During a year a large firm may have to make up on average two or more replacement blends for its brands. The procedure outlined above applies to the whole range of brands. It should be noted, however, that when wine is sold under a varietal name shippers are permitted to blend in up to 15 per cent of wine made from other varieties (e.g. Tinta Negra Mole); all shippers, as far as I am aware, take advantage of this concession except in the case of 15 year old wine. Vintage wines may be bottled in smallish batches (leaving some to age further in cask) or, depending on quantity, all at one time.

Legal controls

At this point, the blender must take into account the further controls on the production of wine carried out by the IVM. The analysis mentioned above is to ensure that the wine conforms to certain norms laid down by law (largely in compliance with the standards set by the OIV).[5] However, the blender will probably also measure other values in his analysis. Certain importing countries (such as Germany, the United States, Canada and Switzerland) impose standards of their own – e.g. an absence of lead or calcium – and the blender has to ensure that the wine conforms to the requirements of all recipient countries. Some countries, such as Canada and Switzerland, restrict the upper alcohol limit of wine.

The most important current standards are the following:[6]

Degree of alcohol	17–22 per cent at 20°C†
Degree of sugar	Very Dry: 0–0.5° Baumé
	Dry: 0–1.5° Baumé
	Medium-Dry: 1–2.5° Baumé
	Medium-Sweet: 2.5–3.5° Baumé
	Sweet: over 3.5° Baumé.
Volatile acidity	1.2–1.5 grams per litre (acetic acid)§
Fixed acidity	2.5 grams per litre (tartaric acid)
Total extract	No limit
Non-reducing extract	Over 12 grams per litre
pH	3.3 to 3.5
Malvina	15 milligrams per litre

† Exceptionally, madeira can be exported at as low as 15.5 per cent to countries which impose special limitations on alcoholic strength.
§ At present, over 10 year old wines are permitted to have a volatile acidity of 1.5 grams per litre, and until April 1999 madeiras made before 1980 may have a limit of 1.8 grams per litre. Thereafter the limit of 1.2 grams per litre will apply to all wines.

It is important that the blender gets his analysis right, because the

IVM does not normally carry out its own analysis until the wine is actually in bottle and ready for export. If the IVM's analysis shows divergences from the above norms, the wine will have to be decanted from the bottles – a hugely expensive and wasteful operation which encourages the shipper to ensure that his madeira will not be rejected.

Once the blender is satisfied that everything is correct, the wine will be bottled. Normally commercial blends will be cold stabilized by being held at between −5° and −7°C for about six days, so that tartrates are precipitated, and they may also receive a light sterilization filtration. Some firms, such as Henriques & Henriques, use cold stabilization only for their 3 and 5 year old madeiras, whilst others, like the MWC, use it for the entire range up to 15 year old wines. All bottling, corking and labelling is carried out automatically nowadays (except by Barros e Sousa), although wicker-covered bottles may require to have their labels applied by hand. Once the wine has been approved by the IVM, a paper strip called a *selo de garantia* is glued up one side of the neck of each bottle, over the top of the cork and down the other side of the neck; the capsule is then applied.

The *selo de garantia*, each one individually numbered, is issued by the IVM. It was redesigned in 1992 and was for a time coloured light blue, but now it is again white. The numbers of the *selos* allocated to every batch of wine are registered, and random checks are occasionally made to ensure that number and label correspond. To the exporter it means a tax of 1.5 escudos per bottle. To the consumer it is the IVM's guarantee that the wine conforms to the standards required by law, and fits the description on the label, which is itself subject to a number of legal requirements. First there are the IVM's requirements, which include conformity to the use of descriptive terms mentioned in the categorization of the wines. Then there are the requirements of importing countries, which can differ widely and are a continual headache to the exporter, who has to have different labels for different destinations.

At this stage, when the wine is bottled and labelled, a representative from the IVM visits the shipper's lodge and randomly chooses four bottles. A wax seal is then superimposed by the IVM representative on the cork of each of these bottles, and from this seal a cotton ribbon is led to the label, over which another seal is placed, in such a way that any attempt to open the bottle or tamper with its label and appearance would be immediately obvious. One of these four bottles remains in the hands of the producer, while the other three are removed by the IVM representative: one for analysis, one to serve as a tasting sample, and the third to be kept as a reserve bottle.

The IVM, in addition to analysing the sample, carries out an organoleptic test to confirm that the wine is of the 'requisite quality' referred to in the legislation. This is done by submitting the wine to a tasting panel drawn from a permanent group of acknowledged experts, which includes oenologists and wine-makers from the shippers' firms and other experienced tasters – such as one from the local brewery! The panel, which normally consists of six members, meets periodically to taste several samples, which are presented blind with an indication of the category of wine to which they aspire to belong. In the (relatively rare) event that a wine fails to find acceptance by the panel, it can be resubmitted using the shipper's reserve bottle, and with one of his representatives present. However, if the wine fails the appeal – as in the case of failing the analysis on appeal – and is rejected, it has to be decanted from the bottles and re-blended to overcome the objections which have been made. If all goes well, however, an EU form (the *documento do acompanha-mento da Comunidade Económica Europea*) is issued in duplicate (one copy for the importing client, one for the Customs), as is a Certificate of Origin authorizing the issue of *selos de garantia* and recording their individual numbers. The *selos* are fixed by the shipper. In the case of *granel*, the shipping containers are filled and then sealed in the presence of a representative of the IVM. The shipper reports the sale (with the serial numbers of the relevant documents) to the IVM and the current accounts of the wines used in the blend are adjusted.

In addition to adhering to the procedures outlined above, the shipper has to fulfil other legal obligations (introduced in 1957).[7] One of the most important of these is the maintenance of minimum stocks. The system is similar to that in Oporto, and has the aim of stabilizing commerce and keeping fly-by-night operators out of the market. The minimum stock level is sufficient volume to cover the export of wine for 18 months, based on the average actual exports during the previous three years, or 600 hectolitres, which-ever is the higher.[8] No shipper may export more than is compatible with the maintenance of his minimum stock unless he has given notice to the IVM that he is winding up his business. In addition, each shipper has an obligation to buy grapes at the next vintage. His obligation is based on 75 per cent of his exports during the year up to the 31 July immediately before the vintage, except that (in broad terms) he may have to buy more or less, depending on whether his stock level is below or above the minimum required.

12

Today's Madeiras

The characteristics of madeira

In this chapter I shall try to describe the qualities of madeira and how it should be assessed. Like any wine, madeira has to have the balance of components appropriate to its character, and in assessing it the professional will find this out by looking at it, smelling it, and finally by tasting it. The analysis of its attributes is a factual matter. In some cases (like colour and sweetness) it is a question of what is appropriate, but mostly the taster is looking for a large number and high degree of the positive characteristics, and a low number and low degree of negative characteristics. In the case of madeira, these can be illustrated diagrammatically by the table of opposites shown on page 144.

By considering these factors the taster will acquire an overall impression of quality. The best sort of glass to use for tasting and drinking madeira is a plain, medium-sized, tulip-shaped glass. Small, traditional port glasses are hopeless: they do not give one the opportunity to swirl the wine and release its bouquet. The wine should always be at room temperature and, except for the cheapest extra-dry and dry qualities, never chilled. As with any wine of quality, decanting helps the wine to breathe and prevents any sediment from getting into the glass.

Madeira, of course, has very distinctive characteristics which make it fairly recognizable even to unpractised tasters. These are the aromas which arise from wood ageing and the distinctive tastes mostly associated with caramelized sugar. When the wine is very old, however, these characteristics become very similar to those of other wood-aged wines – such as port and sherry – of a similar age, and it is not at all impossible to mistake one wine for the other.

COLOUR

Pale   Dark
(−) Dull (turbid)   Bright (+)

BOUQUET

(−) Acetic   Clean acidity (+)
(−) Simple   Complex (+)

PALATE

(−) Light   Weighty (+)
Dry   Sweet
(−) Fruitless   Fruity (+)
(−) Flavourless   Flavoursome (+)
(−) High acidity   Low acidity (+)
(−) Coarseness   Finesse (+)
(−) Simple   Complex (+)
(−) Unbalanced   Balanced (+)

FINISH

(−) Short   Long (+)
(−) Simple   Complex (+)

Indeed, although it is often said that madeira is unique, this is not entirely true. The people who say so are usually referring to the uniqueness of the *estufagem* process, but technically there is nothing to choose between a *canteiro* madeira and a *colheita* port: both are fortified to much the same level, and both are slowly matured in quite similarly sized casks at ambient temperatures. What differentiates them is that the grape varieties used in making them are, except in the rare cases of bastardo and moscatel, completely different.

The flavours and aromas associated with oxidation can be divided into several types: those associated with wood, such as pinewoods and eucalyptus; phenolic flavours, such as vanilla and turpentine; caramel flavours, such as black treacle, toffee, barley sugar, honey, coffee and chocolate; spicy flavours, such as cloves, cinnamon and saffron; nutty flavours, particularly almonds and walnuts; dried fruit flavours, such as apricots, plums and raisins; citrus flavours, in particular orange; and others less easy to classify, such as yeastiness and smokiness.

Excessive acidity and volatility with evident overtones of vinegar were common enough features of cheaper madeiras until quite recently but, having tasted my way through every shipper's commercial range while I was preparing this book, I have to say that the level of volatile acidity was remarkably low in all but a few cases, and the acid balance was generally good. Some people have a higher tolerance of acidity in wines than others. Mine is relatively low, so faults in the acid balance of these wines would have been particularly evident to me. Nor did I often find the stewed flavours which used to be an equally common manifestation of poor *estufagem*. It is clear to me that the general standard of making the commercial wines has greatly improved within the last five years.

The wines made from traditional varieties have individual characteristics which may be briefly summarized here.

Sercial. The palest of madeiras, its colour is similar to that of a very mature Sauternes or a Tokay: a kind of orange-gold tawny. Rather pungent when young, the smell is characterized by aromas of oranges and dried fruits. The oranges carry through to the taste, which develops a certain nuttiness with maturity, while the smell mellows and evolves overtones of turpentine. Very old Sercials seem to fade more readily than other varieties, but develop wonderful balsamic qualities with a patina of age which really defy description. Sercial is generally (and rightly) regarded as an aperitif wine, but it can be drunk with hors d'oeuvres. Old Sercial makes a good palate-cleansing end to a meal for those who do not like to finish on a sweet note.

Verdelho. In colour there is little to choose between this and Sercial, but Verdelho may be a degree darker. Less brusque than Sercial when young, the nose tends to be honeyed and slightly chocolaty, and the taste is reminiscent of candied citrus fruits, but more gently rounded than Sercial. With age Verdelho develops considerably in intensity, and is the favourite variety of many madeira drinkers. It can be drunk (as indeed can all the other varieties) at any time of day. It is pleasant as a pick-me-up in mid-morning, as an aperitif, and is traditionally an accompaniment to turtle soup.

Boal. The darkest of all varieties, Boal has a tawny colour approaching the darker hues to be found in tortoiseshell. Its smell is akin to barley sugar, and a rich mixture of caramel and dried fruit flavours, such as apricot, predominates on the palate. With age the sweetness which is so obvious in young Boal tends to be modified and it can taste similar to old Verdelho. Strictly a dessert wine, it makes a pleasant accompaniment to nuts and fruit, but I prefer to drink it by itself, without the distraction of food.

Malvazia. In former days the cheaper Malvazia look-alikes were sold, as the cheaper sweet blends are today, with the darkest colour (because of market demand, the shippers say). However, genuine Malvazia, until it has considerably matured, is perceptibly a shade lighter than Boal, although of the same general tone. The open and expressive bouquet, even when young, is unmistakably like vanilla cream toffee, sometimes with a hint of meatiness. The taste is also idiosyncratic, combining hints of caramel and barley sugar with marmalade, and, as with Boal, its pronounced sweetness is attenuated with age. Good Malvazia is never cloying, and deserves to be enjoyed by itself at the end of a meal.

Generic madeiras

The most disgusting madeira I know is the free welcoming glass served on presentation of the menu in Funchal's tourist restaurants. For many visitors new to Madeira, venturing out for dinner on the evening of their arrival and knowing nothing of the wine, it must be a traumatizing experience. Far from tempting them to find out more about madeira, it may well put them off it for life. The local word for this substance is *mistura*, indicating that it is a mixture of the remnants of production. Much comes out of plastic containers, which is illegal, and I suspect is bootleg madeira made from direct producers. As it is given away rather than sold, the wine is difficult for the authorities to control, but some way must soon be found, for it is the worst advertisement for madeira there could possibly be. It is ironic that this gesture of hospitality should work so potently to undermine the image of increased quality which the industry is struggling to build.

The very cheapest legal madeira, *granel*, appears mainly on the shelves of continental European supermarkets. Every shipper will tell you that his is of higher than average quality, whilst that of his rivals is unspeakable rubbish. I have had the opportunity of tasting several *granels* on the island. None of them was rubbish exactly, but none had many of the distinguishing marks of madeira. They were universally bland and characterless: not disagreeable, just boring.

3 year old madeiras

The port enthusiast does not, on the whole, find much to interest him among young ruby ports, and the same is true of the younger madeiras; the real madeira aficionado is unlikely to get worked up about 3 or 5 year old blends of Tinta Negra Mole. They are mostly well enough made, but there is a limit to what can be done in such a short time. Part of the trouble is that Tinta Negra Mole, whatever its versatility, is a grape with a certain asperity, and this is difficult to disguise in wine so young (even after *estufagem*). The 3 year old wines, therefore, almost always have a rather harsh edge to them, and this is perhaps why they seem to be generally more acceptable in their sweeter than in their drier versions. They are also more fragrant in their sweeter forms – the drier ones tend to have a smell reminiscent of wet cardboard. Moreover, they lack anything more than a whisper of an approximation to the varietal characters of the grapes after which they were until recently named, and which they are still presumably intended to resemble. That said, they are popular with the public: one shipper told me that he sells a hundred bottles of his 3 year old blends for every bottle of a 5 year old blend. At best, they are an honest drink, but without sophistication; at their (now happily infrequent) worst, they are unlikely to give pleasure to even a relatively unsophisticated palate. What is truly grotesque is the use of the English word 'Finest' to describe this category of wine. The wine is the lowest of the bottled qualities on the market, but it is described by a word implying that it is the best, under legislation introduced, may I remind the reader, 'to protect consumers against the confusions to which labelling so often gives rise'.

5 year old madeiras

When we turn to 5 year old wine we naturally find some advance in quality, though hardly a marked one. Two years is not an immense period of time in the world of wine. The situation is complicated by the fact that two shippers (Barbeito, MWC) use traditional varieties, whilst the rest (Borges, Henriques & Henriques, Justino Henriques and Pereira d'Oliveira) use Tinta Negra Mole. In their case I have to say that many of the remarks made about 3 year old wines equally apply. The asperity is only marginally less apparent, and there is still not much by way of convincing simulation of the traditional varieties (if that is still the aim) – though with the change in labelling laws there is no reason why there should be.

As far as the 5 year old traditional varieties are concerned, Verdelho is perhaps the most successful, being the variety which tends to mature quickest. Rainwater is therefore usually an agreeable, if light and undemanding, drink. The sweeter varieties can also be attractive, and they have much more individuality than their Tinta Negra Mole equivalents. I have not, however, found a Sercial in this category which I have liked. It has always been recognized as the most awkward variety when young, and used to have to be a minimum of 7 years old before sale. I wonder if it is worth the effort of trying to produce it. There is, after all, no fundamental reason – apart from tidiness – why a shipper should produce all four traditional varieties in a particular age range.

10 and 15 year old madeiras

Apart from Pereira d'Oliveira, all the shippers use classical varieties for their 10 year old blends. In my opinion it is only at this point that commercial madeiras start to become of interest to the serious madeira drinker, for here we are dealing with individual varieties which have had enough time to show their true characters. The wines generally have more fragrance, more weight and style, and begin to hint at the glories which older wines can achieve. It is salutary, perhaps, to reflect on the fact that these wines are not only twice the age of the next range down, but are older than most of the madeiras sold in the eighteenth and nineteenth centuries.[1]

Although they are not cheap, these are the wines for everyday drinking. One hopes, therefore, that the trade will find a way of opening the public's eyes to their delights. Because of evaporation during maturation, the cost of a 10 year old wine is always going to be considerably more than that of a 5 year old wine. However, if in the course of replanting and restructuring the vineyards the proportion of traditional varieties in comparison with Tinta Negra Mole can be increased, the differential in the cost of grapes will probably diminish.

15 year old madeiras are produced by Henriques & Henriques

and the MWC, who only make them from classical varieties. Pereira d'Oliveira is intending to introduce them. I can be unreservedly generous in my praise and enthusiasm for 15 year old madeiras. They are, in a sense, junior vintage wines, and act as a bridge between 10 year old wines and the vintages. Five more years in cask produce an enormous difference in maturity and an almost exponential leap in quality. For the drinker who jibs at the price of vintage wines, but who requires something of their quality, they are the answer. Indeed, being blended for immediate drinking, they lack the rawness of some young vintage wines, and may even be preferable.

Old soleras

Only one shipper – Borges – has thought it worthwhile to start a solera under the current rules. However, stocks of old solera wines may be sold off *provided they are already in bottle*. For a while not even this concession was available. The sad fact is that the status of madeira soleras was overlooked during negotiations with the EU, and this led to much subsequent confusion and beating of breasts. Some shippers are sorry, particularly if they have stocks of unbottled soleras; others are not. Richard Blandy's view is that it is wrong to sell bottles with a date from last century on them, when there is nothing like wine from last century in them.

One cannot disagree with that, for the public at large perhaps does not fully understand that the date on the bottle simply indicates the vintage of the wine with which the solera was started. The fact remains, however, that old soleras did seem to work from the point of view of quality, and that some old soleras are amongst the most delicious madeiras you can hope to taste. I remember with fondness three of Blandy's old wines – Verdelho Solera 1822, Bual Solera 1826 and Sercial Solera 1835 – which, when I was warden of a university hall of residence in the 1970s, were regularly sold in the Junior Common Room bar at under £2 a bottle. I recently tasted a Cossart Gordon 1860 Solera Sercial which was of superb quality, and the famous Cossart Gordon Solera 1808 Malmsey is favourably assessed in Chapter 13.

What is their secret? Part of it, I suspect, lies in their approachableness. Unlike very old vintage wines, which can arrive at formidable levels of concentration in cask, *soleras* sometimes appear to have a better balance, more freshness and more elegance.

This may be due to their being frequently refreshed with younger wine and, for the drinker who is overwhelmed by the weight of some vintage wines, soleras can be the answer. Whereas a small glass of an old vintage can sate the drinker, soleras offer more drinkability. And unlike even the 15 year old wines, which are blended as nearly to a standard as possible, soleras have considerable individuality. However, no more are being made, and unless the regulations are relaxed to enable unbottled stocks to be put on the market, they will eventually disappear. Bottles of older soleras appearing at auction are now commanding prices akin to those of vintage wines. *Pace* Richard Blandy, the discriminating public knows a good thing when it sees it.

Vintage wines

The discussion in this section concerns vintage wines in the sense in which they have always been understood: that is, as *garrafeira* wines with a minimum cask age of twenty years. These wines are the glory of madeira, and the yardstick by which it is judged to be a world class wine. I have already quoted from George Saintsbury, in whose opinion good madeira is comparable only to burgundy. His enthusiasm is not unique, however, and it is shared by many contemporary wine writers such as Michael Broadbent and Jancis Robinson. The fascination of vintage madeira arises not only from its apparent capacity to survive over centuries as a wine which can be drunk with pleasure, but because at its best it is capable of making such a strong statement about the wine potential of the grape.

The traditional method of indicating the contents of bottles of vintage madeira has been, and still is, by hand-stencilling the bottles with white paint. This has a striking appearance. Some shippers are now using machine-cut stencils (which I think cheapen the appearance of the bottles) or industrially pre-painted bottles (which, being quite deceptive, look much better). The information will typically include at least the grape variety and vintage, and generally the shipper's name.[2] In some cases *velho* or *velhissimo* is tagged on to the grape variety in addition to a vintage date: thus, *Boal Velhissimo* (Very Old Boal). Older bottles occasionally display in addition two or three initials, which indicate the person who originally owned the wine or from whom it was inherited. *R.A.V.*, for example, might signify Rui Abreu Vasconcelos, and a bottle bearing such initials would typically be passed down through the Vasconcelos family or its relatives, identifiable as having belonged once to their ancestor Rui Abreu. Occasionally a place name is used instead of, or in addition to, a grape variety. *Cama de Lobos* is certainly the most famous and most frequent of these, but others met with include *Campanário*, *Ponta do Pargo* and *São Martinho*. In the United States it is not uncommon to find madeiras named after the ships which carried them out during the nineteenth century.[3]

Labels have also quite often been used for vintage wines since the end of the nineteenth century, sometimes by themselves, sometimes in conjunction with stencilling. Shippers now have to supplement stencilling with back labels giving the additional information about volume, alcoholic strength, etc., which they are obliged to impart by law. In the United States, when old stencilled bottles are imported, the retailer has to add his own label, specifying volume, alcoholic content, (supposed) chemical content (e.g. 'contains sulphites'), and a health warning.

High-quality wines almost without exception have driven corks, which are covered with a wax seal. Most of the corks encountered in older bottles of madeira are astonishingly short, in comparison not just with long vintage port corks but also with those used for table wine. Many are barely two centimetres in length, suggesting either perpetual cork shortages or more-than-Scottish meanness, but they do their job adequately if they are periodically changed. Just occasionally, stopper corks (with a crimped plastic or metal top) are encountered in bottles of vintage wine. They make me think that the producer cannot have had a very high opinion of his wine or he would have chosen a less mass-produced-looking presentation for it.

By far the greater part of all madeira is now sold in standard shaped 75 cl bottles. Vintage wine is not obtainable in half bottles (as some cheaper blends are), but some producers, mainly during the twentieth century, have occasionally put vintage wines in dumpy bottles. These are easily distinguished from old hand-blown bottles by their regularity of shape. Needless to say, vintage wine is not sold in wicker-covered bottles, nor in the grotesquely misshapen bottles with dents and twisted necks that have recently appeared as a tourist gimmick.

Traditionally, bottles for vintage wine have tended to be on the heavy side and, to shield the wine from excessive light, have been made from densely coloured green glass. Sadly in my opinion, there is now a trend towards the use of table wine bottles made from much more translucent glass, and lighter in weight too. In presentational terms they do a disservice to old vintages, which need and deserve more *gravitas*.

The present situation regarding the sale of vintage madeiras is that in 1973 the Delegation of the JNV established *contas correntes* for existing stocks held by shippers, and by private individuals who chose to register them. These accounts were based purely on their owners' declarations, and no supporting documentation was required to authenticate the wines or their ages. They were, so to speak, taken on trust. Since then, only those vintage wines which were declared, and those made since 1973 (very few of which are yet mature enough for sale), can be legally sold on the island. The consequence is that over the last quarter century these registered vintage wines have been diminishing in quantity and are getting scarcer and scarcer, although visitors to Madeira are regularly astonished by the number of old vintages still being sold by the shippers. It is true that there are still considerable stocks of old wines in private hands. Occasionally they surface at auction.[4] One shipper told me that he could take me to a private cellar with over sixty old vintage wines in cask, 'each one better than the last'. One should not however become too excited about such news, simply because there is no way at the moment that shippers, if they acquire unregistered stocks, can sell them as vintage wines. The stock of marketable old vintage wines is therefore diminishing fast.

Many tourists are mesmerized by the dates on the bottles, and a surprising number of expensive vintages are bought as suitable presents for Uncle Henry and Aunt May on their birthdays. One-day visitors from cruise liners like the *Queen Elizabeth II* and the *Oriana*, which regularly stop at Madeira, descend like gannets and make huge inroads into the available vintages, forcing the MWC to make frequent defensive price increases to conserve its irreplaceable stocks. Inevitably, this pressure on stocks is beginning to show itself in the appearance on the market of vintage wines which are just on the twenty-year limit of being legally marketable. When I first began going to the island in the 1970s, about the youngest vintage available was 1940 and most were forty or more years old. Shippers would nurse their vintages until they felt they had reached their optimum development – different in each case – before bottling them and putting them on sale. Some still do, but others, reluctant perhaps to keep their capital tied up for longer than is necessary and finding their older vintages running out, put their wines on the market as soon as the law permits.

It will be sad if this becomes the general rule, because no vintage wine has reached its full development at twenty years; or rather, if it has, then it is not of the potential which used to be considered as absolutely indispensable for a wine to be considered of vintage quality. To put the matter in perspective, although a 20 year old tawny port is only half-way up the range of officially recognized categories for port (which extends to over 40 year old tawnies) – and in such a context cannot be considered as being so very special – a madeira which has been matured in wood for twenty years is at the acme of quality recognized in the official regulations for madeira. One hopes, therefore, that in their efforts to maintain and improve quality, shippers will continue to mature vintage madeiras for much longer than the minimum period required by law – even if such wines when they eventually appear on the market will inevitably have to carry a very large price tag.

Having said that, the ageing aspect of madeira can be exaggerated. It is certainly true that, like Tokay, madeira appears to be capable of indefinite life, and André Simon was right to say that 'no other wine will be not merely acceptable, but superlative a hundred years after it was made'.[5] However, it is certainly not true that greater age necessarily means better to drink. In the notes on various vintage wines in the next chapter, the reader will note how many disappointments there were amongst the really old vintages and, conversely, how many splendid wines are to be found amongst less venerable vintages still obtainable on the island. Age is not in itself a guide to quality. Madeira can dry out like any other wine, and eventually does; and like vintage port, after more than about a hundred years in bottle there is a risk of madeira becoming spirity. It is always happier in cask than it is in bottle. Although, when properly looked after, madeira may well be able to live indefinitely in cask, in bottle it is subject to many of the same hazards as other wines, though it may take much longer for madeira to react to them.

Sadly, perhaps, we live in an age of vintage-year worship; dates fascinate us and we are apt to pay too much attention to them. The oldest extant vintage known to me is 1715. The fact that this is some thirty years before the fortification of madeira became common must put in doubt the ability of wine of this vintage to have survived into the present century. It is of course just possible that it was fortified thirty or more years after it was made. Fortification as part of the process of vinification did not become common until well into the nineteenth century, and before that fortification was carried out just prior to shipping. Another theory I have heard is that the wine might have been made on Porto Santo, where the climate produces grapes with high degrees of potential alcohol.[6] When I recently opened a bottle purporting to be Moscatel 1715, I was curious to see if I could establish the probability of its authenticity and sent off a sample for gas chromatography analysis by a chemist who had previously examined around a dozen early nineteenth- and late eighteenth-century madeiras. The result showed two interesting things. Firstly, the level of alcohol was 17.35 per cent by volume, indicating that the wine must certainly have been fortified. Secondly, the levels of the numerous volatile esters and aldehydes were unusual for a madeira of such a great age and suggested a much younger (nineteenth-century) wine. The disappointing conclusion was therefore that, although clearly very old, this was not likely to be an authentic 1715 wine. That said, it also has to be pointed out that analysts on the island are usually very reluctant to put too specific a date on old wines submitted for analysis, and that 'over sixty years old' is about the limit to which most of them will commit themselves.

Carrying this thought further, it is probably only the oldest-established shippers who have proper records that can verify with reasonable certainty the *bona fides* of their vintage wines. Such shippers may have made the wines themselves, although in the case of wines which predate the establishment of the firm they will have been obtained from elsewhere (such as from other shippers, shippers going out of business, the stocks of the original makers, or from the cellars of private families). Wines which have come from family cellars are occasionally from a particular vintage by repute or family tradition. Even the appearance of a date stencilled on a bottle is no guarantee that what is inside comes from that vintage. With really old bottles there is always the possibility that it is the date of bottling, or even the date of a *solera*. All of which leads me to urge the reader to resist, to some extent, the lure of dates. What is important, at the end of the day, is what is inside the bottle.[7]

Another reason for not letting oneself be hypnotized by vintage years is that, in order to be bottled as a vintage at all, the quality of a madeira already has to be extremely high. This makes the question of whether it is from this or that vintage much less important than it is for a table wine. Yet another important factor which influences the quality of the wine is how long it has spent in cask before being bottled. As was explained in the section on the maturation of madeira, the wine ages while it is in wood, but this development is arrested when it is put in a container through which it cannot breathe. A madeira from a remote vintage year which was bottled after thirty years in wood, and has spent twice that time in bottle, will not be as 'old' a wine, in terms of cask ageing, as a madeira from a more recent vintage which has just been bottled after spending sixty years in wood. This illustrates how important it can be to know the bottling date of a vintage madeira: information which sadly is not available from all shippers, and seldom available for bottles bought from other sources.

Because madeira in a bottle can breathe a little through the cork, it is not quite true to say that its development is totally arrested: it is, however, all but arrested. This has the consequence that when the bottle is opened madeira requires a long time to re-oxygenate itself (breathe) before it relaxes and starts to give off the aromas and to show all the flavours it had in cask. These become dormant in the bottle and it takes time for the wine to come to life again. The longer the wine has been in bottle, the more time it takes to recapture these qualities; a madeira which has been in bottle for upwards of sixty years may require two, three or even four days to regain its composure. I can only echo the words of Noël Cossart on this subject: 'The period of allowing old wine to breathe cannot be overdone in the case of madeira'.[8] Sadly, the contents of many old bottles are consumed before the wine has had an opportunity to get back into condition. Sometimes, when a wine has been in bottle for more than about fifteen years, it gives off a turpentine-like bottle stink when opened. Normally this will clear after a short time, particularly if the wine is oxygenated a little by decanting it once or twice. But when a madeira has been in bottle for more than half a century and has as it were gone into hibernation, it can develop a rather papery smell which is difficult to describe, but instantly recognizable, and all its qualities seem muted. In this case the wine is 'bottle sick'. Normally, if you are lucky, this will disappear as the wine recovers its health (which may, as mentioned above, take several days), but this does not always happen.

Bottle sickness must be carefully distinguished from bottle age. Unlike the shippers themselves, some madeira drinkers actually prefer their vintage madeira to have spent some time in bottle. This taste is parallel to the fashion which used to exist for bottle-aged sherry. When I first started to drink madeira I belonged to this band, but more recently, having had opportunities to compare wine from cask with the same wine out of bottle, I am less sure. The main characteristic of bottle age is a certain austerity and dryness which the madeira, particularly if it is a sweet one, develops on its finish. The wine is somehow more elegant, with a better defined, leaner profile. It is not necessarily better, however, for that is ultimately a matter of personal taste.

The custom on the island is to keep bottles standing upright instead of binning them horizontally. The main reason for this is because madeira attacks corks rather rapidly, and the wine is able to breathe a little better when the air inside the bottle is next to the cork. The general humidity of the island appears to help the corks from drying out, but in well-kept cellars it is common to recork bottles every thirty years or so. In some cellars a back label gives the recorking history of old bottles – Henriques & Henriques do this for their oldest wines. Less often, old vintage wines are rebottled. In this case it is normal to give the wine a light filtering through muslin to oxygenate it slightly. The advantage of recorking is that it reduces ullage and ensures that the wine is in good condition. Failure to recork will eventually result in the cork drying out and excess evaporation taking place. I have seen really old bottles with corks so shrivelled that they had ceased to adhere to the sides of the bottle and were kept in place only by the wax seal.

It is a pity that this policy of recorking is insufficiently understood by collectors of old madeiras, who are sometimes suspicious of it on the grounds that it might mean that the contents of the bottle had been tampered with. That is an argument only for ensuring that the bottle has a good provenance and that the recorking has been reputably carried out. The quest for authenticity can be carried too far where corks are concerned, and a wine which has been regularly recorked is much more likely to be in good condition than one which has not.

After many years madeira – like all wines which have not been filtered to death – casts a crust which tends to adhere to the bottle. With time, a little sediment, which may remain loose, may also be deposited at the bottom of the bottle. Sometimes this is a fine powder, but mostly it has the consistency of coffee grounds. It is therefore worth taking care while decanting the bottle, which is something I would always recommend.

Despite island custom, some merchants in England do bin bottles of madeira on their sides. Whether this is true of other countries I cannot say. My advice to purchasers of old bottles of madeira is to maintain the regime to which the bottle has been subjected. It is often easy to establish this by holding the bottle up to the light and looking at the pattern of crusting inside the bottle. Just as madeiras mature more rapidly in warmer climates, so the process of crusting occurs more quickly in Madeira than, for example, in England. If the bottle has been stored upright the crusting will start at the level of the wine in the neck of the bottle. If the bottle has been stored on its side the staining on the bottle will tend to be greater on the lower side of the neck, and will continue up to the bottom of the cork. Otherwise, madeira is fairly tolerant of storage conditions, and can (and prefers to) be stored at a higher temperature than is recommended for other wines, provided the atmosphere is not too dry. A warm and humid ambience is fine; a dry and very cold one is not so good.

In the next chapter I shall survey many vintages ranging from the oldest to the youngest, amongst them some very famous madeiras and many that are still available for purchase. I hope it may be useful both to the specialist collector and to readers intending to purchase vintages currently available from the shippers. My survey shows clearly, I believe, that the best of the present is every bit as good as the best of the past, and that the enthusiast does not yet need to be apprehensive that the kind of madeira which so impressed George Saintsbury is now only a memory.

13
Notes on Some Vintage Madeiras

All the madeiras noted in this chapter, with only four exceptions, were tasted between November 1996 and May 1997. I hope that this may have given some consistency to my notes. Some madeiras were from my own collection and tasted with friends; others I was able to taste through the generosity of friends in Madeira and in England, and through the generosity of shippers who allowed me access to their vintage wines. I decided to include four wines which I had tasted previously because of their rarity, and because they were in differing ways so remarkable. I also decided, after much agonizing, to include three wines which are not strictly speaking vintages, but which from their superb quality might well have been. When a wine is currently on sale to the public on the island, this is stated under its name.

The madeiras have all been assessed on a scale of one to five stars. As almost all vintage madeiras are of a high standard – otherwise they would not have been kept for so long – this marking system is comparative *within* what is itself a high-quality bracket. Thus a ★★ mark indicates a wine of a high standard, while ★★★★★ indicates an awesome achievement, at the very pinnacle of vinous excellence. The marking is on the basis of how the wines are now. Some of the younger wines will no doubt improve if kept longer in cask, but it is sheer speculation to predict how they will appear in thirty, forty or more years' time. In bottle they will not develop quickly, and so they have been assessed for what they are now and are likely to remain within my lifetime. I have allowed myself the indulgence of awarding a rosette (✱) to wines which struck me as exceptional, or for which I have a special affection.

One of the dangers of trying to describe madeiras is repetitiveness. Superlatives can too easily be overworked, and descriptions can run to excess. I have tried to err on the side of prosaic description rather than flamboyance (though some readers may find this hard to believe). The privilege of tasting so many remarkable wines in such a relatively short period offered a unique opportunity to make comparisons which are normally impossible, and this alone made it seem worthwhile to try to record the experience here. My notes will also, I hope, enable the reader to infer much about the development of madeiras in bottle.

I have unashamedly purloined one of Michael Broadbent's descriptive terms: 'tangy'. It so aptly indicates citrous acidity that it would be impossible to think of a better word. I also use the terms 'fudge' and 'fudgy', in an idiosyncratic way, to try to pin down the characteristic of butter toffee which characterizes madeiras of all sorts. My use of these terms does not *necessarily* denote sweetness. I often detect in dry wines, however paradoxical it may seem, the taste of butter and caramel allied to a certain texture, without any sweetness.

Descriptions of the colour of wines are naturally dependent on the lighting conditions in which the wine is tasted. In some situations when tasting these wines there was insufficient light, and even reflecting the light off a white surface can, in such circumstances, give misleading results. In general I have used the word 'tawny' as the generic colour term in preference to others. It should be understood as the colour of a wood port which has lost its ruddiness.

The arrangement of the notes is self-explanatory. Where I have had information about the provenance of the wines – much of which has been derived from Christie's wine sale catalogues and is printed here by kind permission – and when it has seemed sensible to record details about the bottles and other circumstantial aspects of the wines, I have done so. (The reader should note that, when it comes to buying old bottles, with or without a shipper's name, it is impossible to over-emphasize the importance of a sound provenance.) The notes are printed in vintage date order.

References to the JNV seal of authenticity require some explanation. Before 1980 quality control was in the hands of the Delegation of the JNV, which in the late 1950s and early 1960s carried out a check on substantial stocks of old bottled wine on the island. Random samples were examined, and if the wine was judged consistent with the variety and date attributed to it, then the remaining bottles were branded with a small seal in brown wax superimposed on the existing wax seal. This seal is rectangular and measures 1.75 x 3 cm. Inside a border it displays at the top the letters 'JNV' slanting downwards from left to right, and at the bottom, separated by a squiggle, the letters 'REF'. I have also come across a round black wax seal, the diameter of a cork, with 'Junta Nacional do Vinho Madeira' encircling a crown with 'Delegação' underneath it. The presence of the JNV wax seal must give the purchaser of old bottles some confidence that the wine has a chance of being genuine.

Vintage madeiras

1715   Terrantez   **'J C A & C'**

Tasted in Gloucestershire in January 1986. In a thick glass burgundy-shaped bottle with a deep punt. Crumbly wax seal. Crudely stencilled 'TERRANTEZ/1715/J C A & C'. Ullaged to mid-shoulder. Dense crust entirely coating the inside of the bottle. Purchased in Funchal in September 1973. I have been unable to identify the shipper. I have seen identical bottles, however, from the celebrated Kassab collection. (Braheem Kassab was a Syrian embroidery merchant who put his personal seal, embossed 'B.A.K.', on the bottles he collected earlier this century, which are therefore easy to identify; what remained of his cellar was sold at a Christie's London auction in June 1986.) The wine initially suffered from bottle sickness, but improved over two or three days.

Dark tawny, with ruby and green glints, and very green rim; subdued, but balanced and attractive bouquet, with a little healthy volatility, but not spirity; faded and gentle, with vestigial sweetness, rounded, slightly toasted, with bitter accents; moderately intense finish, bitterness more apparent, but no great length. Is the date remotely genuine? Patently a very old wine, with all the hallmarks of Terrantez, but it seemed, though faded, *too* well preserved to be true. It drank, basically, like a madeira of the post-fortification era; just possibly it was fortified after having been aged. If so, the spirit was still remarkably well married to the wine. This wine will always remain a puzzle. It would be absurd to award it stars after eleven years, but it certainly deserved several.

1715   Moscatel

Purchased in Madeira in December 1983. In a dark green glass, two-part moulded bottle. Stencilled 'Moscatel/1715'. Healthy moist cork under thick wax seal. Dense crust entirely coating the inside of the bottle. No sediment on decanting. The wine took four days to shake off most of its bottle sickness. Alcohol: 17.35 per cent by volume. This wine is discussed further on pp. 153–4.

Dark tawny with green-yellow substratum; a firm if unassertive bouquet, fudge and black treacle, with the merest whiff of paperiness which disappeared in the glass; fairly concentrated and sweet, rich barley sugar, with considerable but balanced acidity, and a slightly herbal, medicinal character; not as weighty in the mouth as some, but with a clean, long and uncloying finish. Fascinating and very drinkable.   ★★★★

1789   Sercial

From a private island source. Three-part moulded bottle, with stencilled date and original owner's initials. Hard wax seal and sound cork. Ullaged to mid-shoulder. Light crusting.

Pale, amber-gold tawny; after two days it developed a subdued, attractive nutty bouquet with the patina of age, hints of eucalyptus, vanilla, discreetly perfumed soap – too subtle to describe adequately; similar on the palate to the 1795 Sercial, but with less depth and slightly drier; gentle finish of no great length, with an aftertaste of melted snow. Wonderfully preserved.   ★★★★

1789   Verdelho

In elegant, tapered, mid-nineteenth-century punted green bottle. Labelled. JNV wax authenticity seal. Very heavy crusting. Purchased in Funchal in September 1973 for £14.50.

Orange, verging on green, on the dark side for Verdelho; intense, rounded, fudgy nose, no excess volatility, but a hint of mould; delicate, a little faded on the palate, with the patina of age, but the mouldiness becoming increasingly disturbing; quite long but dirty finish. Probably a faulty bottle, but still a major disappointment. ★

1789   Cama de Lobos   **Avery's of Bristol**

Last tasted in Gloucestershire in May 1985. This wine, from the Torre Bella vineyards, belonged to Russell Manners Gordon, the first Conde de Torre Bella. Known in the Cossart family as 'Old Gordon's Madeira', some was sold by Cossart Gordon to Ronald Avery. It was matured in cask until put into 20-litre demijohns in 1900, and was bottled in 1950.[1]

Lively tawny, with russet and green toning; quite fudgy and volatile bouquet, full and open, with a suggestion of toasted almonds; still quite sweet on entry, with a symphony of dried fruit flavours, refined richness, controlled acidity, then a sudden gear-change to relatively austere dryness in the throat; massive length, acidity apparent, but finishing with a heavenly fudginess. No hint of decay. Stupendous wine – but, as will be apparent from the Introduction to this book, perhaps I cannot be wholly impartial about it.

❀ ★★★★★

1790   Malvazia

Thick green glass, punted, two-part moulded, burgundy-shaped bottle. Thick wax seal with JNV wax authentication seal on top. Heavily crusted. Crumbling cork, consistent with being 60–80 years old. Purchased privately in Funchal in 1973 and reputed to have come from the cellar of the Conde de Carvalhal – though this I doubt.

Dark, dense but bright, bronze and amber, with ruddy overtones and very green rim; very alive, fudgy, cigar box, chocolaty bouquet, with well-controlled undertow of acidity; coated the glass; very beguiling, intensely sweet, richly textured, well balanced, with layers of flavour associated with tobacco, vanilla and caramel; immensely long finish, singing on and on. Fantastic wine, clearly very old, but so amazingly well preserved it prompts a doubt: can it *really* be over two hundred years old? A port shipper specializing in old *colheitas* thought it could. Reminiscent of the Henriques and Henriques *Reserva Malvasia (q.v.).*   ★★★★★

1790 Moscatel

Extremely elegant, two-part moulded green glass bottle with deep punt. Stencilled. Wax seal, with JNV seal of authenticity superimposed. Purchased in Funchal in December 1983 from the same source as the preceding bottle.

Mahogany and olive green; bottle sickness dispelled after two days and the wine came to life with a rather spirity, treacly aroma; intensely sweet, Demerara sugar, rather lacking in concentration; moderate length. Very acceptable, particularly in view of age, but not in the top flight. ★★★(★)

1792 Madeira   Blandy

The so-called 'Napoleon' madeira. Bottled in 1840. Mid-nineteenth-century moulded green bottle, with meagre but intact wax seal. Old, short cork, which broke. Irregular, quite heavy crusting, but no deposit. Remains of label. See Appendix 5 for further details of this wine. Bought at Christie's in 1977.

Pale orange-green; rather ethereal, spirity bouquet, hints of malt whisky and fudge; reminiscent of armagnac; elements of a sound madeira detectable, even if a touch fiery and starting to dry out; gentle, faded, and not at all disagreeable; dry, rather short finish. Not quite a ghost, but has seen better days. ★★

1795 Sercial

From a private island source. Three-part moulded bottle. Stencilled with date and original owner's initials. Wax seal and sound cork. Ullaged to top shoulder. Consistent light crusting.

Pale, amber-gold tawny; initial papery bottle stink cleared to leave a balsamic, clean bouquet with lifted volatility, hints of fudge, altogether surprisingly alive and attractive; full palate, extracted, flavoursome, with overtones of cream and butterscotch, dry, and with plenty of supporting acidity; finishes quite gently, but with considerable length. Complete. Delicious and remarkable. ★★★★★

1795   Terrantez   Barbeito

Currently available on the island. For further details see pp. 209–10.

Medium-dark, russet tawny, with amber highlights and olive green
rim; mellow, delicate bouquet with hints of fudge and surprisingly
fruity for age; intense, vinous, quite sharp entry, with bone dry,
characteristically bitter, clean acidic finish of considerable length.
Beautifully balanced and delicious.   ★★★★(★)

1795   Messias   F. F. Ferraz

*Bottle with 'F. F. Ferraz/Madeira' etched on shoulder. Labelled.
Lead capsule covered with waxed raffia, and bearing two JNV wax
seals. Messias is Portuguese for 'messiah', presumably indicating
a wine of messianic quality! Purchased at Christie's in April 1970.
F. F. Ferraz, when asked about the wine, replied that it had not
been shipped by them since joining the Madeira Wine Association
in 1937, so must have been bottled prior to that date. A former
clerk with the company recalled that it was 'as dry as a Terrantez'.*

Amazingly, more pale green-yellow with orange than tawny with
green; harmonious honey and dried apricots on the nose, with gently lifted, cognac-like intensity; bone-dry entry, intensely flavoursome, with hints of prunes, concentrated vinosity; extremely dry,
lingering, rather smoky finish. A shade dried out perhaps, but
otherwise wonderfully integrated and well preserved, with the
patina of a wine of great age. Fascinating.   ★★★★★

1802   Terrantez   Oscar Acciaioly

*Special Reserve. Oscar Acciaioly was descended from Simão
Acciaioly, who came to Madeira in 1505. This wine was sold by
Oscar's sons at Christie's in 1989.*

Very dense, reddish mahogany with yellow-green rim; complex,
highly perfumed, fruity bouquet with some vanilla and pungent,
lifted acidity; heavy and viscous, coating the glass; slightly unctuous, some sweetness, but dominant impression of strong acidity
allied to rich, black treacly flavours; sweet and bitter on the finish,
with great length, the treacle persisting. Balanced and impressive.

                                                      ★★★★★

1808 Sercial

From a private island source. Eighteenth/nineteenth-century blown glass bottle. Wax seal. Stencilled 'SS 1808 MS'. Cork estimated to be 50–60 years old. According to Noël Cossart, the highlight of the collection belonging to Sir Stephen Gaselee – the famous collector of madeiras in the first half of the twentieth century – was an unblended 1808 Sercial from the vineyards of Conde de Carvalhal, bought from Lomelino, who had rebottled it in 1914. He goes on: 'I was told by Dr Alfredo Leal that it was the best Sercial he knew . . . and it is only from this particular bottling that we know that there was a fine Sercial produced in 1808'.[2] There are no means of telling whether this is the same wine. However, a bottle bearing the Kassab seal,[3] but otherwise identical to this one, was sold at Christie's in June 1986.

A darker orange-tawny than is normal for Sercial, with hints of green; a meat extract, yeasty smell took two days to clear, leaving a slightly muted but harmonious, rather generalized madeira bouquet with some volatility; amazingly full palate, quite extracted, faintly herby and very individual, dry and acidic; great length, with refreshing acidity and an aftertaste of Boal. So unlike aged Sercial and akin to Bastardo it astonishes, but it could never become my favourite Sercial.   ★★★★

1811 Malvazia Cândida

From a private island source. Old, machine-made green glass bottle. Labelled. 'P W' stencilled on bottle. Hard wax seal with JNV authentication seal superimposed. The most shrivelled (relatively long) cork I have ever seen, not adhering to the sides of the neck, but kept in place by the wax seal. Heavy crusting. 13.4 per cent alcohol (by gas chromatography analysis).

Extremely pale, amber gold, with greenish hues throughout; very bottle sick; after 24 hours a faded, aged aroma combining vanilla with singed paper, not wholly agreeable, but with hints of former richness; after 48 hours the bouquet developed into a harmonious, quite pungent, sweet vanilla, reminiscent of the smell of a cognac glass after the last drops have evaporated; dried out and hollow, with pronounced smoky, tobacco flavour and the merest hint of acetic acid; slightly dirty, short finish, with lingering acidity on the tongue. What on earth is this? It seems, apart from the bouquet, so far removed from even the ghost of a sweet fortified wine that it is difficult to believe it is really Malvazia. Patently old, but not evidently fortified – though it probably was. Fascinating, if you can conquer the expectations to which the label gives rise.　　　[★]

1822　Verdelho　　　　　　　　　　　　　　　Cossart Gordon

Tasted in January 1994 at a MWC tasting in London. This wine was originally part of the Grabham collection, also mentioned on p. 247.

Dark, dense tawny, almost opaque; lively, complex bouquet, with some volatility and bottle-aged roundness; very concentrated, palate-coating, almost chewy, allied to considerable but not discordant acidity; a long, ravishingly complex finish. Stupendous – a real winner.　　　　　　　　　　　　　　　　❀ ★★★★★

1827　Boal　　　　　　　　　　　　　　　Quinta do Serrado

Matured in cask until 1935, then put into demijohns; bottled in 1988 prior to sale at Christie's in 1989. From Câmara de Lobos.

Intensely dark mahogany, green highlights; a bouquet of great depth and richness, with molasses and vanilla; opulent, mouth-coating, so concentrated it is like a quintessence of madeira, yet quite sweet and with refreshing acidity; amazing length, a kaleidoscope of flavours remaining in the throat. Revelatory of what madeira can achieve.　　　　　　　　　　　　　　❀ ★★★★★

1830　Malvazia　　　　　　　　　　　　　Quinta do Serrado

Matured in cask until 1935, then put into demijohns; bottled in 1988 prior to sale at Christie's in 1989. From Câmara de Lobos.

Mahogany with a green substratum; pungent, aromatic, slightly volatile, rich, toffeeish; very concentrated and complex, mouth-filling, with quite fiery acidity; explosive finish, very long, leaving tongue-tingling acidity. This wine shows its long wood ageing in its concentration, but although impressive, attracts respect rather than love, and is not in my view a very characteristic Malvazia. ★★★★

1834 Malvazia   Barbeito

Currently available on the island.

Medium tawny, and light for the age of the wine; lovely rich, honeyed aromas offset by a clean, slightly varnished, lift – intense and attractive; rich and refined, mouth-filling, butter toffee, with supporting acidity; finishes cleanly, with decent length.   ★★★(★)

1839 Malvazia – Fajã dos Padres   Blandy

One of the few bottles to surface at auction in Britain, this was purchased in 1983.

Orange-green; highly aromatic and wonderfully full, vanilla, toffee apple, with hints of raisin and malt, paradigmatic of Malvazia, and with no unwanted volatility; the sweetness modified by a certain dryness which does not affect the overall richness, with layers of flavour ranging through barley sugar, cream toffee and dried fruits, supremely elegant and balanced; clean acidity and dry, lingering finish. Seductive nectar. Wonderfully preserved. It is easy to understand why the *Fajã* had its reputation, and how deserved it was.   ✿ ★★★★★

1846 Terrantez   Blandy

Tasted in January 1994 at a MWC tasting in London.

Darkish mahogany, but bright, with lively green rim; the bouquet a symphony of aromas, with great depth and complexity; on the palate perhaps the most concentrated wine I have ever tasted (and that just after a Cossart Gordon 1862 Terrantez); intense vinosity, the quintessence of the grape allied to zinging acidity, creating an overpowering impression of richness; a finish of incredible length which went on and on and on. Monumental.   ✿ ★★★★★

1846   Terrantez   Cossart Gordon

Purchased originally from H. M. Borges, and bottled in 1900.
Purchased at Christie's in 1974.

Dark tawny, with a yellow-green rim; characteristic dark-toned
bouquet of dates, herbs, fudge, agreeable volatility; lean, compact,
but with considerable extract, bitter-sweet; dry, long, smoky finish.
A sophisticated, mellowed, stylish wine of wonderful quality, but
without the memorable qualities of the Blandy bottling described
above.   ★★★★

1846   Campanário   Blandy

This wine, named after the area in which it was produced,
once belonged to the collector Sir Stephen Gaselee.⁴ Purchased in
England in January 1970 for £5.10.0d. In three-part moulded
bottle.

Dark tawny, with pronounced green rim – almost green with tawny
highlights against strong sunlight; fragrant, Boal-type bouquet,
without much volatility; elegant, balanced, flavoursome rather than
assertive, with overtones of Malvazia, still some sweetness,
although quite dry; moderate finish. By no means a blockbuster, but
nonetheless impressively complete. Delicious.   ★★★★(★)

1846   Verdelho   Avery's of Bristol

Reserva Velhissima around 1846. Produced by the Visconde de Val
Pariso at Porto Moniz. Bought in cask by Noël Cossart from his
son, Dr John Bianchi, when he was Portuguese ambassador in
Washington, and bottled in 1936. Noël Cossart's verdict:
'Magnificent'.

Quite dark tawny, with lively highlights; astonishing and intensely
resinous bouquet of crushed geranium leaves, rather unpleasant;
amazingly powerful and concentrated on the palate, vinous, a
little dried out and spirity, with the resin flavour coming through
strongly; assertive but short aftertaste; wholly unattractive and
disappointing.   [★★]

1862   Terrantez   Avery's of Bristol

This wine was aged in cask until 1905, when it was put into demijohns. It was bottled in 1936. Made from grapes grown on the properties belonging to João Alexandrino Santos, from whom it was purchased in cask. Purchased from Avery's.

Dark tawny, ruby and orange highlights, orange-green rim; astonishingly full and assertive bouquet, quite volatile, showing candied peel, coconut and kiwi fruit; immensely weighty on the palate, intense, with layer upon layer of rich, smoky, concentrated extract, and then some, but behind the opulence, a steely backbone of acidity which holds it all together; almost medicinally dry, with a bitter finish and a length which goes on and on and on. Sensational. A giant amongst giants. Cossart's view that this is 'the best Terrantez ever vintaged – surpasses all others' is challenged only by Blandy's Terrantez 1846.   ✽ ★★★★★

1863   Boal   Barbeito

Currently available on the island.

Dark tawny – the darkest of all Barbeito's current vintage wines – showing olive green on rim; moderately powerful, toasted bouquet with rich, clean volatility; fairly sweet palate with some depth but not much complexity; clean acidic finish of moderate length. ★★(★)

1864   Sercial

From a private island source. Early twentieth-century machine-made bottle. Label indicates that the wine originated in Câmara de Lobos, and was inherited from Dr Francisco E. Henriques. This may be the same Sercial 1864 that was purchased by Sir Stephen Gaselee from Dona Eugenia Bianchi Henriques, who inherited it from her grandfather, Barone Carlo de Bianchi.[5]

Orange-yellow, shot with lime green; rather ethereal, patinated, soft old Sercial bouquet, similar to the 1875 Sercial but with deeper toning, gentle but satisfying; clean, slightly honeyed, nutty flavour with a little depth; a little acidity but not much length. Very refined, subtle, rather faded but still positive. Delicious.   ★★★(★)

1870   Malvazia – Fajã dos Padres

A clear glass, hand-blown, cognac-type bottle. Labelled. Rebottled in 1950. Private island source.

Very light amber, yellow and orange, with green rim; still bottle sick after 48 hours, but much improved by oxygenating the wine in the glass; restrained, rather spirity nose, light and lifted, faintly rubbery, but a harmonious, slightly citrus, 'old malmsey' aroma still detectable; very sweet, not very concentrated, lacking acidity, but very elegant; dry, rather short but clean finish. Pleasant but unremarkable.   ★(★)

1870   Terrantez   Blandy

At least fifty years in bottle. Unfortunately, I have been unable to establish anything about the origins of this wine, which was purchased in England.

Dark tawny, orange highlights, greening rim; complex, rich, fudgy nose, quite acidic; positive, bitterly acidic entry, weighty, lots of extract, mouth-filling; clean, fresh acidic finish with considerable length and a hint of sweetness at the end. A wine of sophistication and character.   ★★★★(★)

1870   Bastardo   Blandy

Originally from the cellars of Padre Henriques, vicar of Estreito de Câmara de Lobos. Some of this wine was sold to Sir Stephen Gaselee and acquired by Avery's of Bristol after his death.

Medium-dark tawny, orange-green highlights; dry, volatile marmalade nose, a bit varnishy; some glycerine on the palate, but high acidity and a dry, citrous zing do not disguise some lack of depth; long, intensely tangy finish.   ★★(★)

1875   Sercial

From a private island source. Three-part moulded bottle.

Mature, orange-yellow; extraordinarily fragrant, almost sweet aromas, with hints of linseed oil and almonds, but ultra-refined and with an evident patina of age; gentle and faded on the palate and not bone dry, with a slightly flat flavour of hazelnuts, and some remaining supportive acidity; modest, unassertive, clean finish. Subdued maybe, but gracious, refined, evocative, and in its way delicious. ★★★

1875 Moscatel   Pereira D'Oliveira

Currently available on the island.

Very dense, dark mahogany, with virgin olive oil green rim; on the nose, treacle and chocolate, a little raisiny, powerful but without much lift; weighty, complex and concentrated, quintessence of barley sugar; acidity masked by the intense sweetness; persistent without being throat-filling. The most powerful Moscatel madeira I have encountered, and impressive. Remarkable of its kind, but something of a curiosity. ★★★★(★)

1879 Verdelho   Torre Bella Estate

From Câmara de Lobos. Recorked in April 1987. Sold in the Captain David Fairlie sale at Christie's on 24 November 1988.

Pale, medium orange-gold, greening on the rim; fragrant, balanced nose with no exaggerated acidity; concentrated, citrus orange, slightly smoky, very dry; refined and subtle strength; good length, with acidity to the fore. Delicious. ★★★★

1882 Verdelho   Cossart Gordon

Currently available on the island. Bottled in December 1984.

Really dark mahogany, with russet tints, but very bright; steely, focused bouquet, concentrated, with overtones of marmalade and fudge; complex, clean fruit offset by intensely tangy acidity, producing delicious balance; medium-sweet finish, clinging, with tanginess predominating. Attractive. ★★★★

1883 Tinta
Blandy

Bottled in 1936 or 1937. Made with grapes from the Porto Moniz vineyard of the Visconde de Val Pariso. Purchased from Avery of Bristol in June 1967 for £3 0s. 7d.

A light golden colour, yellow, gold, orange and green throughout in strong natural light; fruity, slightly sweet and fudgy, rounded Boal-type bouquet, lacking volatility; at first flat, one-dimensional, dried out and somewhat woody on the palate, with a rather astringent, long, dry finish; but after 48 hours settled down a little and developed more of a Boal character, with more apparent residual sweetness and depth; but, sadly, the wine has dried out a little, and a papery taste on the finish was still evident. Not wholly agreeable when first tasted, but more enjoyable later.   ★★(★)

1885 Verdelho
Barbeito

Currently available on the island.

Medium-dark tawny with yellowish green rim; weighty, deep-toned bouquet without much liveliness; notable lack of intensity on the palate, but finishing with nice, persistent, tangy acidity.   ★★

1890 Verdelho
Pereira d'Oliveira

Currently available on the island.

Very dark, glowing, russet mahogany – amongst d'Oliveira's densest wines; toasted, brûlé, pungently volatile bouquet; big, concentrated layers of flavour, balanced with strong acidity; long, tangy finish.   ★★★★

1890 Boal
Artur de Barros e Sousa

Medium-dark tawny, with green rim; very pungent, rich and concentrated nose, hints of coconut; explosion of concentrated fruit, apricots, layer upon layer of flavour; mouth-filling, with long, long, slightly tangy finish. Astonishingly big and weighty, but structured and balanced. Close to perfection.   ★★★★★

1890   Moscat Velho   Artur de Barros e Sousa

Mahogany shot through with green; rather volatile, with some
treacle; very sweet, soft, a little hollow and not particularly
flavoursome; initially throat-filling, but no great length. Seems to
lack any special Moscatel character.   ★★★

1892   Sercial   Cossart Gordon

At least thirty years in bottle.

Very mature Sauternes, orange-yellow; pleasant, clean, fragrant and
lifted volatility; explosive on the palate, flavoursome, with hints
of coconut and dates, bone dry and with searing acidity; a long,
cleansing, acidic finish. Bracing but balanced.   ★★★★

1897   Boal   T. T. da Câmara Lomelino

Mahogany, with red glints and a yellow rim, like very mature claret;
pungent bouquet, a little varnishy, showing candied sugar, chocolate and roasted almonds; mouth-filling, very intense, rich
but refined and focused, with controlled acidity; long, fairly acidic
finish. Fine specimen of a Boal.   ★★★★

1899   Terrantez   Cossart Gordon

*Currently available on the island. Bottle stencilled 'AO–SM', indi-
cating the wine belonged (until 1984) to Aníbal d'Oliveira–São
Martinho. 5.5° Baumé, 1.5 volatile acidity.*

Dark orange with hints of green; could easily be mistaken for
Malvazia from the bouquet, which is rich caramel and butter toffee,
very forthcoming; explosive entry, mouth-filling, concentrated,
complex and for Terrantez surprisingly sweet; long and dry on
the finish, but lacks the whiplash intensity of the best Terrantez.
Wonderful to drink, but more interesting than typical.   ★★★(★)

1900   Boal   Adegas do Torreão

Medium-dark tawny, hints of gold; full, slightly burnt-sugar nose;
restrained sweetness, lacking a little in power, but balanced and

of decent quality; dry finish of moderate length. Elegant and pleasing. ★★(★)

1901 Malvazia Barbeito

Currently available on the island.

Tawny with pale orange tones; rather flat and dirty, meat extract smell (a bottle stink, perhaps, which never quite cleared); rich, butter toffee, vanilla, quite concentrated and palate-coating, with refreshing acidity; finishing quite dry with moderate length. A second bottle had no stink and was much more attractive.

(★)/★★★(★)

1901 Malvazia Adegas do Torreão

Heavily crusted bottle.

Dark tawny, yellow glints; full, generous, cream toffee, classic Malvazia bouquet, considerable volatility; mouth-filling, rich and concentrated butterscotch, sweetness cut by acidity; exhilarating intensity in the throat, quite long acidic finish. Still youthful, and a little four-square and lacking in elegance, but its sheer power overcomes such criticism. ★★★(★)

1903 Boal Pereira d'Oliveira

Currently available on the island.

Very deep tawny; rich, variegated, deep-toned vanilla bouquet; hugely concentrated barley sugar, sweet, but with a wonderful acid balance; big, lingering finish. The weight of this wine does not, however, submerge its Boal character. Excellent; combines power with charm. ★★★★★

1907 Malvazia Pereira d'Oliveira

Currently available on the island. (The birth year of both the parents of the d'Oliveira brothers, and therefore for many years the family celebratory wine.)

Almost opaque, dense ruddy mahogany, even darker than the 1912

Verdelho, with brilliant amber glints; pungent, with characteristic butter toffee varietal bouquet; glass-coating; so concentrated on the palate that one has to work at it, almost a wine to chew; sweet but, with high controlled acidity, not in the least cloying; persistent, but without the full finish one expects. A blockbuster wine, commanding respect rather than love, of which a few sips suffice. Tasted a second time six months later: on this occasion noted for the treacly character of the nose and treacly concentration on the palate – neither easily recognizable as Malvazia. ★★★★

1908 Boal   Cossart Gordon

Currently available on the island. Bottled in 1984 after 76 years in cask.

Dark mahogany with russet tints, not showing much age on the rim; forthcoming aromas of burnt sugar, coffee and chocolate, lively, but focused and refined; powerful, vinous, concentrated, with high but integrated acidity; clean, full palate finishing very long. Very good, satisfying wine. ★★★★

1910 Sercial   Barbeito

Currently available on the island.

Lively medium tawny with amber glints; fairly intense, fresh and harmonious bouquet, characteristic, with attractive acidity; full palate, clean and balanced; moderately long finish. A long-time favourite of mine. ★★★★

1910 Sercial   Cossart Gordon

Currently available on the island. Bottled in 1984.

Golden-orange; moderately assertive bouquet, rounded and nutty, hints of orange peel and fudge, stylish and well bred; powerful entry, considerable depth, full but delicate; deliciously complex, clean, bone-dry finish of moderate persistence. Very fine. ★★★★

1912 Verdelho   Pereira d'Oliveira

Currently available on the island.

Dense, ruddy mahogany, with olive green rim; intensely perfumed, complex, flowery nose with an exhilarating but refined volatile lift; a full palate – concentrated vinosity, hints of fudge – opening out to a powerful, lingering aftertaste of black treacle devoid of any sort of cloying sweetness. Another winner.   ★★★★★

1920 Malvazia   Lomelino

Dark mahogany; pungent volatility, burnt sugar and toffee apple; sweet, concentrated, mouth-filling, raw acidity; tangy, tonsil-tickling finish. Clumsy, crude, lacking balance and any clear Malvazia character. Still too young?   ★(★)

1920 Malmsey   Cossart Gordon

Said by Noël Cossart to be the last vintage made from Malvasia Cândida, and from grapes from the Fajã dos Padres (but see p. 101).

Dark tawny with green toning; very aromatic, with the unmistakable cream toffee bouquet of genuine Malvazia; concentrated, with hints of treacle, sweet and luscious; long finish. A wonderful Malvazia, if still too young-seeming.   ★★★★(★)

1922 Boal   Pereira d'Oliveira

Currently available on the island.

Dense, ruddy mahogany, with yellow-green rim, just beginning to coat the glass; the bouquet grew and opened in the glass, a rich symphony of aromas like *crème brûlée* and roasted nuts; very concentrated and sweet, but with good balancing acidity; powerful and persistent finish. A reference wine.   ★★★★★

1927 Bastardo   Adegas do Torreão

Tawny with green, yellow and orange tones; faintly Malvazia on the nose, and rather volatile; intense, austerely dry, and very acidic on entry; long, dry, acidic finish. Contrasts strongly with the sweeter, typically MWC Bastardo style – like a Sercial with lots of body. Not better, but very different. Impresses mainly because of its concentration. ★★★(★)

1934 Malmsey · Henriques & Henriques

Currently available on the island. Bottled over 20 years ago.

Dark mahogany, with striking yellow toning; rich, quite lifted bouquet; rich, layered and concentrated, intensely sweet; but the sweetness is cut by the tangy acidity of the long-lasting finish. A fine wine. ★★★(★)

1937 Sercial · Pereira d'Oliveira

Currently available on the island.

Dark tawny with orange-gold highlights; pungent and characteristic bouquet with hints of fudge, varnish and strong acidity; explosive fullness on palate, big but rounded, with an astringent, very long finish; totally dry, with a deliciously lingering fudge flavour. ★★★

1954 Verdelho · Justino Henriques

Currently available on the island.

Fairly dark tawny with amber-orange and olive green tints; nice restrained caramel aroma, with a bit of lift, balanced; distinctly sweet, but harmonious and concentrated; good length. Attractive, with overtones of Boal. ★★

1954 Bastardo · Blandy

Bottled in 1992.

Tawny with gold and orange glints; quite volatile nose, a little dusty, with hints of barley sugar and dried fruits; apricots and caramel on palate; sweetness cut and balanced by considerable, but unaggressive, acidity; a touch raw, but stylish; medium length with agreeably fruity finish. ★★★

1957 Boal   Barbeito

Currently available on the island.

Medium tawny; modest but delicate bouquet, with harmonious volatility; quite rich, nutty, full palate with adequate acidity; finishes a little disappointingly. Needs further development. ★★

1958 Boal   Cossart Gordon

Currently available on the island.

Dark orange-tawny; high-toned, focused aroma of dried fruits; rich, textured, considerable acidity; long acidic finish with toffee-ish aftertaste. Promising.   ★★(★)

1959 Boal   Blandy

Currently available on the island.

Medium tawny; lacking power, but otherwise complete and satisfying bouquet; similar palate to the 1958 Boal, but much more delicate; moderate finish. Modest but attractive.   ★★

1964 Boal   Justino Henriques

Currently available on the island.

Extremely dark tawny with orange highlights and a glint of gold on the rim; attractive aroma, typical of Boal, sweet, but a little lacking in power and with a hint of varnish; a big mouthful, quite tangy, with an agreeable barley sugar aftertaste. Finishes well. Attractive.   ★★★

1966 Verdelho   Pereira d'Oliveira

Currently available on the island.

Dark tawny with russet-orange highlights; focused, well-bred but unassertive bouquet; ripe, concentrated and flowery on the palate with a tangy, dry finish.   ★(★)

1968 Boal   Pereira d'Oliveira

Currently available on the island.

Dark tawny with ruddy tints; forthcoming and harmonious blend
of singed aromas, already well developed, with a slight volatile lift;
fruity palate, its sweetness cut by considerable acidity, finishing
rather dry and quite long.   ★★

1969 Bastardo   Cossart Gordon

Currently available on the island. Bottled in 1982. 3° Baumé.

Medium-dark orange tawny; harmonious, quite lifted, toasted
aroma of dried apricots; slight sweetness, masked with an
astringent hint of almonds; toffee-ish, with slightly bitter
overtones, reminiscent of Terrantez; longish, quite dry finish, not
too astringent. Elegant and powerful, but hardly medium-sweet
as described.   ★★★

1971 Sercial   Cossart Gordon

Currently available on the island.

Pale amber tawny; candied peel, rather muted and clumsy with
hardly any vibrancy; brittle, nervous, without much depth. Rather
ordinary.   ★

1972 Verdelho   Madeira Wine Institute

Currently available on the island.

Pale, medium orange gold; rounded, rather clumsy nose, not particularly pungent but showing some volatility; biting acidity on the
palate, even raw; finishes short.   ★

1972 Verdelho   Cossart Gordon

Currently available on the island.

Orange tawny; rather subdued nose; tongue-tingling acidity and
some intensity of flavour; modest finish. Still very young and
undeveloped.   ★★

1974   Terrantez   Cossart Gordon

Currently available on the island. 2.5° Baumé.

Pale orange tawny; young, crisp, undeveloped Verdelho-like
bouquet; quite sweet, rounded, rather lacking in characteristic
bitterness, but finishes long and quite dry. Needs a long time
to develop.   ★★(?)

Non-vintage wines

Malvazia – Solera 1808   Cossart Gordon

*Made into a solera in 1873 and not topped up after 1953.[6] The best
wine, in my opinion, at a Cossart Gordon tasting in 1979, beating
in quality all the vintage wines shown on that occasion. Tasted on
this occasion against the 1920, 1870, 1839 and 1830 Malvazias
discussed above.*

Very dark tawny, slightly ruddy, hints of green; bottle stink took
three days to clear; rich, harmonious, characteristic Malvazia toffee
aroma, with slight volatility; unctuous entry, the sweetness discip-
lined by quite sharp acidity, luscious, considerable depth of flavour,
rather malty, but does not flower in the mouth as it should; slightly
burnt finish, moderately persistent but leaving the tongue tingling.
This wine grows on one, and its attraction is perhaps the blend of
obviously aged characteristics with youthful zest – which is possibly
what shows that this is a solera wine. Misses being of the very top
quality only by a whisker.   ★★★★(★)

Grand Old Boal   Henriques & Henriques

*Currently available on the island. Old bottled, and recorked in
1927, 1955 and 1975. Bottle absolutely black from interior
crusting. Thought to date from the first quarter of the nineteenth
century. For further details see p. 194.*

Darker than medium tawny, with orange tints, and showing olive
green towards the rim; very rich and pungent on the nose, without
any excess volatility, and a mature fudgy aroma – Boal at its most
typical; rich, concentrated, with vanilla predominant, but balanced;

wonderfully focused long finish, persistent black treacle aftertaste, going on and on, but nevertheless dry. A lovely wine. Classic. ★★★★★

Reserva Malvasia   Henriques & Henriques

Currently available on the island. Rebottled in 1964 and similar in age to Grand Old Boal.

Very dark tawny, golden highlights, shot with olive green; complex, nutty and fudgy, ethereal bouquet, redolent of age and maturity, totally captivating; hugely concentrated, many-layered wine with an explosive entry and almost chewy consistency; ravishing, intense, but controlled and uncloying sweetness; an exceedingly long, very intense and lingering finish. The quintessence of Malvazia and, for me, perfection. ❀ ★★★★★

PART III
The Shippers

14

The Shippers

===

Artur de Barros e Sousa, Lda[1]

This small firm came into being at the instigation of Dr Pedro José Lomelino (1864–1930),[2] who came from an important if not particularly wealthy Funchal family. Although prominent in public life – he was for a time Funchal's Deputy District Civil Governor and for many years Director of the Municipal Superior Primary School – he continued to practise medicine. Being fond of wine, Dr Lomelino bought parcels of good madeira when he could and, according to family tradition, he often got paid with wine for his medical services.[3] He thus amassed a sizeable collection, and when, early in the 1920s, his nephew Artur de Barros e Sousa had to return from Brazil because the climate was unsuitable for his asthma, Dr Lomelino offered him work sorting out the wines. Artur was so successful in this that shortly afterwards Dr Lomelino offered to set him up in the wine business. The resulting company was first registered in 1921 under the name of Lomelino (not to be confused with the other firm of this name which became part of the Madeira Wine Company), but was re-registered the following year in the name Artur de Barros e Sousa, Lda. Artur had a daughter Virginia who married Edmundo Menezes de Olim, and it is their three sons who currently own the business: Artur and Edmundo, who have an active role, and Rui, who is a sleeping partner. Artur is the wine-maker and Edmundo is principally on the sales side.

Barros e Sousa have never had a very high profile as madeira producers. Although registered with the IVM as exporters, their activity in this sector now consists of despatching orders abroad to individual customers who have visited their lodge. (Many years ago they exported to Trinidad and Venezuela.) So far as I am aware, their existence has never before been acknowledged in any book about madeira in English, whereas in Portuguese wine books and guides they are accorded an important place. Even their lodge in the Rua dos Ferreiros (next door to that of Pereira d'Oliveira) is inconspicuous and easily missed, unless you happen to peer into its shadowy doorway and your eye is caught by their trade sign. Once inside, however, you pass through a time warp into a setting which cannot have changed very significantly since the firm first occupied these premises more than 75 years ago, and whose quaintness is more suggestive of the nineteenth century than of the end of the twentieth. A cobbled passage leads to a wider area which serves both as a workplace and shop, and beyond this is the office. To the right a door leads into a small yard off which there is a modest three-storey wine store. Whereas the old-world atmosphere is maintained in other establishments largely as a part of their marketing image, in the case of Barros e Sousa it is just how things happen to be. Hardly anything is mechanized – a pump is used to take wine to the upper floors of the store – but otherwise one has entered a world of traditional artisan craftsmanship, totally removed from the frankly industrialized wine production met with elsewhere on the island. Not only do Barros e Sousa carry out all the processes of production, bottling, labelling, etc. by hand, but they are the only firm on the island not to use any *estufagem* in the maturing of any of their wines. Such is their pride in this that on some of their labels there is a printed offer of £1,000 to anyone able to prove that their everyday drinking wines are not products of the *canteiro* system. It is partly this avoidance of *estufagem* which has earned Barros e Sousa the reputation they have in Portugal for the quality of their wines. Sadly, some larger firms scoff at this claim and look down their noses at a little firm so rooted in the past. I, on the other hand, find it heartening that a small enterprise of this kind – consisting of the Olim brothers and a cellar hand – with a clear commitment to traditional values continues to flourish in a brutal commercial world.

The Olim family used to own vineyards on Porto Santo, but apart from some Listrão Branco must which they bring over from the island, all their grapes are now bought from growers in Madeira. The company's wine-making facilities are at the Rua dos Ferreiros, where the must (the result of mechanical pressing) is received and fermented in wooden pipes. The firm is the only one prepared to take the trouble to vinify varieties like Terrantez, Bastardo and Moscatel in quite minuscule amounts. Unlike, for example, the MWC, Artur opts for a bone-dry style of Terrantez and Bastardo, which he thinks best shows their characters. All varieties are fermented off the skins except Moscatel, which is allowed to macerate for several months. No filtration is ever used, and the health of the wines is maintained by regular racking and washing out of casks. In the case of Moscatel, however, the first lees are put into a fine-grained bag, then hung up and allowed to drip – a very traditional procedure, and the nearest thing to filtration to be found here. Clarification is carried out only prior to bottling: gelatine for Sercial, egg whites for Verdelho, Boal and Malvazia, and milk for Terrantez and Moscatel. Bastardo, apparently, never requires clarification.

Artur uses Tinta Negra Mole of course, but for the standard blends he prefers to use Complexa, which he buys from São Jorge in the north. This, he finds, is particularly good for sweet wine, but also satisfactory for medium-sweet and medium-dry. Most of the wines which Barros e Sousa sell as Reservas (which by law have to be a minimum of five years old) actually have an average age of ten or more years. 'Five year old wine is no good to me,' Artur says. This may be why other firms have voiced suspicions about the 'no *estufagem*' claim, for the wines certainly have a roundness and maturity which could not be achieved in five years without *estufagem*. How is it possible to sell such wines in competition with the larger firms which do use *estufagem*? Part, at least, of the answer must lie in the smallness of the scale of the operation: no advertising, no back-up staff, very little capital investment apart from the wine itself.

Barros e Sousa sell a full range of the standard qualities, together with some relatively young vintage wines. They have never had anything to do with *granel*, the bulk wine for export. They aim uncompromisingly at quality, and I find their wines well made, honest and attractive. Sadly, they do not at the moment have much really old wine for sale – which is in my opinion the true barometer of quality – but they do offer a number of comparative rarities. They are the only firm to sell a Listrão. It has about five or six years of ageing, an attractive if not very complex aroma, and is medium-sweet: in short, a pleasant, even elegant wine of decent quality. Their Terrantez Reserva (about ten years old) is very dry and offers a straightforward example of the variety: again without much complexity or weight, it is well made, balanced and displays the true Terrantez style, with a slight bitterness on the finish. For me, however, their Bastardo Reserva Velha holds most fascination. It is a blend of several vintages averaging more than twenty years. Heralded by an attractive, fairly full bouquet, it turns out to be an extremely dry, characterful wine of some depth, almost like a dry Boal (if one can imagine such a thing) with a crisp, dry finish. It makes an enjoyable aperitif.

Quite recently the firm suffered – but survived – problems arising from the death of Sra Virginia de Olim and the wish of the sleeping partner to withdraw from the business. The need to cope with this crisis, however, appears to have led to a more go-ahead sense of marketing, with the use of machine-painted bottles and more modern label design. Looking to the future, Barros e Sousa would like to move away from the lesser quality blends to producing only higher quality wine, with ten years as a minimum age. That, they think, is the way forward for them, and for madeira as a whole.

H. M. Borges, Sucrs., Lda

Henrique Menezes Borges began as a food importer, but he ploughed his profits into the purchase of old wines of which he built up a large stock. In 1877, therefore, in addition to running his importing business, he became a *partidista* and thereby founded the firm which now bears his name. He supplied many firms,[4] but was particularly associated with Krohn Brothers, who specialized in exporting to Russia. Henrique Menezes Borges died in 1916, leaving two sons, João and Henrique, and a daughter, Maria da Conceição. The company, which was situated in the Rua do Seminário, then became styled H. M. Borges, Sucessors, Lda. In 1922, when the firm itself began to export madeira, it moved to its present lodge in the Rua 31 de Janeiro, which had previously been a flour mill. In 1925 Borges acquired a company called the Adega Exportadora de Vinhos da Madeira. Maria subsequently married João Henriques Gonçalves, proprietor of a madeira firm of the same name, which was merged with Borges in 1926. In 1932 Gonçalves bought the Borges firm from Maria and her brothers, but retained the name, and in the same year Borges merged with another firm, Araújo, Henriques & Co. João Araújo (now dead) became a partner in

Borges. Finally, in 1935 Borges Madeira, Lda, was created as an associate firm of Araújo Henriques and H. M. Borges.

João and Maria Gonçalves had two sons and a daughter. Jorge Eduardo Borges Gonçalves, the eldest, is presently the senior member of the family involved in running the business. He, assisted by one of his daughters, Isabel, is the wine-maker. There is no oenologist, but technical advice is obtained from the IVM when required. Dr Helena Borges – one of the daughters of Fernando, Jorge's brother – is in charge of the company's administration. In all, four people work in the office and eleven in the winery.

The company's lodge is small and compact. In front, next to the street, is the characterful tasting room to which tourists are welcomed. Next to this is the office, and next to the office (but out of sight) is the laboratory. Behind all three is the *adega* and bottling line. The company owns no other premises, but rents storage space from the IVM (just across the street) to mature some of its wine.

Borges do not own any vineyards as a company, but members of the Araújo family who are shareholders own vineyards at Quinta do Jardim da Serra in Estreito de Câmara de Lobos, and this is where the company obtains its Sercial. Verdelho is purchased in Estreito de Câmara de Lobos and Ribeira da Janela, Boal in Campanário, and Malvazia in São Jorge. All together, the firm buys grapes from about a hundred farmers and makes an average 5,000 hectolitres of wine a year. There is a total storage capacity of 10,000 hectolitres. Jorge Gonçalves's methods are traditionally straightforward. Storage is in large satinwood vats of around 35,000 litres capacity, and stainless steel containers are used only for blending the wine. Traditional varieties are fermented in cask and kept in lodge pipes in a store which is fairly warm but not artificially heated.

Borges's main export markets are Sweden – where their very competitively priced 3 year old wines dominate – Germany, Japan, Belgium and Britain. Most wine is sold under the Borges label, but those of the older amalgamated companies are also still used. The house style is characterized by the relatively low acidity of the wines, even the old ones. Half of Borges's production is *granel*. Of the other half, about 20 per cent is made from traditional varieties, and 80 per cent from Tinta Negra Mole. The firm offers a full range of 3, 5 and 10 year old wines, some of them (unusually) in half bottles. The 3 year old wines are curiously numbered *1, 2* and *3*, indicating 'sweet', 'medium-sweet' and 'dry'. This is a relic of war-time exports to Brazil. 'The numbering system made it simple for them', Jorge Gonçalves will tell you with a smile. Only the 10 year old wines, which sometimes have a greater average age, are made from traditional varieties. I like the 5 year old sweet madeira and all the 10 year old wines. The stock of extremely good vintage wines which Borges used to sell is unfortunately now exhausted, but there are some younger vintages which are still maturing, and these will eventually come 'on stream'.

H. & M. Borges is a relatively small family company whose better quality wines have been, in my opinion, of a consistently high standard over the years. The company adds considerably to the diversity of the madeira market, and I hope it will continue to do so in future.

Henriques & Henriques – Vinhos, S. A.

Everyone bearing the Henriques name is descended from Dom Afonso Henriques, the first king of Portugal (1139–85), whose father, le Comte Henri, arrived in Portugal from Burgundy in 1094. The Henriques were large landowners in the Câmara de Lobos area from the second half of the fifteenth century; the branch of the family which had the greatest number of vineyards in that area was extinguished in 1968 when the last Henriques died at the age of ninety.

In 1850 João Joaquim Henriques started a wine company. His own vineyards supplied its needs – as they continued to do until the 1974 Revolution, after which tenants were able to purchase the freehold of their land. This left only about three hectares of vineyards near the company's lodge at Belém in Câmara de Lobos. In founding a company, therefore, João Henriques was not so much breaking new ground as formalizing in business terms what had already been a family activity for a considerable time previously. The reason he decided to form a company is not known, but it may have been because changes in the inheritance laws in Portugal – which had adopted the so-called 'Napoleonic Law' – brought about the progressive division of property holdings, and the formation of a company was one way of keeping land holdings intact.

João Henriques had three sons. The eldest was Francisco Eduardo, and the youngest, named after his father was another

João Joaquim – later known familiarly as João de Belém, which conveniently distinguishes him from his father. The middle brother, António Eduardo, lost his inheritance because he made a pact with his younger brother that the first to get married would lose his inheritance to the other: as things turned out, he was the first to do so. It may well be that the threat of property division lay behind this odd agreement, since its effect was to enable the family to keep its possessions intact. According to John Cossart, whose godfather the youngest son was, the joking nature of the contract would have been completely in tune with his sense of humour and his shrewdness. Perhaps the youngest brother guessed that his middle brother was more likely to marry. At any rate, the middle brother founded his own madeira firm, António Eduardo Henriques. Ironically, it is now incorporated in Henriques & Henriques, having been bought by the the youngest brother from his widowed sister-in-law.

After their father's death, the firm was inherited by the eldest and youngest brothers and was reconstituted in 1912 as Henriques & Henriques. In due course the youngest brother, João de Belém, inherited his eldest brother's share in the business. He invited two of his friends to join the firm; Alberto Jardim (known to everyone as Bertie) and Carlos Nunes Pereira. He then took in Peter Cossart, the younger brother of Noël Cossart of Cossart Gordon. The reason why Peter did not join his own family's firm was because in 1938, despite Noël's opposition, his mother advised him not to. She was convinced that war was coming, and believed that if it did the family firm would be badly affected. She advised Peter either to start a company of his own, which he could not afford to do, or to go in with someone else as an interim measure. As João de Belém had been a great friend of his parents, and had become virtually a surrogate father to Peter Cossart when his own father had died, he said, 'Look no further – come in with me'. The 'interim measure' became permanent.

Before his death in 1968 Joaquim de Belém made provision for his three friends, whom he also considered as his partners, by dividing the shares in the firm between them. At the same time he put into the firm all the productive land and several buildings that were his personal property. Bertie's children did not come into the company, although his daughter's husband was in the firm until July 1997. Carlos Nunes Pereira's nephew Lúis, the only child of his father's generation of the family, has been with the company for some thirty years and is now the wine-maker, while Peter Cossart has been succeeded by his son John.

Until 1995 the centre of operations for Henriques & Henriques was in the Rua da Ribeira de São João in Funchal, in a building close to the English cemetery. A separate building, the Casa dos Vinhos da Madeira in the Rua dos Ferreiros, provided tasting facilities and a sales point for tourists. In 1990, however, the company decided to take advantage of EU grants and invested 900 million escudos (about £3.5 million) in making a double move. Of this sum, the EU grant comprised 249 million escudos (about £996,000). The company built a new vinification centre at Quinta Grande, where it also established a ten-hectare vineyard with bulldozed terraces on land which had belonged to the Henriques family since the sixteenth century. And it developed the site of its original lodge in Câmara de Lobos as a new wine store, office and tourist reception centre. When these were ready, Henriques & Henriques moved their operations out of Funchal altogether.

The new vinification centre at Ribeira do Escrivão, Quinta Grande, is set in its vineyard and built like a Douro *adega* to take advantage of the sloping hillside site. There are six autovinifiers – three large and three small, to make it possible to vinify small quantities of traditional varieties – which were manufactured on the island by a French firm because this proved to be more economical than having the tanks manufactured on the mainland and shipped to Madeira. The centre's total vinification and *estufagem* capacity is 15,000 hectolitres, and the company has a total storage capacity of 30,000 hectolitres, of which a third is wood storage at Belém. At Ribeira do Escrivão the 50,000-litre storage tanks, all of stainless steel, are situated in an immense hall on the lower level of the building, and at the south end of this hall there is a separate *estufa* room. After its second *estágio* the wine is taken, generally speaking, to the company's stores at Belém to mature.

The new lodge at Belém stands at the western edge of Câmara de Lobos. It is an extremely attractive five-storey concrete building clad with red tiling, with a wall of glass facing south through which a large number of smartly painted casks can be seen. One is immediately reminded of an old *armazem do sol*. On entering the reception hall, which is on the second floor, the visitor is greeted by an old wooden *lagar*. This level of the building contains offices, laboratories, tasting rooms and the glass-fronted cask store, with notable vintages back to Bastardo 1927 (not yet on sale) and some soleras which, because they were still in wood when the embargo on sales was imposed, cannot at present be sold. The tradition at Henriques & Henriques has been to mature vintages for many years before marketing them. Some of the casks here are very old. Those with 'J J G H' branded on them date from before the founding of the firm in 1850. They do not leak, and are still in excellent condition. This is also where many of the company's large vats made from mahogany, or satinwood from Brazil or Angola, are situated.

On the floor above the entrance there is a cask store in which vintages from the 1970s onwards (including Terrantez and Moscatel) are ageing. It provides an atmospheric setting for a tourist reception area, adjacent to which there is a retail wine shop decorated with wine memorabilia and old photographs. Offices occupy the top floor, while on the floor below the entrance is the bottling and despatch area. Henriques & Henriques are fortunate in having two bottling lines, one of which was brought from their old premises in Funchal. Bottling is only done on demand. On the basement floor (two floors below the entrance) there is an assortment of stainless steel tanks, including four with a 29,000 litre capacity and internal paddles, which are used for blending. Others are holding vats, particularly for wine destined to be exported in bulk. A single cooper has established himself in a corner, where he repairs pipes and reconditions those which are surplus to requirements. These are sent to Scotland, where they take on a new lease of life holding (and flavouring) whisky.

Like most of the older shippers, Henriques & Henriques has associated companies. These are Carmo Vinhos, Lda, established in 1928; Belem's Madeira Wine, Lda, and Casa dos Vinhos da Madeira, Lda, both established in 1932; and António Eduardo Henriques Sucrs, Lda, established in 1960. Some of these names are still used on labels, though they are not necessarily targeted at specific markets. Casa dos Vinhos da Madeira, for example, makes wine which is sold under the Sandeman label by the Seagram group, and is the market leader in Canada. Until January 1996 Henriques & Henriques also supplied Harvey's of Bristol with their madeiras, but this long-standing link has now been severed.

The company produces a full range of wines in a style which they believe has been fairly constant for over a century, and tends to be weighty and concentrated. In the commercial range I particularly like the Special Dry and Medium Dry amongst the 3 year olds; the Verdelho, and to a lesser extent the Sercial, Boal and Malmsey, in the 10 year old range; and the 15 year old Sercial and Malvazia. However, some twentieth-century vintages apart, the special glory of their offering, in my opinion, is a range of old bottled wines which, although they have no specific vintage year, were reckoned to be old wines in 1850! They are very expensive, but are textbook demonstrations of the peaks which old madeira can scale.

Currently Henriques & Henriques are in a somewhat transitional state. A move of the sort they have recently undertaken from Funchal to Belém and Ribeira do Escrivão can never be easy, and the inevitable stress turned to angst when their contractor went bankrupt half-way through the construction of their new premises. This gave rise to very costly problems which are only now being resolved. At the same time they have undertaken a total restructuring of their British and American markets, while Canada, Denmark, Sweden and (especially for bottled wine) Germany remain important destinations for their exports. Henriques & Henriques share with Barbeito joint position as the second largest exporters of bottled wine, with approximately 15 per cent of the market.

For the time being the company is settling down after its move, taking stock of its situation, and positioning itself to take advantage of the opportunities which its new facilities, and particularly its winery, offer.

Madeira Wine Company, SA

Some of the history of this firm, originally known as the Madeira Wine Association, has been told already.[5] In 1981 its name was changed to the Madeira Wine Company (MWC), prompted by the fact that the word 'Association' has no legal significance in Portuguese law. The change was therefore purely nominal and did not mark any alteration in either the ownership, structure or running of the firm.

Essentially a single company, during most of the second half of the twentieth century the MWA traded under a large number (though not all) of its associated companies' names. This meant that a complete range of each company's blends, with whatever variations of these were demanded by different markets, had to be produced, and that these were marketed throughout the world through a network of different agents. A more cumbersome and, as it finally turned out, unworkable way of selling madeira could hardly be imagined. Even the general manager, who travelled the world to sell the company's madeira, had to maintain the fiction by having a series of trade cards appropriate to each firm he represented. Ferdinando Bianchi, who was general manager in the 1960s and early 1970s, told me about the situation in the 1950s: 'I travelled quite a lot in Germany. We had seventy or eighty agents. When I travelled there it was a most difficult time for me, because I had to produce different cards. I remember once that I went to Frankfurt, and I travelled under the name of Welsh. The following day I was going to Mainz – that is a distance of about forty or fifty kilometres – and I was travelling under the name of Leacock. And it happened that our agent who came from Mainz wanted me to visit his colleague in Frankfurt who dealt with Welsh. I was so embarrassed to explain to him that I couldn't go there, because I had been there the day before.'

I remember going to the MWA during my first visit to the island in 1973. In the centre of the laboratory there was an island of shelving with an immense number of half-empty bottles. These, I was told, were the reference samples of the entire range of the company's blends. Once opened, they were kept for two years! Latterly, in the 1980s, this crazy system was simplified a bit, and the company traded in the names of only nine companies: Blandy, Cossart Gordon, Ferraz, Freitas Martins, Gomes, Leacock, Lomelino, Miles and Power Drury (although the labels of some of the other companies were still used). The company's oenologist at this time, Ivo Couto, recalls that even with this simplification the task of providing all the required blends, which came from the common stock of the company, was immense.

The MWA was put in a very serious position when all Portuguese banks were nationalized after the 1974 Revolution. The company dealt with only one bank, and the committee of workers which ran it was more interested in using money to promote socially worthwhile projects than to age stocks of madeira. All lines of credit were suddenly cut off and difficult labour problems arose. The older generation of directors, rather bewildered by events, decided to leave the company. At this time the Blandys and Leacocks were the principal (and equal) shareholders, and within a period of two years Richard Blandy, William Leacock and Anthony Miles entered the company to represent their respective families. The three formed an executive committee to deal with the situation, chaired by Anthony Miles.

Rationalization of the company was long overdue. It badly needed further capitalization, but the shareholders had no faith in the future and held back. Blandy's wanted to develop the company and invest in it: Leacock's did not. A stalemate of some four years ensued, resolved only when Blandy's acquired Leacock's shares and thereby a controlling interest. Meanwhile, although the company had found another bank and loans were secured against stocks, this was a difficult time to trade. In the late 1970s and 1980s the escudo was undergoing devaluation at 12 per cent per annum, bank interest rates rose to 29 per cent per annum and there was at one time 36 per cent inflation per annum. Against this, sales were stagnant and interest repayments rose to over 20 per cent of revenue. For a number of years, therefore, the company did not make a profit.

Under Blandy's control some progress was made, and the financial problems were eventually resolved. But it was a turbulent period for the company, and not just because of adverse trading conditions. During this time there were five different managing directors, four financial directors and four production directors – which hardly suggests a continuous forward direction or an established policy – and as a result, the required radical rationalization did not take place.

Blandy's were well aware of these problems, and they saw others looming on the horizon. During this period multinational companies not only began to buy the best-selling brands but also their distributors, who frequently did not wish to carry what they regarded as fringe, low-volume products – amongst which they numbered madeira. Lines of world-wide distribution began to look shaky. Also, in the run-up to Portugal's entry into the EU, it was becoming clear that the methods used to make madeira were not in line with the best wine-making practice, and that the EU would insist on standards more stringent than those then observed on the island. With all these problems in mind, Blandy's decided to look for a business partner to help resolve the situation and take the company forward.

The Symington family, who own six port firms, were approached by Blandy's and became shareholders in the MWC in 1988. As Richard Blandy points out: 'There is an identity of interests between us: we are both family firms; we have the same outlook on life and the same way of doing business; and we are both in very similar businesses. In addition, the Symingtons were able to provide the MWC with considerable wine expertise and a wider distribution network than we already had.' So this was, in many ways, a marriage made in heaven. Following the Symingtons' entry into the company, the other shareholders, taking advantage of an offered premium, disposed of their interests to the Symingtons, who now have a controlling interest in the firm.

The necessary rationalization of the company soon followed, though not without hiccups. Appalled, they say, by the general standards of viticulture and vinification on most of the island – 'We did not know how bad things really were until we arrived', one of the directors told me – the Symingtons immediately began to reform the technical processes of the company's wine-making. A new, Oporto-trained oenologist was soon appointed, and with him came a conscious intention to make a wine with a more open, fruity character (partly achieved by reducing the amount of *estufagem*). The results were fairly swift. So was the reaction of the trade, from whom the Symingtons received a generally hostile reception. The company was accused of trying to turn madeira into a kind of port, and for a while the IVM tasting panel consistently rejected the new style. However, an accommodation has since been reached. The present MWC style is still marked by a strong fruit character, but nobody, I think, would ever mistake the wine for port. Its vindication, in the company's view, is its enthusiastic acceptance by the market.

In organizational terms, the company now benefits from the Symington distribution network and confines itself to marketing four brands – Blandy, Cossart Gordon, Leacock and Miles – while maintaining some other company names purely as labels in markets where they have become familiar, and which there is no point in upsetting by needless change. Of these four brands, Blandy's has been and is the most important, and it is probable that in time, for several reasons, two or even three of the other brands will disappear. The first reason is that the Symingtons have always been keen to promote a family image for their port products – not only of themselves, but also of their six companies – and they wish to do the same in Madeira. The second reason is that, although the six Symington port companies are separately run and to some extent in healthy competition with each other, the madeira market is so small that competition with oneself is rather self-defeating. And the third reason is that, since Blandy's are not only the sole family from the original Association to survive as actual owners of the company, but also its most successful brand, it is a natural step to build the future of the MWC round them.

To madeira drinkers Blandy's is pre-eminently a firm of shippers. What is less widely known is that, from the late nineteenth century onwards, Blandy's has been a group of companies with a wide range of interests besides wine. John Blandy established himself in Funchal in 1811 as a general trader, and with his sons Charles Ridpath and John founded John Blandy and Sons. After phylloxera, wine began to lose its dominance in their concerns, whilst shipping (repair, servicing with coal and water, tugs, lighters and coastal vessels, Lloyd's agency) assumed an ever larger place. Offices were opened in London in 1838 and the Canary Islands in 1886. In the twentieth century these interests became astonishingly diverse, including running a bank, and currently they embrace a travel agency, a shipping company and agency for visiting cruise liners, flour milling, running the local newspaper (with the largest provincial circulation in Portugal), commercial and residential property development, the export of orchids and an interest in a new luxury hotel. (Reid's Hotel, which Blandy's had owned since 1936, was sold in 1996.)

It would be wrong, however, to conclude that Blandy's lost interest in madeira in the midst of this commercial empire. Indeed, it was Blandy's determination which eventually pulled the company through the very difficult post-Revolution period and ensured its survival. Although the Symingtons are now in the driving seat, the company is run on a partnership basis, and the commercial emphasis is firmly on Blandy's Madeiras, Lda.[6] Indeed, the present structure of the company belies the umbrella-like character of the original Association, which led to the adoption of the generalized, company-neutral name 'Madeira Wine'. It would perhaps be appropriate, in the course of time, to drop this name altogether and re-personalize the firm. That would certainly fit in with the Symington trading philosophy.[7]

'A cathedral of wine' is how a rival shipper has described the São Francisco lodge, situated on the Avenida Arriaga in the centre of Funchal. This is one of the two sites occupied by the MWC and it is visited by 250,000 people a year. Originally part of the site of the São Francisco monastery,[8] which was on the adjacent São Francisco Gardens, the buildings enclose one of the oldest mediaeval streets in Funchal and incorporate some walls of the original sixteenth-century buildings. The expulsion of religious orders from Portugal in 1834 brought about the destruction of the monastery and the transformation of the site. The Blandy family purchased a house at 8 Rua de São Francisco and acquired the spacious wine stores which already existed there. In 1925, when Blandy's became part of the MWA, the new company was established in these premises and has remained there ever since. In 1996 and 1997 the fabric of the building was comprehensively renovated, with the installation of smoke detectors and emergency lighting, but without disturbing its character.

The lodge is indeed atmospheric, consisting of a cluster of old buildings round a cobbled central courtyard with, exotically, palm and banana trees. It is geared to receiving tourists and, in addition to a tasting room decorated with a famous mural painting on madeira wine themes by Max Romer, has an indoor museum of documents and wine artefacts (including an early seventeenth-century wooden *lagar* from Porto Santo); a semi-outdoor area where the company's three coopers have their workshop and where an old wooden *lagar* from Quinta Grande bearing the emblem of the Jesuits, together with branding irons and cooperage tools are displayed; a souvenir shop and a wine shop. There is also a special bar where vintage wines can be sampled (on payment) by the glass. But although welcoming tourists is an important aspect of its function, this is a working wine lodge, and most of its space is devoted to a series of rooms and attics for *canteiro* maturation of the wine in wood (casks and vats), without a steel tank to be seen. Four of the stores, named after the four companies, hold casks and demijohns. At the top of the building is the Sotão de Amêndoas (the Almond Attic), where the natural temperature reaches 28°C and mainly Blandy's madeiras are kept, while at ground level, next to the tasting room, is the store with the oldest wines still in cask (back to Boal 1920). Above the tasting room on a specially reinforced floor are twenty-five huge satinwood vats holding about 10,000 litres each (weighing 250 tons overall), while elsewhere, at ground level, there are some of the largest vats on the island, including one made of mahogany which holds 50,000 litres, used for maturing Tinta

Negra Mole for 3 year old blends. The total storage (all in wood) of the São Francisco lodge is 7,200 hectolitres. Guided tours of the lodge and museum are given every working day.

The MWC's second centre, called Mercês after the street which runs behind it, stands on a site which the company acquired when Lomelino and Miles joined it. Mercês is situated at the top of the Rua dos Ferreiros, and is as unglamorous as the São Francisco lodge is charismatic. Before it was started in 1963, everything was done at the São Francisco lodge and at a small *adega* the company used to own at Estreito de Câmara de Lobos. Mercês is very much the MWC's operational centre, and here in two buildings we find the company's offices, vinification plant, *estufas*, laboratories, stores and more space for ageing wine.

The eight stainless steel autovinifiers, with a total capacity of 300,000 litres, are the first thing to meet the eye, being situated in the open air in the angle between the buildings. They are covered with a scrim canopy which gives them a rather makeshift look, though they have been here since 1985. They can deal with up to 100,000 kg of grapes per day, but increasing quantities of white varieties will shortly lead to their being supplemented by further tanks, which are already *in situ* but not yet in use. Inside the *adega*, the *estufas* are mainly concrete tanks with epoxy linings and internal serpentine heating pipes, having a total capacity of 350,000 litres. Several older wooden *estufas* with the same serpentine arrangement provide back-up facilities. An *armazem de calor*, with water pipes for heating round the walls, is no longer heated artificially, and casks of wine mature here at ambient temperature. Most of the storage, however, is in large vats: 80 per cent are made from American oak and 20 per cent from Brazilian satinwood. The Mercês lodge has 15,000 hectolitres storage capacity in wood, approximately 25,500 hectolitres storage in concrete tanks, and 1,050 hectolitres in stainless steel, making with São Franciso a total storage capacity of 49,000 hectolitres – the largest on the island. Finally, at the opposite end of the building from the *estufas*, there are more concrete tanks (used for *estágio*), a bottling line and a despatch area.

If things had gone according to plan, the Mercês installations would by now have been replaced by a new EU-assisted winery on a spectacular site at Cabo Girão. Alas, at an advanced stage of planning it was discovered that the company had unhappily chosen, as one director put it, 'the one spot on Madeira that wasn't solid rock'. The cost of stabilizing the site would have been prohibitively expensive, so this plan had to be abandoned. The company is therefore faced with revitalizing the rather old-fashioned and run-down installations at Mercês it had hoped to do away with. The present plan is to modernize and maintain Mercês for at least another ten years, leaving the possibility of moving to another site open for the time being.

The MWC makes around a third of all the madeira produced on the island, and is the largest producer. It exports in bulk to eight countries, of which France, Belgium and Switzerland are the most important markets. However, bottled wine – of which the company is the largest shipper – is its most important export, accounting for about 55 per cent of the island's total. This goes in any one year to more than two dozen countries. The company's most important market for bottled wine, in terms of both quality and quantity, is Britain. This is followed in order of volume by the United States, France, Japan, Finland, Holland, Sweden, Canada and Denmark. All four of its brands go to the United States and Denmark; most of the other markets receive, on average, only three; while France, apart from Blandy, is mainly BOB, 'Buyer's Own Brand'. Of the other labels, Santa Luzia goes to Finland and Hong Kong; Victoria to Holland; Welsh and Donaldson to Japan; and Lomelino to Belgium.

The style of the company, as has been remarked, is now towards fruitier, fresher and (in colour) lighter wines. From the entire range I particularly like Blandy's 5 year old Verdelho, Cossart Gordon's 10 year old Bual, Blandy's 10 year old Rich Malmsey and Leacock's 15 year old Superlative Medium Rich Bual. A Blandy 10 year old Terrantez, which is quite delicious, is also available (1997), but is not one of the standard range. When we turn to vintage wines, the company has a splendid selection to offer, and some of these are assessed in Chapter 13. The MWC has also paved the way for the production of table wines for the island's tourist trade. In 1992 'Atlantis' was introduced: first as a rosé made from Tinta Negra Mole, and then in 1994 as a light white wine made from Verdelho. Both are pleasant enough, but lack any remarkable qualities.

It seems that with the Symingtons at the helm the company has now settled down on a steady course. With exports showing steady increases of as much as 5 per cent a year, the MWC is certainly helping to revive interest in madeira world-wide.

Pereira d'Oliveira (Vinhos), Lda

This is a small, long-established family firm. It was founded in 1850 by João Pereira d'Oliveira, the owner of property, including vineyards, at São Martinho. At that time it was a separate village to the north-west of Funchal, but nowadays it has been absorbed by urban growth. The d'Oliveira vineyards, which amount to almost 15 hectares in eight parcels, are still owned by the family and are amongst the relatively small number to have survived in this area. Aníbal and Luís, representing the fifth generation of the family, took over the running of the firm from their father and uncle, and Aníbal's son has recently joined them. Aníbal, who joined the firm in 1958, is the wine-maker and Luís, who joined the firm in 1968, runs the marketing side of the business.

Pereira d'Oliveira incorporates two other firms. The first is Júlio Augusto Cunha, dating from 1820, which was purchased by the two brothers' grandfather (another João) at the beginning of the century when the Cunha family ran out of heirs. The other company is João Joaquim Camacho, which became part of the firm through the brothers' mother, to whose family it had belonged.

The company's present headquarters is a very beautiful and atmospheric lodge in Funchal, just around the corner from the Praça do Município in the Rua dos Ferreiros. The date 1619 above the door indicates the age of the building rather than the firm; apparently it was a school in the eighteenth and nineteenth centuries. Pereira d'Oliveira moved here at the beginning of the twentieth century, having started off in premises (which they still own) in the Rua Santa Maria and the Travessa do Forno. By the time this book is published, however, the firm will have opened a smart new lodge at premises it owns near the central market in the Rua Visconde de Anadia, which will provide another central sales outlet and more space for ageing wines.

The family vineyards, in which Sercial, Verdelho and Tinta Negra Mole are grown, all on *latadas*, are insufficient to meet the company's needs. Pereira d'Oliveira prefers in any case to buy its grapes, because that way it can control the quality better, and it deals with about forty farmers each year. One of the São Martinho properties contains an *adega* with a wine press, and the company's wine-making is done there. A crusher (dating from 1984) is used, and the musts are fermented in stainless steel tanks. This equipment is beginning to show its age and replacements, which will save on manpower, are already on order. After the Tinta Negra Mole has undergone *estufagem* it is taken along with the traditional varieties to Funchal to age in wood. The company will vinify Terrantez when it is obtainable, but has not been able to do so since 1991. On average, about 1,500 hectolitres of wine are produced every year.

Pereira d'Oliveira is blessed with an unrivalled stock of old wines, dating back to 1850, the year of the firm's foundation. All the wines have come from family companies, rather than by purchase from other firms or *partidistas*, although in the 1970s and 1980s Pereira d'Oliveira did sell some of their wines to other firms (including the MWC). Wines of up to about eighty years old are, in general, still in cask, while older wines are now kept in demijohns. In my opinion, the house style of the Pereira d'Oliveira vintage wines is character-ized by the sort of weight and concentration which indicates long cask ageing and minimal refreshing; they say they do none at all.

There is, of course, a range of everyday madeiras. Unusually, the 10 year old wines are not single varieties, but blends with about 50 per cent Tinta Negra Mole. Luís d'Oliveira believes that in the future all standard madeira wine will have the simple fourfold sweetness classification. 'Because we can find a balance between several – two, three or four – grapes does not mean that the wine is of less quality, if the grapes are of good quality.' A 15 year old range just about to be introduced will follow the same policy. Within the present range I particularly like the 5 year old sweet and the 10 year old medium-dry madeiras.

The firm exports in a modest way to a large number of countries: Britain, Germany, Belgium, Austria, Switzerland, Sweden, Canada, and the United States. It intends to go on being a small firm dedi-cated to quality and hopes to maintain a good, in-depth stock of old vintages. Madeira enthusiasts will say 'amen' to that.

Silva Vinhos, Lda

Silva Vinhos is the youngest of all the madeira shippers. It was founded in 1990, at a time when Europe was still going into reces-sion and the fortunes of madeira were not particularly encouraging.

The two owners of the firm, João Alexandre and José Olavo da Silva, are the sons of João da Silva senior, who had his own wine firm and worked as a *partidista*. It had always been his dream to export wine and Silva Vinhos is the outcome of that ambition – though, sadly, he died in 1990 before he could see the project come to full fruition. Neither of his sons had started off life in the wine trade, but had pursued separate careers – José Olavo as a international professional footballer and João Alexandre as a bank manager – before the new enterprise brought them together. They must be credited with courage and enterprise in launching a new company of madeira shippers at such a critical time, as well as with considerable shrewdness. Silva Vinhos was the first to make use of the capital grants available from the EU, and the company was therefore able to build the first modern vinification facilities on the island. João Alexandre is the managing director of the company, but the two brothers take an equally active part in running it. The oenologist of the company is Ivo Couto, who formerly worked for the MWC.

The activities of Silva Vinhos all take place under one roof in a custom-built winery situated a short distance from the church at Estreito de Câmara de Lobos, down the old road towards Funchal. Built on a slope, it is the converse of the traditional Douro *adega*, with the grape reception and vinification facilities at its lower end and the storage, bottling and loading facilities at its upper end. This is not as perverse as it sounds. Pumps make the traditional dependence on gravity to move wine an irrelevance, and the height of modern stainless steel tanks is better accommodated where the building is tallest. In fact, the winery, which has a potential storage capacity of 1,500,000 litres, is rationally and compactly designed to make the fullest use of a relatively small site.

The upper level of the winery has a bottling line, stockroom, laboratory, offices and reception area for tourists. On the lower level, six 10,000-litre fermentation tanks are situated outside the building. Currently only Tinta Negra Mole is vinified, and in 1996 the company purchased 200,000 tonnes, mainly in the Estreito area. From here the new wine is pumped through underground pipes into stainless steel storage tanks, and after *estágio* pumped into three insulated 10,000-litre *estufagem* tanks. Stainless steel tanks are used for storing *granel* and for blending and sterilization, the other wines being matured in wood. Current storage capacity is 750,000 litres, of which 400,000 are in wood (principally four very large satinwood vats). There are plans to use the full potential of the building by doubling this within the next two years.

Silva Vinhos has as yet only a small range of products for sale. When it first started in 1990 it sold 3, 5 and 10 year old wines, largely depending for the older wines on stocks which had belonged to João da Silva senior. These, however, were quickly exhausted. Currently only a 3 year old quality is sold, though casks of the 1990 vintage are maturing, and Silva Vinhos plans to offer a 10 year old wine again in the twenty-first century. Rather philosophically, however, they are reconciled to the fact that by far the greatest demand is for their cheapest blends, and whether they will start to vinify classical varieties is in doubt. Of their 3 year old range I prefer the sweet wine.

Ironically, the launch of Silva Vinhos more or less coincided with the demise of Veiga França, another respected family firm, founded in 1944, which had its *adega* in Estreito de Câmara de Lobos almost within a stone's throw of the Silva Vinhos winery. Shrewdly, Silva Vinhos purchased the right to use the Veiga França label and acquired its list of foreign clients, to whom it continues to export wines under the old name. In 1996 *granel* was exported to Switzerland, France and Holland, and bottled wine to Japan, Germany and the United States. Between 1995 and 1997, however, bottled wine exports were increased by 20 per cent and the exports for *granel* fell correspondingly. Bulk sales to France have now stopped, and the company hopes that within a further two years it will achieve its aim of exporting exclusively bottled wine.

Despite its rather low profile on the island, Silva Vinhos is a medium-sized firm in terms of volume of exports – though the efficiency of its modern plant means that it employs relatively few people. It appears to have established itself securely at the cheap end of the market.

Vinhos Barbeito (Madeira), Lda

This company was officially founded in 1948 by Mário Barbeito, but it really began in 1946 when Barbeito started to trade in wine as a private individual. He was very much a self-made man. Born in 1905, he trained himself as an accountant whilst working full time and eventually became a partner in H. &. M. Borges. Just after World War Two, Barbeito went to Brazil in search of new customers and returned with an order for 5,000 cases, but a difference of opinion with his partners led him to set up in the wine business on his own. In the post-war climate of uncertainty, it was perhaps a courageous decision. He was evidently quite well off by this time, for not only did he acquire substantial stocks of wine in cask, but right from the start he began to make his own wine. He acquired a building close to Reid's Hotel on the Estrada Monumental which had originally been established as a sugar mill by Pedro Pires in 1887,[9] and started off his new business there.

Mário Barbeito died in 1985. Sadly, our knowledge of how the company developed in its earlier years is somewhat sketchy, for few written records were kept. We do know, however, that he quickly built up exports to Denmark and Sweden, and a little to Norway, both in cask and in bottle. Barbeito was a complex and cultivated man; quite apart from his wine interests, he was a considerable scholar and collector of books, of which he amassed a collection of 23,000. They occupied all the available space in his house, which had to be extended to accommodate them. His special interest was Christopher Columbus, about whom he gathered a notable collection of books and memorabilia over a period of sixty years. These now constitute a small museum to Columbus situated in the basement of Barbeito's retail outlet, Diogo's Shop, in the centre of Funchal.

In 1972 Mário Barbeito's daughter, Dona Manuela de Freitas, began to help her father with running the business. The first two of her five children were at school and she wanted something to do. She went abroad to find new business, building up the export side of the firm. A gifted and charismatic businesswoman, she proved to be immensely successful and quickly became a popular figure in the trade. In 1980, when her father was seventy-five, Dona Manuela more or less took charge of the company, which she continued to run single-handedly after his death in 1985. In 1991 two of her sons, Miguel and Ricardo, entered the firm, and in the same year the family decided to sell 50 per cent of Barbeito to Kinoshita Shoji Company Ltd, a large firm of wine and spirits distributors which handles its exports to Japan and also runs an extensive chain of delicatessen stores there. This was more than a purely commercial marriage, because during the more than twenty years of their business relationship the two families behind the companies had got to know each other well – and coincidentally, both companies are now managed by the third generation of their respective families. Their agreement to join forces, Ricardo de Freitas says, was on both sides as much a matter of the heart as of the head. Although the entry of Miguel and Ricardo into the company secured the family succession, Dona Manuela felt that the company needed an injection of new blood; and so, with Portugal's entry into the EU, Kinoshita Shoji were happy to establish a stronger link with Europe. Dona Manuela retired from the company in 1992.

The new arrangement leaves the day-to-day management of the company in the hands of Ricardo, who acts as general manager, and Miguel, with whom Ricardo consults every morning but who is in charge of other family businesses (motor cycles, office renting and banana production). Ricardo de Freitas, a history graduate, worked for a year as a schoolteacher before deciding to enter the family business. He exudes energy and enthusiasm for his job. The Japanese partners monitor the performance and financial affairs of the company, are kept fully and constantly informed of all relevant developments, and participate in all important decisions regarding marketing strategy and sales. A great deal of behind-the-scenes reorganization has taken place since 1991: management procedures, accountancy methods, investment in new equipment and the appointment of an oenologist. Nor can it be an accident that Barbeito, with their Japanese connection, are now probably the most sophisticatedly computerized of all madeira firms. Nevertheless, the ambience of the company has not changed. As Ricardo de Freitas says, 'Every day I realize that a part of my grandfather is still here.' To make the point, he opens the drawer of his grandfather's desk – at which he works – to show that Mário Barbeito's box of pens and clothes brush are still there.

The lodge in Funchal is the centre of operations. Here we find the company office, storage and *estufagem* facilities, laboratory, bottling line and tasting room for tourists. The total staff, including directors, is twenty-five, and the general workers are expected to turn their hands to whatever job needs doing. Until 1990 the company bought some of its wine from other people, but now all its requirements are supplied from the wine it makes in its vinification centre in Estreito de Câmara de Lobos. The arrangements here are conventional. There are four 15,000-litre concrete fermentation tanks lined with epoxy resin and some stainless steel tanks, but none have any means of temperature control. When necessary, small quantities (up to 1,000 litres) of traditional varieties are fermented in cask. There are also facilities for keeping wine in *estágio* prior to being taken to the *estufas* in Funchal. These are large wooden vats with internal hot water pipes, but they have the advantage of being computer controlled so that finely tuned heating is possible. After *estufagem* the wine is either stored at the lodge in Funchal or in Estreito, where it undergoes its second *estágio*.

However, 25 per cent of the total production, consisting of classical varieties and some of the best Tinta Negra Mole, does not go to the *estufa*, but is sent to a large store in the grounds of Dona Manuela's house at Barreiros, where it is matured in cask. Here there is a kind of *armazem de calor*, without artificial heating but with a roof designed to prevent natural heat from escaping. In 1993, with an eye to the future, the company decided to invest in larger quantities of classical varieties. This is where they are stored, along with potential vintage wines dating back to the 1970s.

Barbeito do not now own any vineyards, though until 1979 Mário Barbeito personally owned several parcels of vineyards in Caniço, surrounding a house that for a time functioned as a restaurant called Jardim do Sol. Mário Barbeito acquired them after going into the wine business and planted them himself. Ricardo de Freitas has no regrets that the company no longer owns them. Owning vineyards is not part of his business philosophy: although they can be an important aspect of a company's image, he thinks, this does not justify the unwelcome complications to which they give rise. It is better, he thinks, to work throughout the year with the farmers from whom you buy, giving them advice and help when required, instead of getting directly involved oneself. That way you can give your undivided attention to making and marketing the wine.

Barbeito have between 120 and 140 producers who are looked after by two agents, one in Estreito de Câmara de Lobos and the other in São Vicente – which, with Câmara de Lobos, is where they mainly buy their grapes. Sercial comes from Câmara de Lobos and Jardim da Serra; Verdelho and Boal come from São Vicente; and Malvasia is from São Jorge.

As one might suspect from Kinoshita Shoji's involvement in the firm, Japan has long been by far the most important market for Barbeito, who first began exporting there in 1965. Mateus Rosé, the first firm to export wine to Japan, was already established by then, and its flask-shaped bottle was familiar to the Japanese. Barbeito sought permission to sell their madeira in identical bottles, which was granted on condition they were covered in wicker. It was thus that Barbeito's wicker bottles – now a major part of their image, particularly in Japan, and since copied by other firms – came into being. The production of these bottles is a major logistic operation. They are covered manually with wicker and plastic by sixty women in Machico and Ribeira Brava, working at home. Weekly production averages 3,000 bottles; a minimum of 16,000 is permanently held in stock; and 80,000 are either in stock, awaiting delivery or on order. The cost of each bottle, including labour and materials, is 230 escudos – all this only to be discarded as unwanted packaging by the Japanese as soon as the contents have been drunk.

Barbeito share with Henriques & Henriques the honour of being the second largest exporters of bottled wine from the island, each having roughly a 15 per cent share of the total. Apart from Japan, Barbeito's most important markets, in decreasing order of size, are Taiwan, Great Britain and Portugal (third equal), the United States, Belgium and Holland, Korea and Singapore. In the east they also export to Hong Kong, and in Europe to Denmark, Norway and France – although these are still developing markets for the firm. In 1993 Barbeito was the first company to stop exporting wine in bulk. It was a brave decision – they had no idea how it would affect them, especially during the following year – but they have never regretted it from a commercial point of view. The removal of this burden has enabled them to devote more attention to the quality of their bottled wines.

The style of Barbeito's madeiras is characterised by slightly more acidity than those of other houses. Barbeito sell a complete range of 3, 5, and 10 year old wine, the two latter being made of classical varieties. Of these I particularly like the 5 year old Verdelho (Rainwater), Boal and Malvazia, and the 10 year old Verdelho and Malvazia. Sales of the older wines have been increasing. Barbeito also sell a range of vintage madeiras, of which the glory is undoubtedly the Terrantez 1795. This wine originally belonged to the Hinton family, from whom it was acquired by Oscar Acciaioly. On his death his stock of wines was divided between his two sons by his first wife (who later sold them at Christie's) and his second wife, who sold them to Mário Barbeito. The 1795 Terrantez was by this time in demijohns, but Mário Barbeito took the unusual decision of returning the wine to wood. Of the little now remaining, fewer than a dozen bottles, eagerly awaited by enthusiasts, are sold each year. Occasionally some of Oscar's other wines are also on sale.

Ricardo de Freitas summed up his attitude to the market, and to Barbeito's place in it, thus: 'We don't want to be a big company; we want to be a company from which people wish to buy wine'.

Vinhos Justino Henriques, Filhos, Lda

Until recently Vinhos Justino Henriques operated from a charmingly old-fashioned office in the Rua do Carmo in Funchal. In common with Henriques & Henriques – there is no connection, despite the similarity of name – it has recently moved its operations entirely out of Funchal; in this case to Cancela, a modern business park just north of Caniço, where it has a purpose-built winery partly funded by EU grants.

Justino Henriques, founded in 1870, was originally a small family firm. In the 1930s its trade was almost exclusively with Brazil, but the company ran into financial difficulties and in the 1940s and 1950s developed a market in Canada. By the early 1960s ownership was diffused widely amongst the descendants of the family, and as often happens when there is a large number of owners getting small dividends, they decided to sell the company.

Justino Henriques then belonged for a time to the owners of the Companhia Vinícola da Madeira (which has since gone out of business). In 1981 it was acquired by Sigfredo da Costa Campos, an extrovert Lisboetan of considerable energy and determination with a wide range of sporting interests. A colonel in the Portuguese air force during the troubles in Angola, he commanded a parachute regiment and was being groomed for high command. But he felt his destiny lay in another direction and decided to abandon his military career, later entering the wine trade almost by accident.

Sigfredo da Costa Campos decided that he must expand the company and almost immediately began to cultivate export markets in Europe, the United States and Japan. Having achieved this aim with considerable success, by 1993 he felt that Justino Henriques had arrived at the point where, in order to develop the company, expand its markets and modernize its premises and wine-making technology, an injection of capital was required. To achieve this without undue financial risk, da Costa Campos sought an alliance with the large French import and distribution group La Martiniquaise. At this time they not only handled about half his entire export trade, but were the largest importers of madeira into France.

This, in conjunction with EU grants, made it possible for him to move the company out of the centre of Funchal – where, in addition to the offices and store in the Rua do Carmo, it had a vinification plant and bottling line in the Rua do Ribeirinho. The difficulties of operating in these old buildings with increasingly out-of-date facilities were exacerbated by the city's traffic congestion, and so it was with relief that in 1994 the whole operation was put under the single roof of a purpose-built modern winery. As a result, production costs have been reduced and quality has improved. Sigfredo da Costa Campos is fiercely defensive of the traditions of madeira, and has no wish to change the product. For him, the advantage of moving to his new winery is that old ways can be more efficiently carried out by modern means, and he does not disguise his contempt for innovators who wish to transform madeira into an aperitif – 'or port', he adds, making no secret of the target of his criticism. Two of the traditions he specially emphasizes are the avoidance of maceration in fermenting the wine and the maintaining of a constant 50° during the full three months that the wine is undergoing *estufagem*.

Justino Henriques is the second largest producer of madeira on the island, with around a 25 per cent share of the total. The new winery, which in architectural terms is similar to the other buildings on this industrial estate, is designed to be completely functional. The grape reception is outside the building. From there, the grapes are pumped to an Italian press which separates the must from the skins and pips. For quantities of white grapes of less than 16 tonnes, however, it is necessary to use a smaller press brought from the former winery. There are four stainless steel, thermostatically controlled fermentation tanks, each of 55,000 litres capacity, and eight 100,000-litre stainless steel storage tanks for *estágio*. The *estufa* tanks are also made from stainless steel. A normal vintage is around 10,000 hectolitres; 1996 was rather large at 13,000 hectolitres. The total storage capacity of the winery is about 20,000 hectolitres in stainless steel, and rather less than half that in wood.

Most of the winery is on one floor, but upstairs there are offices, and in one section of the main hall there is storage space for bottles (many of which are pre-painted) and cartons, etc. There is also a bottling line – the only one in Madeira to use self-adhesive labels – which can be operated by three employees. There are no facilities for receiving tourists. The dominant impression of the winery is one of compactness and logical arrangement, and this is reflected in the relatively small staff required to run the business – twelve, including Sigfredo da Costa Campos himself.

Justino Henriques are not involved in the local or national market, though their wines are obtainable in Funchal at Wine and Wicker, a shop opposite the Savoy Hotel. They concentrate instead on foreign markets and supply about 35 per cent of all bulk exports from the island. Their most important bulk market is of course France, followed by Belgium and Germany. For bottled wine, which accounts for about 5 per cent of their total exports, their most important markets in order are the United States, Britain, Belgium and Germany. Japan is becoming increasingly important.

It may seem strange, given Justino Henriques's pre-eminence in the bulk sector, that the company is undisturbed at the prospects of reform. Sigfredo da Costa Campos would like to see future bulk sales confined to 'modified' wine sold solely for cooking purposes, and the remainder replaced with bottled wine of a higher quality than is at present sold as *granel*.

The company offers a full range of madeiras, including a number of vintage wines which previously belonged to the Companhia Vinícola da Madeira. The style of the house is exactly as one would expect from Sigfredo da Costa Campos's determination to preserve the traditions of madeira. The wines have a baked and toasted character which seems quite old-fashioned, and contrasts with the fruitier styles coming into vogue elsewhere. In the commercial range the 10 year old Boal and Malmsey are the ones I like best.

Other firms

One other firm of exporters is registered with the IVM – P. E. Gonçalves, Lda – but at present it exports only bulk wines and it bottles very cheap blends solely for the local market. Ten firms of *partidistas* are registered, but only three or four are active in the market. One, the Adegas do Torreão, was in business until 1994, when its owner Vasco Loja died, and at that time a range of very good vintages was obtainable from it. The firm re-emerged on to the market in 1996 with a range of commercial madeiras. Another firm of *partidistas* of note is J. Faria & Filhos, Lda, who appear to be the main suppliers of P. E. Gonçalves. This firm was originally a manufacturer of *aguardente*. It started making madeira only in 1994 and sells cheap bottled wine on the local and national markets only.[10]

It is worth mentioning that Madeira continues to produce *aguardente*, a brandy (or rum) made out of sugar cane. Ten firms are registered with the IVM, the oldest established being the Companhia dos Engenhos do Norte. *Aguardentes* range in strength from 40 to 50 per cent alcohol, and most are pretty rough. They can be clear or light tawny in colour, and the best (a very comparative term in this context) have been aged in oak casks. Various other alcoholic drinks are manufactured: rum and honey; *poncha*, which is *aguardente* with lemon, honey and sugar; *aguardentes* at half strength, mixed with passion fruit and other fruit juices; and liqueurs made from tropical fruits. The production of *aguardente* is small at the moment and destined for local use, but the IVM believes that it might in future become an export.

PART IV
The Future

15
The Future

We have seen that since Portugal joined the EU, a great deal of development has occurred in Madeira and a big investment has been made in the wine industry. But after a century during which the popularity of madeira has declined, and in which trade has been stagnant for several decades, how is the industry going to enter the new millennium? In this chapter I shall review some of the problems facing the trade and look at some of the directions it may now take.

One of the most worrying problems for the future must be the fact that the island's vineyards are all labour intensive. Here, as in rural areas on the mainland, there is a gradual exodus from the land of the younger generation, for whom agricultural work in tough conditions for little reward has increasingly less charm. According to the 1989 General Agricultural Census, 52 per cent of all agricultural enterprises are run by people over the age of 55 and less than 10 per cent by people under 35.[1] If this, despite some mechanization, remains a problem for the Douro, think how much more of a threat it poses to future grape production in Madeira, where as yet only two mechanized bulldozed vineyards exist. I doubt whether further mechanization along these lines will solve the problem, though it will undoubtedly help. For one thing, much of the vineyard terrain in Madeira, which has steeper slopes than the Douro, is not suitable for making into *patamars*. It is also said that the soil in Madeira, which is not as compact as in the Douro, is less suitable for this treatment, particularly when steep gradients necessitate terraces with shoulders up to 4 metres high. Some of the older *patamars* in the Douro are already suffering from soil erosion, and in Madeira there has been enough erosion in some places to expose the roots of some vines planted close to the shoulders of bulldozed terraces. It seems likely, therefore, that shortages of labour will not be fully compensated for by mechanization, and that rising costs might one day threaten the competitiveness of madeira on world markets.

Another problematic area has been the export of bulk wines. For many years this has been both the economic mainstay and, in quality terms, the nadir of madeira. The market is very competitive and margins are wafer-thin, so bulk exports represent a great deal of trouble for very meagre profits and several shippers have wanted out of the market for some time. As this book goes to press, the decision to stop all future bulk sales is being discussed by the island's government, and it is likely that they will be discontinued by 2001. If bulk exports do end, there will be a collective sigh of relief, but it may take some time for the export markets to readjust. Sigfredo da Costa Campos expects that, just as with the switch to sweetness indicators in 1993 – when the market dipped and then more or less recovered within three years – there will be some market resistance to the change but acceptance will soon follow. Much may depend on whether a new low grade of cooking madeira, bottled on the island, is introduced, or whether these markets will be asked to accept 3 year old wines in their place.

The problem of what to do about the continuing dominance of the direct producer varieties at present preoccupies the IVM. We have seen that the efforts to regraft or replant the vineyards to increase the production of recommended varieties has so far made only a small impact. The ratio of the so-called traditional varieties to total grape production remains pitiably small, and this, one would think, is where the biggest effort to increase production should be made. According to the shippers, that is what they want. One can see why. It is basically no more difficult to make wine with the traditional varieties than it is with Tinta Negra Mole, and the use of these varieties should of itself make possible a big overall increase in quality. However, there are difficulties, not all of which are easy to overcome. The north of the island, it is frequently said, is not climatically suited to the intensive production of the traditional varieties. While this may be true of exposed sites, it has to be said that in the nineteenth century a great deal of Verdelho was grown in the north, while Santana produces almost all the Malvasia (de São Jorge) grown on the island. A bigger problem is the inertia of most of the growers, who are quite content to go on as they are at the moment, and have a ready use for their direct producer grapes for *vinho seco*.

These problems have led the IVM to seek another solution quite unconnected with the production of madeira. Even if the direct producers could be got rid of in favour of recommended varieties, it is (to say the least) unlikely that sales of madeira would grow sufficiently to absorb almost twice the present grape production. But perhaps the vineyards could be restructured to provide a better table wine than *vinho seco*. After all, there is a persuasive model already available in the Douro, where wine not made into port is sold as quite acceptable table wine. Moreover, the island welcomes close on half a million largely wine-drinking tourists every year, and 40,000 hectolitres of table wine has to be imported (mainly from mainland Portugal) to meet their requirements. Would it not therefore make sense to make this table wine locally, solve the excess grapes problem, improve the economy of the island, and complement the tourist's image of Madeira with an attractive local product?

I have to say that, despite the IVM's commitment to this idea, the shippers do not appear to be very enthusiastic about it. They point out that such wine might be rather expensive, and that it would probably be cheaper to continue to import table wine for the tourists. There is also some scepticism about whether suitable table wine varieties can be found to adapt to the climatic rigours of the north and still produce drinkable wine. Again, *vinho seco* is now so much a part of local culture that I doubt if anyone will persuade the islanders to change their tastes. My prediction, therefore, is that although this scheme will certainly get off the ground – legislation to govern this new wine-producing sector is currently in the pipeline – it is unlikely to be as comprehensive or as successful as the IVM hopes, and it will take longer to establish a viable table wine industry on the island than the three years at present anticipated.

The contrast between the enthusiasm of the governmental agencies for this project and the relative indifference of the trade and the farmers highlights what seems to me one of the greatest difficulties for the industry: lack of communication. The lines of communication are attenuated. Between the shippers and the Divisão de Viticultura, for example, the line is from the shippers to ACIF, from ACIF to the IVM, from the IVM to the Direcção Regional da Agricultura, then down to the Direcção de Serviços de Produção Agrícola, and finally to the Divisão de Viticultura. Even the shippers, although they meet monthly on the wine panel of ACIF, are surprisingly ignorant about each other. I was told by some shippers about practices (such as vinification processes) which they thought were unique to themselves but which in fact are done by others; and I was told of things that other shippers were alleged to be doing which in fact they had long since given up.

What is lacking most of all is any sense of being part of a joint enterprise. As one shipper put it, 'There is no spirit of co-operation among the companies: everyone criticizes but no one has ever presented a plan.' The wine section of ACIF – which in conjunction with the IVM ought to be the power house helping to build trade – is itself in disarray, the MWC (the largest exporter) having withdrawn from it in June 1996, frustrated by its ineffectiveness in promoting madeira. The situation was neatly summed up in the crisp words of another shipper: 'It's not a problem of Madeira; it's a problem of Madeirans. We don't have a co-operative spirit.'

In addition to being openly critical of the IVM – whose efforts at promoting madeira are also sometimes perceived as misdirected – some shippers regret the division of responsibilities between the IVM and the Regional Directorate of Agriculture, the former for wine-making and the latter for vineyards, and believe that the wine industry would have a better chance of meeting future challenges with a firm sense of direction and leadership if these functions were to be united under one authority. It is difficult to say how much of a difference this would make, but quite certain that such a reform is unlikely in the near future. In the meantime, there are reforms which the existing authorities should, in my opinion, undertake without delay.

It is surprising that, although this was one of the sixteen specific responsibilities laid on the IVM at its formation in 1979,[2] there is still no *cadastro*: a list of all growers, with the extent of their holdings and a record of all the vines on their properties. A *cadastro* was in fact started by the Delegation of the JNV just after World War Two, but it was not kept up to date and rapidly became useless. Sentiments are divided on the usefulness of a *cadastro*. Some shippers are very enthusiastic and see this register as a necessary tool in the effort to improve the quality of the wine. The Associação dos Agricultores da Madeira, the professional body to which many viticultors belong, is decidedly unenthusiastic. It sees a *cadastro* as unnecessarily restrictive in its implications and believes that self-regulation is best. The IVM, as its tardiness in pursuing the project (which is just getting under way) makes plain, is fairly satisfied with existing controls and thinks the claims made for a *cadastro* are overstated. However, the Direcção Regional da Agricultura does appear to be enthusiastic, and its director is at the moment negotiating with the EU to see if it will finance the work involved in making a *cadastro*.

I have already pointed out some of the absurdities and confusions in the regulations relating, for example, to grape varieties and labelling, and how the trade operates under proposals which have never become law. If I have sounded scornful, that is because I am. I would like to hope that the embarrassment of having these matters paraded in public may lead the authorities to rethink them and to produce legislation which is relevant to the present situation and needs of the industry. One matter, I believe, must be attended to quickly: the way the integrity of *garrafeira* (or vintage) wines is being undermined by the marketing of wine from harvests less than twenty years old in bottles which, marked with a vintage year, are indistinguishable from the former.[3] Within a short period of time it will become impossible to know which of two bottles with identical dates contains wine which was over twenty years old when it was bottled, and which does not.

The situation could be quickly remedied if it were made mandatory to indicate the date of bottling on the bottle. Such labelling is becoming more frequent. However, for small bottling lots this proves to be quite an expensive operation, and not all shippers are sympathetic to the idea. I am not so much arguing against the practice of selling wines from a particular vintage before they are twenty years old. This certainly used to be done in more distant times, and might constitute part of the flexibility for which part of the trade yearns. What I am arguing for is a clear way of distinguishing between early and late bottlings of single harvest wines before the integrity of *garrafeira* wines is compromised.

Some shippers, foremost amongst them the MWC, think that the official categories governing the sale of madeira are unduly restrictive. They would like to see Tinta Negra Mole, for example, elevated to the status of a recommended variety, just as Verdelho was made into a *casta nobre* (as the traditional varieties used to be called) at the beginning of the twentieth century. This would mean that wine made from Tinta Negra Mole could be bottled under its own name. The reformers would also like to see more flexibility in the categories, particularly for old wine, under which madeira can be sold. Now that the vintages registered in 1973 are beginning to run out, a way must be found of marketing the older stocks of wine which still exist in private hands on the island but which at present could only be marketed legally as 15 year old wines. This is unrealistic, because a very old wine so described could not command a commercially realistic price. It is also urgent to find an acceptable way of marketing old soleras which are still in cask.

There are a lot of traditionalists on the island, most of whom are happy with things as they are. I also count myself a traditionalist, and I would not like to see everything changed overnight. But I think even traditionalists have to admit that – as the historical part of this book shows – throughout the centuries madeira has always been a developing wine, and has become what it is today only through evolution. Why does that evolution have to stop now? Part of the wine's misfortunes this century have arisen from an undue conservatism, treating madeira almost as a museum piece, something which has reached its final stage of perfection. While the IVM is quite properly the guardian of tradition and quality, this should not mean that it stifles innovation and commercial enterprise – which, after all, have also been an important part of the madeira tradition.

The IVM is certainly aware of the problems, and there are rumours of changes in the law to meet some of these points. It is to be hoped so, for the future development of madeira must surely depend on new initiatives. However, the IVM seems for the moment implacably opposed to permitting Tinta Negra Mole to figure on a wine label. It is difficult to see why, for two reasons. In the first place, I believe that the use of the name Tinta would perhaps, through time, help to dispel some public suspicion that the dropping of the names of the classical varieties from the labels of wines made from Tinta Negra Mole is indicative of a reduction in quality when, if anything, the reverse has happened. And, secondly, Tinta is a name with a long and honourable history in Madeira. To recognize it again would not be breaking new ground, but reviving a lost tradition. Indeed, other traditions might also be revived. For many years it was quite common for madeiras to be sold under the name of the area from which they came – Cama de Lobos, São Martinho, Ribeira Real – but this is now, if not actually illegal, greatly discouraged.

There may be further battles to be fought. It is known that the OIV is unhappy with *estufagem* and has said that the heating of the wine cannot go on for ever. The IVM, on the other hand, believes that the recognition of *estufagem* is secure, that it is established as a necessary step in the manufacture of the wine. That is hardly true: it is established only as a part of making non-*canteiro* wine – that is, the cheaper blends. Abolishing it would effectively mean another two years of maturation in wood to achieve the same result. Whether that would greatly improve its quality is rather a moot point, but it would add appreciably to the cost of its production. Nevertheless, this is something which may have to be resolved in the future.

It is clear that, if the madeira trade chooses to rest satisfied with the commercial *status quo*, trade is likely to shrink further. A certain complacency, a contentedness to go on ticking over, is its greatest enemy and must be overcome. More positively, despite the many problems which still beset the industry, much of note has recently been achieved. The arrival of the Symingtons may have ruffled some feathers, but their determination to succeed in everything they do can only produce beneficial results for madeira as a whole. The large investments which have been made in modern plant since the entry of Portugal into the EU are testimony to a determination not only to expand trade in madeira but to apply modern production techniques to increase the quality of the cheaper blends. Indeed, the almost universal commitment to making a better product, and the emphasis on quality rather than quantity, are already bearing positive, tastable results.

Fashions change. I can recall in my youth when, despite its cheapness, wine merchants could hardly sell a bottle of Château d'Yquem. Madeira, I believe, will also regain its recognition one day. The best-quality madeira will never be cheap – it never was – and it will probably never be a really popular drink. But what a glory it is, and how lucky are those who are in on the secret.

Maps

Map 1
Madeira

Vine-growing areas

— — — *Concelho* (Council) boundary

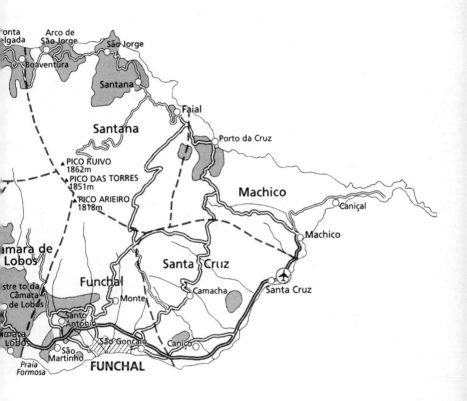

Map 2
Madeira showing the vineyards *circa* 1580 according to Fructuoso, including small vine-growing properties mentioned by him.

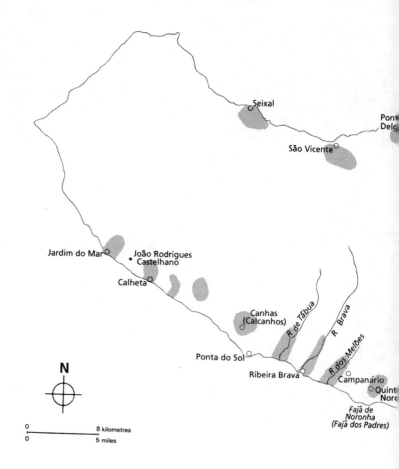

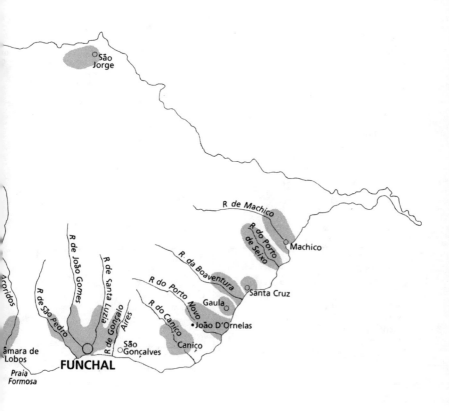

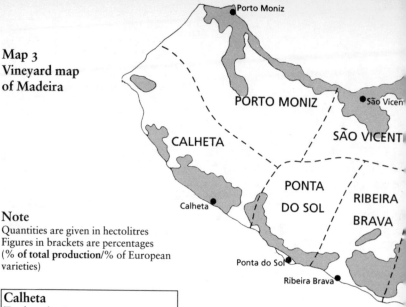

Map 3
Vineyard map
of Madeira

Note
Quantities are given in hectolitres
Figures in brackets are percentages
(% of total production/% of European
varieties)

Calheta
Total production: 782.95
  Direct producers: 376.5 (48.19)
  European varieties: 406.45 (51.91)
Verdelho: 16.42 (2.09/4.03)
Boal: 291.57 (37.24/71.73)
Malvasia: 1.81 (0.23/0.48)
Others: 96.55 (12.34/23.75)

Câmara de Lobos
Total production: 22,867.17
  Direct producers: 2,493.82 (10.91)
  European varieties: 20,373.35 (89.09)
Sercial: 91.42 (0.41/0.46)
Verdelho: 3.19 (0.01/0.01)
Boal: 86.27 (0.38/0.42)
Malvasia: 52.78 (0.23/0.26)
Others: 20,136.98 (88.06/98.84)

Machico
Total production: 121.53
  Direct producers: 120 (98.75)
  European varieties: 1.53 (1.25)
Boal: 0.03 (0/1.96)
Malvasia: 1.5 (1.25/98.04)

Funchal
Total production: 1,154.05
  Direct producers: 836.35 (72.47)
  European varieties: 317.80 (27.53)
Boal: 15.7 (1.36/4.94)
Malvasia: 34.15 (3.04/10.75)
Others: 274.92 (23.82/86.51)

Ponta do Sol
Total production: 511.84
  Direct producers: 331.20 (63.63)
  European varieties: 180.62 (36.37)
Boal: 17.16 (3.35/9.5)
Malvasia: 8.5 (1.46/4.71)
Others: 154.96 (30.27/85.79)

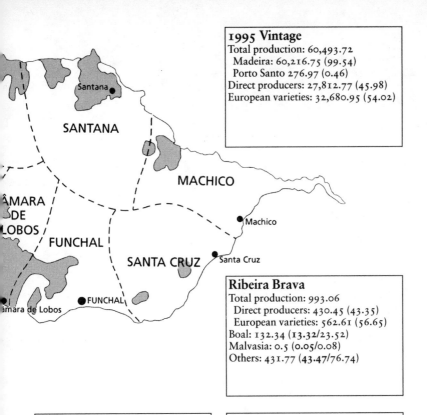

1995 Vintage
Total production: 60,493.72
 Madeira: 60,216.75 (99.54)
 Porto Santo 276.97 (0.46)
Direct producers: 27,812.77 (45.98)
European varieties: 32,680.95 (54.02)

Ribeira Brava
Total production: 993.06
 Direct producers: 430.45 (43.35)
 European varieties: 562.61 (56.65)
Boal: 132.34 (13.32/23.52)
Malvasia: 0.5 (0.05/0.08)
Others: 431.77 (43.47/76.74)

Porto Moniz
Total production: 5,554.76
 Direct producers: 4,825.03 (86.86)
 European varieties: 729.73 (13.14)
Sercial: 359.12 (6.28/49.21)
Verdelho: 171.96 (3.09/23.56)
Boal: 1.5 (0.02/0.2)
Malvasia: 19.77 (0.36/2.71)
Others: 196.98 (3.54/26.99)

Santana
Total production: 8,039.41
 Direct producers: 6,654.63 (82.88)
 European varieties: 1,384.78 (17.22)
Sercial: 47.01 (0.58/3.39)
Verdelho: 33.15 (0.41/2.39)
Boal: 4.9 (0.06/0.35)
Malvasia: 961.8 (11.96/69.46)
Others: 337.92 (4.2/24.4)

Santa Cruz
Total production: 54.24
 Direct producers: 51 (94.03)
 European varieties: 3.24 (5.97)
Boal: 3.24 (5.97/100)

São Vicente
Total production: 20,127.74
 Direct producers: 11,693.95 (58.1)
 European varieties: 8,433.79 (41.9)
Sercial: 137.26 (0.68/1.63)
Verdelho: 295.55 (1.46/3.5)
Boal: 29.36 (0.14/0.35)
Malvasia: 5 (0.02/0.06)
Others: 7,966.72 (39.58/94.46)

Appendices

APPENDIX I

Madeira: Some Basic Information

Geological origins and formation

Of long-extinct volcanic origin, Madeira is the tip of a vast plateau more than three-fifths submerged in the sea. Its terrain is rugged and mountainous, the highest point being 1,862 metres above sea level. Of the total land area, 47 per cent is above 700 metres; 66 per cent has gradients of more than 25 per cent; and barely 11.5 per cent has gradients of less than 16 per cent. By far the greater part (about 80 per cent) of the coastline consists of cliffs, and 30 per cent of these are considerably over 100 metres in height. The highest cliff is Cabo Girão, just west of Câmara de Lobos: at 580 metres, it is said to be the second highest in the world (but the guide books never tell you which is the highest).

A central, east–west spinal ridge has a shallow convex orientation towards the south-west, its extremities curving slightly in opposite directions. The central region, the principal area of volcanic activity, consists of spectacular rocky peaks with a conical formation reminiscent of Java. The summits here (Pico Ruivo, Pico do Arieiro, Pico da Torre) are over 1,800 metres in height.

To the west of this central region, the island is divided from north (São Vicente) to south (Ribeira Brava) by extended re-entrants which are connected at the pass of Encumeada (1,004 metres), over which the main road connecting the north and south of the island passes. Further to the west again there is an extensive plateau, only a little lower than the peaks (Paúl da Serra, 1,400 metres), while to the east the mountains gradually give way to less accentuated slopes.

On both the north and south sides of the island, the central mountain ridge is marked in places by considerable erosion, giving indentations or basins separated from each other by vast shoulders of land. Where there are small rivers, their rate of descent can be as steep as 10 per cent.[1] In consequence, the rapidity of their torrential winter flow precludes any alluvial deposit and their paths are marked by deep valleys or ravines with steep, wall-like sides.

Three other features of the landscape are worthy of special note. Where beds of lava in the uplands have been exposed by erosion, they often form mini-plateaux, known as *achadas,* on the slopes of mountains and the sides of valleys. Occasionally – and especially between Paúl da Serra and the south coast – rivers with almost parallel courses have between them level or slightly convex areas that slope gently towards the sea; these are called *lombos* or *lombadas.* Finally, both along the coast and inland, erosion has caused landslips at the foot of cliffs, and the resulting tongues of land, known as *fajãs,* are noted for their fertility. All these terms are frequently used in place names.

On account of this geomorphic formation, populated areas are mainly confined to the coastline – especially where there are basins (generally the sites of towns and villages) – to those valleys and re-entrants which have hospitable contours, and inland to *achadas, lombos* and *fajãs.*

Climate

The island's climate is largely determined by the north-westerly winds, which prevail for almost the entire year, and the central mountain ridge, which shelters the south coast from the winds to which the north coast is directly exposed.

During the summer these winds carry anticyclonic air masses from the Azores, thereby ensuring a long dry season. This nevertheless remains temperate owing to the cooling effect of the surrounding ocean – except when occasional east winds from Africa produce suffocating conditions by suddenly increasing the temperature and reducing humidity to dramatically low levels (13 per cent). At other seasons, Madeira can be subject to westerly winds, sometimes violent, whose cyclonic character produces abundant rain. The passage of the seasons, however, is less evident at coastal level than at higher altitudes, where seasonal differences become more marked the higher one gets.

Typically, the centre of the island is covered with cloud for much of the year. Temperatures are generally relative to altitude, and as the land temperature along the south coast increases each day, so masses of air rise from the valleys, provoking condensation and cloud formation at about 500 metres in winter and slightly higher in summer. In the middle of the day this cloud barrier reduces the heating effect of the sun and helps to maintain, even in summer, a moderate temperature. In the evening the air cools and the process is reversed, as winds push the humid masses into warmer zones where the clouds rapidly dissipate.

On the north coast, however, the dominant wind pushes the humid masses of air against the mountain barrier and they are obliged to rise rapidly. The resultant cloud forms at about 400 metres or even lower. This affects both the local temperature and humidity – the former being on average 1.5°C lower than on the south of the island and the latter as much as 10 per cent higher. The clouds also ascend to 1,200–1,400 metres and give rise to precipitation, which approaches 3,000 mm each year. The central peaks and Paúl da Serra often remain above cloud level, surrounded by a white tablecloth of cloud, and for that reason are much drier than the areas only slightly below them.

Nevertheless, the irregularity of the island's relief gives rise to many microclimates. The hottest areas are the *fajãs* of the south coast. Snow on the peaks is not uncommon in winter. Temperature varies with altitude and exposure, ranging from an average of 15.7°C in February to 22.2°C in August, giving an annual average of around 19°C on the south coast and 17.5°C on the north. Precipitation also varies with altitude, and normally ranges from 500 mm on the south coast, through 1,200 mm on the north coast, to 3,000 mm in the central part of the island. In Funchal, for example, 63 days of rain would be a *typical* annual figure. However, the number of rainy days varies widely from year to year. Thus, in Funchal over a thirty-year period the total ranged from 26 to 111 days, while during the same period the total precipitation ranged from 200 mm to 1,138 mm – a clear reminder that we are dealing with a climate that in some respects verges on the tropical, and which has since the eighteenth century subjected the island to thirteen catastrophic floods.[2] Relative humidity varies from an average 65 per cent in March to 72 per cent in July, with an all-year average of 69 per cent.

Population

The population of Madeira is much the same as it was fifty years ago. According to the 1991 census, the total number of inhabitants was 248,720, compared with 247,000 in 1940.[3] In 1960, however, the total rose to 265,432. The main reason for the decline since then has been a falling birth rate. Emigration may also have played a part, though it must be remembered that emigrants frequently come back to the island in retirement, and even second generation emigrants often return home (as has recently happened from South Africa).

The *concelho* of Funchal, the capital, is the largest nucleus of population with nearly half the total: 115,403 (46.4 per cent). This is followed by other *concelhos* along the south coast: 31,476 (12.66 per cent) live in Câmara de Lobos; 23,465 (9.43 per cent) in Santa Cruz; and 22,016 (8.85 per cent) in Machico. Only 21,429 (8.62 per cent) live in the north of the island (Santana, São Vicente and Porto Moniz).

Political organization

The RAM (Região Autónoma da Madeira) – which includes the whole of the archipelago – was established under the 1976 Constitution as an autonomous region within the Republic of Portugal. It is divided into eleven *concelhos* (councils): Funchal, Câmara de Lobos, Ribeira Brava, Ponta do Sol, Calheta, Porto Moniz, São Vicente, Santana, Machico, Porto da Cruz and Porto Santo. Councils are further subdivided into *freguesias* (parishes).

The autonomous region is governed by a Regional Legislative Assembly, elected for a four-year term by direct universal suffrage on the basis of proportional representation. Each of the eleven councils elects a deputy to the Legislative Assembly for each 3,500 electors (or fraction over 1,750). The Regional Government is formed by a President, nominated in the light of the electoral results, and by the Regional Secretaries of each government department. It is competent to legislate on a wide range of regional concerns, but in national matters the Lisbon central government prevails. The island is a net recipient of finance from Portugal.

APPENDIX 2

Control of the Wine Industry

Government control

There are two regional governmental bodies concerned with wine. The Direcção Regional da Agricultura (Regional Directorate of Agriculture) is concerned with all matters relating to vineyards and viticulture, while the Instituto do Vinho da Madeira (Madeira Wine Institute, referred to as the IVM) has global responsibility for the making and marketing of madeira and other alcoholic products, such as *aguardente*, as well as the control and sale of imported wine and spirits.

At the top of an elaborate chain of responsibility is the Secretaria Regional Agricultura, Florestas e Pescas (Regional Secretariat for Agriculture, Forestry and Fishing), which is controlled by the Regional Secretary, a member of the government. The Secretariat consists of four regional departments, one of which is the Direcção Regional da Agricultura (Regional Directorate of Agriculture). This is at the same governmental level as the IVM and consists of six sub-departments called Direcções de Serviços (Directorates of Services), one of which is the Direcção de Serviços de Produção Agrícola (Directorate of Agricultural Production Services). Finally, this is sub-divided into nine sub-departments which cover fruit, flowers, bananas, horticulture and vines. The last of these, which is the one we shall be concerned with, is the Divisão de Viticultura (Viticultural Division). Its activities have been described in more detail earlier in the book.[1]

The Instituto do Vinho da Madeira

The Instituto do Vinho da Madeira (IVM) – which is more immediately involved in wine matters than the Direcção Regional da Agricultura – began to function on 1 January 1980, inheriting the role of the Junta Nacional do Vinho, the previous regulatory organ. In addition to controlling the production and marketing of madeira – which has already been explained in detail – it supervises the production, import and sale of all other alcoholic drinks on the island. Its structure comprises a directorate (consisting of a president – currently Dr Constantino Palma – and two vice-presidents) which supervises its three service divisions: administrative and financial management; wine promotion; and a laboratory. The Câmara de Provadores (tasting panel) is a specific department not under the directorate. There is a council of directors of five (the directorate plus representatives of the wine producers and shippers), and a general council of fifteen members, which has a consultative role and approves the budget and accounts.[2]

The work of the three divisions is self-explanatory. Apart from running the Institute, the administrative division (which has four principal and five subsidiary staff members) helps to operate the legal controls on the industry and is responsible for public relations, the promotion and development of the madeira trade and support for initiatives abroad. The wine promotion division (which has a staff of seven principals and eight subsidiaries) shares in the implementation of the legal controls, undertakes technical studies, promotes liaison between viticultors and commerce, and gives technical assistance and support to the industry. This division also runs a small winery (making single-variety madeiras from the harvests of the experimental stations run by the Divisão de Viticultura of the Serviços de Produção Agrícola) and offers storage facilities for shippers' overflow stocks. The laboratory, with a staff of five, also assists in controlling the authenticity and quality of madeira. It analyses samples of wine prior to marketing; it analyses samples of must during the vintage; it controls the quality of the alcohol used in making madeira; it offers technical advice and assistance to all sectors of the wine trade; and it undertakes research projects in conjunction with university departments. Currently it is trying to establish the chemical make-up of the wines made from the four classical varieties.

The IVM occupies a rather exotic building in the middle of Funchal, originally the house of Henry Veitch, the British consul at the turn of the eighteenth and nineteenth centuries. Veitch carried out his wine trade there, and since then the building has from time to time housed other shippers – including Isidro Gonçalves, Cossart Gordon and the Companhia Vinícola da Madeira – and was the headquarters of the Delegation of the Junta Nacional do Vinho between 1940 and 1979. The basement houses a small museum, open to the public. There are two warehouses with a large storage capacity. One of these has recently become redundant as a result of the EU-funded development of large *adegas* for three of the shippers, who therefore no longer need to store their surplus stocks with the Institute. There are plans to develop the warehouse into additional office space and a tasting room and reception centre for the public.

APPENDIX 3

Exports during the Nineteenth and Twentieth Centuries

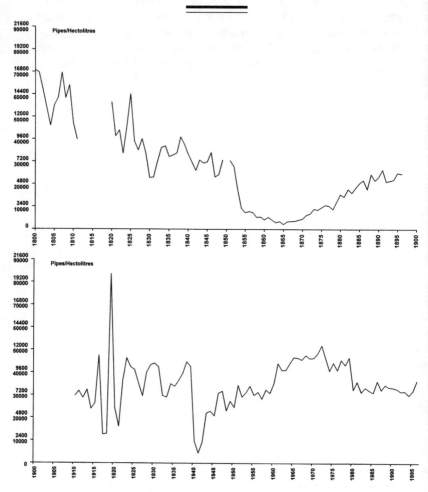

SOURCES 1800–1811, and 1820–1896 (Biddle, p. 194); 1910–1942 (Tavares, pp. 34–5); 1943–1988 (Lemps, p. 119); 1989–1996 (supplied by the IVM).

APPENDIX 4

Production and Exports: 1980–1995

TABLE I Production of must from 1980–1995

Year	1980	1985	1990	1995
Number of growers	3,916	3,150	3,566	2,284
Sercial			893.7 (1.16%)	627.52 (1.03%)
Verdelho			427.2 (0.55%)	520.29 (0.86%)
Boal			524.45 (0.68%)	583.5 (0.96%)
Malvazia			945.56 (1.22%)	1,085.83 (1.79%)
Other European varieties			37,466.69 (48.58%)	29,863.81 (49.36%)
European varieties sub-total	37,702.59 (32.79%)	20,866.94 (36.08%)	40,257.8 (52.19%)	32,680.95 (54.02%)
Direct producers	77,259.49 (67.21%)	36,954.84 (63.92%)	36,866.85 (47.81%)	27,812.77 (45.98%)
Total	114,962.08	57,821.78	77,124.65	60,493.72

Quantities are given in hectolitres.
Percentages indicate the proportion of the total production.
Figures supplied by the IVM.

TABLE 2 Summary of exports from 1980–1995. The trend is indicated by a breakdown of figures at five yearly intervals.

Country	Total amount imported (A)	% of total (A)	Total amount in bottles (B)	% of (A)	% of (B)	Total amount in bulk (C)	% of (A)	% of (B)
1980	32,506	100	3,659	11.26	100	28,847	88.74	100
France	11,048	34.0	44		1.2	11,004	33.9	38.1
Germany	5,838	18.0	63	0.2	1.7	5,775	17.8	20.0
Britain	2,870	8.8	127	0.4	3.5	2,743	8.4	9.5
Denmark	2,620	8.0	24		0.7	2,586	8.0	9.0
Sweden	1,739	5.3	364	1.1	9.9	1,375	4.2	4.8
Belg./Lux.	1,660	5.1	127	0.4	3.5	1,533	4.7	5.3
Switzerland	1,443	4.4	10		0.3	1,433	4.4	5.0
Holland	1,393	4.3	148	0.5	4.0	1,245	3.8	4.3
USA	1,174	3.6	1,166	3.6	31.9	8		
Japan	294	0.9	294	0.9	8.0			
Others	2,427	7.6	1,292	4.0	35.3	1,145	3.5	4.0
1985	31,182	100	4,355	13.97	100	26,827	86.03	100
France	13,299	42.6	12		0.3	13,287	42.6	49.5
Germany	3,558	11.4	71	0.2	1.6	3,487	11.2	13.0
Belg./Lux.	3,244	10.4	180	0.6	4.1	3,064	9.8	11.4
Britain	2,858	9.1	348	1.1	8.0	2,510	8.0	9.4
Sweden	1,831	5.9	331	1.1	7.6	1,500	4.8	5.6
USA	1,472	4.7	1,457	4.7	33.5	15		
Denmark	1,360	4.3	35	0.1	0.8	1,325	4.3	4.9
Japan	837	2.7	837	2.7	19.2			
Holland	736	2.4	67	0.2	1.5	669	2.2	2.5
Switzerland	714	2.3	16		0.3	698	2.2	2.6
Others	1,273	4.2	1,012	3.2	23.4	272	0.9	1.1

1990	33,417	100	8,441	25.26	100	24,976	74.74	100
France	14,180	42.4	908	2.7	10.8	13,272	39.7	53.2
Germany	4,335	13.0	139	0.4	1.6	4,196	12.6	16.8
Britain	2,825	8.5	2,821	8.5	33.4	4		
Belg./Lux.	2,695	8.0	240	0.7	2.8	2,455	7.3	9.8
Sweden	1,612	4.7	212	0.6	2.5	1,400	4.2	5.6
Japan	1,587	4.7	1,587	4.8	18.8			
Spain	1,226	3.7	2			1,224	3.7	4.9
Denmark	1,128	3.4	259	0.8	3.1	869	2.6	3.5
USA	960	2.9	941	2.8	11.1	19		
Holland	849	2.5	47	0.1	0.6	802	2.4	3.2
Others	2,020	6.2	1,285	3.8	15.3	735	2.2	3.0

1995	30,070	100	10,151	31.65	100	21,919	68.35	100
France	12,530	39.0	857	2.7	8.5	11,673	36.4	53.3
Germany	4,803	15.0	494	1.5	4.9	4,309	13.4	19.7
Britain	3,485	10.9	3,118	9.7	30.7	367	1.1	1.7
Belg./Lux.	2,220	6.9	223	0.7	2.2	1,997	6.2	9.1
Japan	2,044	6.4	2,044	6.4	20.1			
Sweden	1,599	5.0	323	1.0	3.2	1,276	4.0	5.8
USA	1,193	3.7	1,169	3.6	11.5	24		
Holland	1,158	3.6	357	1.1	3.5	801	2.5	3.7
Denmark	1,004	3.1	458	1.4	4.5	546	1.7	2.5
Switzerland	727	2.3	7			720	2.3	3.3
Others	1,307	4.1	1,101	3.5	10.9	206	0.6	0.9

Quantities are given in hectolitres. Figures supplied by the IVM.

APPENDIX 5

The 1792 Vintage and the Napoleon Madeira

═══════

Undoubtedly the most celebrated of all madeiras is the so-called 1792 'Napoleon' vintage. Several mid-nineteenth-century moulded bottles have survived into this century. They bear a small cream label, generally scuffed and often no longer legible, measuring about 8.6 cm across and 4.8 cm deep; it reads 'BLANDY/*Madeira*/1792–1840'. The first date is that of the vintage and the second is the date of bottling. The bottles have undoubtedly been recorked from time to time and have wax seals.

The connection with Napoleon was first mentioned in print by André Simon in *Madeira, Wine, Cakes and Sauce*, published in 1933. It was also touched on by Rupert Croft-Cooke and Noël Cossart in their books on madeira, and has been recounted, more or less inaccurately, many times since. According to Simon, he was told by Michael Grabham on his ninety-third birthday in January 1933, when the 1792–1840 madeira was drunk, that 1792 was the year his father had been born. The story continued: 'When, in 1815, Napoleon I called at Madeira, on his way farther south to St Helena, this 1792 wine was picked out as likely to become very fine with age,[1] and it was bought for the fallen Emperor, to help him forget the duress of exile. But, as you know, they found out that he suffered from some gastric trouble – some said that it was cancer of the stomach – and they would not let him drink this wine. As a matter of fact, the Emperor died in 1820, and this 1792 was hardly ready by then. The curious thing about it was that nobody had paid for the wine. That is to say, the English Consul at Funchal, a Mr Veitch, had paid the merchant who had put the wine on board His Britannic Majesty's ship, in 1815, but he, Veitch, had never been able to get the money refunded. So he did the next best thing. He claimed the pipe of 1792 as his own, and he got it back in Madeira, in 1822, when he sold it to Charles Blandy. His son, John Blandy, bottled the wine in 1840, and that happens to be the year when I was born. I married his daughter; that is how the wine came to me, and why I can give it to you today.'²

The story, even if true in essentials, is certainly wrong in detail. Charles Blandy was only ten years old in 1822 – when, according to Grabham, Veitch sold him the pipe of madeira. John Blandy, who is said to have bottled the wine in 1840, only joined the firm in 1841. It may have been a fabrication. Croft-Cooke, basing his opinion on a letter written by Grabham's son Walter, thought it was; Cossart, on the other hand, did not. The fairest thing to do, therefore, is to let Walter Grabham and Noël Cossart speak for themselves.

In a letter to Graham Blandy dated 13 November 1941, Walter Grabham wrote: 'I am afraid that during his last years, my father embroidered some of his statements ... This Blandy, 1792–1840 Madeira wine of which my father in 1930 still possessed about 15 dozen bottles, never had any association with Napoleon. In a letter dated 30 Aug. 1930, to Col. Arthur Cossart about some wines he was selling, my father referred to this wine: "1792–1840: a grand old wine; our family wine, the dates strangely coinciding with the birth year of my father and myself." There is no taint of Napoleon about that, and he would hardly have omitted it if it had been a fact. I never heard my father associate Napoleon with this wine but about the same time there was a younger wine, either 1902 or 1923 or both, which he referred to as "Faraday wine". When I taxed him with this perversion, he just replied that it pleased him.'

In a letter to Richard Blandy dated 26 July 1982, Noël Cossart put his point of view: 'In my book I am telling the story as I heard it from Uncle Michael, Uncle Arthur, and confirmed by André himself. When André left Pommery & Greno in 1933 he was P.R. to the M.W.A for a short time, and that is when he got the story. I remember having a long discussion about the Blandy 1792–1840 with him at the Academy of Ancient Madeira Wines at Water Lane in 1959. Walter had a peculiar quirk of discrediting his father whenever possible, I presume because he had always been suppressed by him. He was a wicked old man, but I am convinced his story is true. The fact that in his letter to Uncle Arthur he did not mention the Napoleon connection was because Uncle Arthur knew it.'³

My own view inclines sharply towards scepticism. All the evidence points to Michael Grabham having been the sole source of the story. In another letter to Richard Blandy, dated 12 July 1982, Cossart says: 'In their notes both uncle Michael Grabham and my grandfather say that it was John who bottled the famous Blandy "Napoleon Madeira" in 1840 . . .' In the absence of these 'notes' there is no independent confirmation of the story, so when Cossart writes, 'I can guarantee the story he told about his 1792 madeira was no leg pull and is fact',[4] he appears to overstate his case. The truth, I believe, is that Cossart was a good raconteur who enjoyed a good story, and he was convinced by this story because he wanted to be.

Other discussions about the Blandy 1792–1840 have left considerable confusion in their wake. The first thing to be clear about is that, in addition to the vintage wine, there is also a Blandy 'Extra Reserve – Solera 1792'. The first mention of the solera is by Vizetelly (1877): 'A powerful choice old reserve from the same district [Cama de Lobos], the solera of which was founded as far back as 1792.'[5] It seems probable that this solera was created from the same 1792 vintage, part of which was bottled in 1840, though the only evidence to support this is negative: Blandy's have no records of a second wine. It seems a little unlikely, however, that there would have been two different 1792 vintages, one of which was bottled in 1840, the other being used for the solera. The final bottling, which finished off the solera, was in 1957. The bottles have embossed lead capsules, body labels and neck labels, and typed or printed back labels which state: 'This famous old Solera was laid down in the year 1792 and matured in its original casks. In 1957, the year of the State visit of Her Majesty Queen Elizabeth II and the Duke of Edinburgh to Portugal, the remainder of this wine was drawn from the casks and bottled.' There was a total yield of 1,228 bottles, each individually numbered.

The labelling of neither the straight vintage nor the solera indicates from which grape variety the wine was made, suggesting that it was (like most eighteenth-century madeira) generic. Vizetelly's mention of Cama de Lobos might suggest a fairly rich, Boal type of wine. Cossart, possibly following Vizetelly, also refers to both wines as from Câmara de Lobos,[6] but the labelling does not support this. Nor does it support the not infrequent description in auction catalogues (since 1977) of both the vintage and solera wines as Boal.[7] Nor is there any evidence that Blandy's ever marketed a 1792 Boal in addition to the 1792–1840 madeira.

Despite the fact that Christie's, in a sale on 25 September 1980, listed as Lot 383 'Sercial – 1792. Blandy. Bottled 1840', I am disinclined to think either that the 1792–1840 madeira was a Sercial or that there was a separate 1792 Sercial (coincidentally bottled in 1840). This mention is unique, apart from Croft-Cooke's assertion that the wine drunk by Churchill at Reid's in 1950 was a Sercial,[8] which is clearly just a mistake. On the other hand, there is more convincing evidence of the existence of a 1792 Solera Malvazia. Cossart refers to one having been 'bottled [in] 1957 on the occasion of HM the Queen's state visit'. Not only is this at odds with his assertion that the solera bottled for the Queen's visit was from Câmara de Lobos[9] – there has never been any suggestion that two different soleras, one from Câmara de Lobos and the other Malvazia, were bottled for the Queen – but, like the Câmara de Lobos assertion, it is unsupported by the labelling of the solera bottled in 1957. I would dismiss this as a confusion similar to Croft-Cooke's over Sercial, were it not that a Malvazia Solera 1792 was sold at Sotheby's in 1972[10] and Michael Broadbent reports drinking one – the same bottle? – in his *Great Vintage Wine Book*.[11] These are, however, the only references I have been able to find to this wine, and there have never been any other suggestions, so far as I know, that the 1792–1840 vintage might have been made from Malvasia.

All things considered therefore, I am inclined to the view that Blandy's 1792–1840 vintage and Extra Reserve Solera 1792 came from the same source, and that (on the authority of Vizetelly) this was a wine which may well have originated in Câmara de Lobos, although we cannot now say whether it was made from a single grape variety, or if it was, what that might have been.

APPENDIX 6

Vidonia and Vidonho:
An Unsolved Mystery

———

Vidonia was a wine produced in the Canary Islands from the early Middle Ages until the end of the nineteenth century, when it seems to have disappeared, probably as a result of phylloxera. It was extremely popular in England in the eighteenth century, and much of it was fraudulently passed off as madeira. Cyrus Redding wrote in 1824: 'What is called Vidonia is properly the dry Canary wine, best known as Teneriffe. Perhaps it was so called because it was derived from the *vidogna* grape.'[1] Vizetelly, visiting the Canaries in 1877, indicated that it was still much in vogue: 'To-day the favourite vine in Tenerife is the vidueño, or vidonia, as it is sometimes called, the fruit of which is a juicy round white grape, the bunches seldom exceeding a pound and a half in weight. There is also a black variety of the vidueño, but this is very rare, and is mainly grown in the valley of Orotava.'[2] He goes on: 'We tasted a variety of growths shipped under the name of Vidonia (the grape from which they are produced being so called), commencing with the vintages of 1876 and 1875, which, however, had not yet developed any especial characteristics. On the other hand a sample of 1874 proved remarkably soft, and some 1871–72 wine, destined for the Russian market, had acquired an oily richness of flavour combined with considerable aroma.'

From these reports we learn that the Canary Vidonia was a dry white wine made from a grape variety which in its anglicized form is called Vidonia, but which is also referred to as the Vidogna and (in Spanish) as the Vidueño. Other synonyms of the variety which are met with include Viduño (also Spanish), Vidogne (French) and *possibly* Vidonho (Portuguese).

Vidonias were also shipped from Madeira from at least the seventeenth century until the beginning of the nineteenth century, and very probably from as early as the sixteenth century. One of the reasons why it is difficult to determine exactly when the trade in vidonias started is a purely lexicographical one concerning the Portuguese word *vidonho*, which has at least three meanings:[3] (1) 'a new vine shoot which is cut together with a piece of the wood of the mother vine'; (2) 'grape variety'; (3) 'a certain variety of grape'.

The first definition (unknown to Portuguese wine-makers I have spoken to) may be discarded for the purpose of our discussion, which hinges on the other two. The second sense is obsolete or at best obsolescent, having been replaced by *videira* and *cepa*. This is therefore a generic meaning of *vidonho*, indicating a grape variety in general. The word was frequently and clearly used in this generic sense in nineteenth-century writings about wine, as in this example from 1865: 'The varieties (*vidonhos*) which are cultivated on trees are, for the most part, Verdelho, Sercial and Tinta'.[4] The most recent use of the word in this sense I have come across was in 1956. The third meaning of *vidonho* refers to a specific grape variety, and we find it appearing regularly, in its synonyms of Vidogna and Vidogne, in nineteenth-century lists of Madeira grape varieties.

As the following discussion will make clear, part of the problem in determining what vidonia was stems from uncertainty about whether early references to Vidonhos should be construed as indicating a specific type of wine made from a specific type of grape (from which its name was derived) – sense (3) – or as indicating other varieties of wine in a generic way – sense (2).

Vidonhos are first mentioned in the context of Madeira by Gaspar Fructuoso, who died in 1591. On the six occasions when he uses the word, he does so in the plural, and he always speaks of them in conjunction with (and in contrast to) Malvasias. He twice qualifies *vidonhos* with the word *outros*, meaning 'other'. Thus: 'Gaula ... has many vineyards with Malvasias and many other varieties (*outros vidonhos*)'.[5] On the other four occasions when Fructuoso uses *vidonho*s, however, there is no qualifying 'other', and one has the strong feeling that he is not talking about vine varieties in general, but about a specific type of wine (contrasted with Malvazia), and possibly, in addition, one made from a specific grape variety called *vidonho*. Thus: '... above [the João Gomes river] there are many vineyards with Malvasias and Vidonhos, from which two hundred pipes of wine are vintaged each year'.[6] In his description of the contemporary vine culture of the Canaries,

Fructuoso fails to mention *vidonhos*; he mainly mentions Malvasias and *vinhos* ('vines' in mediaeval Portuguese), though he also tells us that at the parochial church of São João, near Terras de Santa Luzia and Ponta Chã, 'there are good vines which are there called Granel and Sabinal'.[7] Nevertheless, we cannot be absolutely sure that Fructuoso was not just using the word *vidonho* generically rather than specifically; still less, if Fructuoso did intend a specific grape variety, can we now identify what it was.

Even if Fructuoso was not speaking of wines made from Vidonho, however, it is clear that in Madeira a type of wine called Vidonho – or in its anglicized version, Vidonia – was being exported from the island by the first half of the seventeenth century. Thus, in the Funchal Câmara registers for June 1641 we find that it was proposed that Vidonho should be valued at 4,000 réis per bica.[8] And whereas in 1620 only 287 pipes of vidonho were exported, in 1650 we find that the export figure for vidonho had grown to an amazing 2,381 pipes.[9]

Bolton, writing at the beginning of the eighteenth century, makes three references to the shipping of Vidonia;[10] and in 1723 the *London Gazette* refers to '31 Pipes ... of ... White Vidonia Madera Wine'.[11] There is one reference in the Condell Innes Notebook, in the entry for 5 April 1809: 'At foot we note the Shipping prices as/agreed upon at the Meeting of Factory on 31 Xbr last/Vidoho. 65/-'.[12] References later in the nineteenth century are to wine made from the Vidonho grape, rather than to wine called Vidonia as such. Thus Jullien, whose *Topographie de Tous les Vignobles Connus* was published in 1816 and translated into English in 1824, includes Vidogne in his list of grape varieties to be found on Madeira and says (rather obscurely) that it makes 'a wine drier than the white *Burgundy*, but not so sharp as the *Rhenish*'.[13] Redding, in his *A History and Description of Modern Wines* published in 1824, also includes Vidogna in his list of Madeira grape varieties,[14] and finally Thudichum and Dupré include it in the list of Madeira varieties given in their *Treatise on the Origin, Nature and Varieties of Wine* published in 1872. 'In [Madeira] lives the genius of the Malvasia and Vidogna grapes', they say, remarking of the Vidogna that it is *similar* to Chasselas.[15]

From these references it is clear that Madeira Vidonia was a type of wine like the Canaries Vidonia which was usually contrasted with Malvazia, which we may surmise was dry,[16] and which was apparently made from a specific grape variety called Vidonho or Vidogna. The question therefore arises: was the grape variety used to make Madeira Vidonia the same as was used for the Canaries Vidonia?

We may take as our starting point Viala and Vermorel's *Ampélographie* published in Paris at the beginning of the twentieth century, where we find the following confirmation of the third dictionary definition of the word: '*Vidonho. Cépage portugais de la Beira Baixa, très répandu à l'île de Madère, d'après certains auteurs identiques à Vidogne ou Chasselas, différent d'après d'autres et bien spécial.*'[17] A further entry under 'Vidogne' confirms its identity with Chasselas, and the entry for 'Chasselas Doré' indicates that this variety was grown in Tenerife.[18]

I know of only one reference, however, which records the presence of Chasselas on Madeira, and this expressly states that 'it is a recently (1921) introduced variety cultivated only in the surroundings of Funchal'.[19] When Thudichum and Dupré mention the Vidogna in Madeira, they compare it, but do not identify it, with Chasselas. The absence of any other evidence to suggest that Madeira Vidonia was *originally* made from Chasselas appears to rule out this possibility entirely, and we must conclude that, even if Canaries Vidonia was made from Chasselas, what was called Vidonia in Madeira was not.

Noël Cossart states that Verdelho 'was also once known as Vidonia'[20] and presumably following him, so do Lemps[21] and Robinson.[22] I believe that from the nineteenth century onwards at any rate, this is true. However, the only evidence I have discovered for making this identification is purely circumstantial. In two cases, writers who mention Vidogne/Vidogna in their surveys of the grape varieties in Madeira, perhaps significantly, fail to mention Verdelho. These are Jullien and Thudichum and Dupré. Both of them list Malvasia, Boal, Sercial and Vidogne/Vidogna. To what then, if not Verdelho, could they possibly be referring? Moreover, Viala and Vermorel say that the Vidonho is '*très répandu à l'île de Madère*'. Again, what could they possibly mean if not Verdelho, the preponderant variety on the island at the time of phylloxera? Nevertheless, I am not convinced, even if Vidonia or Vidogna were alternative names for Verdelho in the nineteenth century – which they pretty evidently were – that we can be certain that references to Vidonia in the eighteenth century and to Vidonhos in the sixteenth and seventeenth centuries were to wine made from Verdelho. Indeed, Cossart himself tells us that the wine made from Verdelho in the mid-eighteenth century was called 'Verdia', not Vidonia.[23]

Convenient though it might be to accept the simple identification of Vidonho with Verdelho in the context of Madeira, there are at least three reasons for caution. Firstly, in listing the grapes grown in Madeira, Redding[24] mentions *both* Verdelho and Vidogna, making it difficult to see how they could be one and the same. (Vizetelly when speaking of the Canaries[25] does the same, but this of course is consistent with the Vidogna in the Canaries being the same as the Chasselas Doré.) Secondly, Viala and Vermorel indicate, without further explanation, that the Madeira Vidonho is thought by some to be *bien spécial* – that is, not to be identified with any other variety, and certainly not with Verdelho, about which they have a lot to say without a hint of identifying it with Vidonho. And thirdly, André Simon, who was an extremely knowledgeable wine historian of this period, clearly distinguishes Verdelho from Vidonia when listing the types of wine made in Madeira when Bolton was writing his letters. Compare 'A smaller quantity of ordinary beverage *White Wine* was made, from the *Verdelho* grape' and 'In certain specially favoured vineyards . . . richer species of grapes, chiefly the *Malvazia* and *Vidonia*, were grown and gathered later than the common beverage grapes'.[26] It is not clear upon what basis Simon asserts that there was Verdelho in Madeira at this time (though there *probably* was); and he may have made the distinction between Verdelho and Vidonia only because, as mentioned above,[27] he appears to have considered Vidonia as predominantly a sweet wine – wrongly, in my view – which he would therefore *have* to distinguish from a dry beverage wine.

It is difficult to know how best to sum up this discussion, let alone devise a theory that will square with all the facts. I am inclined to take as my starting point the clear parallels between Madeira and the Canaries as wine-producing areas. Both were Portuguese in the fifteenth and sixteenth centuries. They both produced Malvazia[28] and dry wines, and were in competition with each other. But although both certainly had Malvasia vines, it *may* be significant that Fructuoso mentions Vidonhos only in connection with Madeira. Although Vidonia latterly became associated more particularly with the dry wine of the Canaries, the term may well have originated in Madeira and later been adopted in the Canaries to indicate a style of dry wine similar to the Madeira Vidonia with which they were in competition. Over the course of time, either in Madeira or in the Canaries, or in both, the use of the word may have become detached from the wine made from a specific grape variety of the same name, and may have instead acquired a more general sense indicating a *type* of wine. It does not take too much imagination to think of the British merchants in Funchal adopting Vidonia as a generic name for dry wines. As it became more general to make dry wines from Verdelho – for the production of Sercial at this time, if there was any at all, must have been extremely small – a reverse transference of the name may have occasionally been made to the Verdelho grape. It would, in these circumstances, be a natural extension of this generalized use of 'Vidonia' to employ the same word as a synonym for Verdelho. A similar thing might well have happened in the Canaries, accounting for the Vidogna there becoming synonymous with the Chasselas and explaining why, by the nineteenth century at any rate, the grape varieties referred to as Vidogna in the Canaries and in Madeira were not one and the same. It appears to be merely an accident that in the Canaries the word Vidonia, signifying a type of wine, lasted much later into the nineteenth century.

Unfortunately, this theory does not easily explain away Redding's mention of both Vidogna *and* Verdelho in Madeira, unless he was confused or misinformed. But given that many grape varieties do have synonyms, confusion is by no means an impossible explanation. If some islanders he met referred to the grape by the one name and some by the other – which is consistent with my theory – it is possible that he could have mistakenly thought they were two separate varieties, especially if they were in fact two separate varieties in the Canaries. It would be like someone hearing about Sercial in one context and Esganocão in another, and not realizing that they are the same variety.

What my theory does not explain, however, is the fate of the original grape variety, or what it was. It may simply have disappeared, perhaps since the publication of Viala and Vermorel's *Ampélographie*, which lists at least eight Madeira grape varieties no longer to be found on the island.[29] It is only by chance, after all, that Terrantez and Bastardo survived into the twentieth century. What I am most confident of, however, is that this is not the last word on Vidonia and Vidonho.

APPENDIX 7

The Condell Innes Notebook

The Condell Innes manuscript is bound into a copy of *Account of the Island of Madeira* by N. C. Pitta, published in 1812. There is no apparent connection between the book and the manuscript, which consists of 254 pages numbered 9–83, 83 (repeated), 85–177 and 179–263. Several of the pages are blank apart from the page number and a date. The information contained in the notebook relates to a shipping company in Funchal called Condell, Innes & Co (later, from 1809, Duncan, Innes, Lewis & Co) and appears to consist of statistical information copied from other sources, including parts of letters to the firm's correspondent in London. The paper on which the manuscript is written bears an 1810 watermark. One may surmise therefore that the notebook was written by a partner of Duncan, Innes, Lewis & Co some time after 1810 and was used to record interesting information concerning the firm, which dealt in corn, cereal and flax imports from the United States and India, imports of foodstuffs from England, and in wine exports mainly to these three countries.

The major part of the text, which starts on page 27, is headed 'Extracts from Madeira' and, apart from fifteen pages concerning trade with the East India Company between 1808 and 1812, comprises a chronologically arranged notebook covering the period from 30 September 1789 to 13 January 1821. There are no entries for 1790. The contents are miscellaneous but maintain a more or less regular pattern, at least for some years at a time. The entries until 1803 are very brief (one or two pages a year), but thereafter they become increasingly longer and more detailed. Apart from the earlier years, the information generally provided includes: (1) a list of exports to the East India Company, which appears to have been the firm's best customer; (2) a list of the prices of the various qualities of wine as decided by the British Factory; (3) the company's stock position (until 1807); (4) extracts from letters covering the prospects for each year's vintage and how it turned out, indications of the state of the cereals market in Funchal, the difficulties and costs of letters of credit drawn on London, and complaints – all occasionally interspersed with pieces of unrelated information, such as the total exports for the year, imports of corn and cereals, lists of merchandise, analyses of the profit structure of the company, comments on noteworthy events on the island (notably the great flood of 1803, the visit of Napoleon), etc.

The Condell Innes Notebook reminds one irresistibly of the Bolton Letters in its scope, and is full of interest to economic historians of the period. It deserves to be published, but as its contents would be of more interest to the specialist than the general reader, this may not happen soon. The Notebook belongs to Blandy's Madeiras, Lda, and I am most indebted to Mr James Symington not only for allowing me unrestricted use of it, but for generously permitting me to quote from it.

APPENDIX 8
Suppliers

All madeiras (including vintage wines) which are currently being shipped may be located by contacting the shipper concerned, who will direct you to his importing agent for your area, who in turn can give you a list of retail suppliers. Artur de Barros e Sousa, Lda, have no overseas agents but will send wine by post, as will Pereira d'Oliveira (Vinhos) Lda. All telephone and fax numbers have the following country prefix: 351–91

Artur de Barros e Sousa, Lda, Rua dos Ferreiros 109–111, 9000 Funchal, Madeira. (Tel: 220622)

H. M. Borges, Sucrs., Lda, Rua 31 de Janeiro 83, PO Box 92, 9001 Funchal, Madeira. (Tel: 223247; Fax: 222281)

Henriques & Henriques, SA, Sítio de Belém, 9300 Câmara de Lobos, Madeira. (Tel: 941551; Fax: 941590)

Madeira Wine Company, SA, Rua dos Ferreiros 191, PO Box 295, 9000 Funchal, Madeira. (Tel: 740100; Fax: 740101)

Pereira d'Oliveira (Vinhos) Lda, Rua dos Ferreiros 107, 9000 Funchal, Madeira. (Tel: 220784; Fax: 229081)

Silva Vinhos, Lda, Sítio da Igreja, Estreito de Câmara de Lobos, 9300 Câmara de Lobos, Madeira. (Tel: 945810; Fax: 945199)

Vinhos Barbeito (Madeira) Lda, Estrada Monumental 145, PO Box 264, 9003 Funchal, Madeira. (Tel: 726434; Fax: 765832)

Vinhos Justino Henriques, Filhos, Lda, Parque Industrial da Cancela, 9125 Caniço, Madeira. (Tel: 934257; Fax: 934049)

Apart from buying directly from someone with a private cellar of madeiras there are, in general terms, three other possible sources of older wines.

Commercial wine auctions are regularly held in Britain, in the USA and in some central European countries, and old madeiras turn up from time to time. In Britain the principal wine auctioneers are Christie's, who also auction wines in Holland, Switzerland and Japan (Tel: 44–171 839; Fax: 44–171 839 1611), and Sotheby's (Tel: 44–171 493 8080; Fax: 44–171 409 3100). Occasional wine auctions are held by Bonhams (Tel: 44–1404 41872; Fax: 44–1404 43137), and Phillips (Tel. and Fax: 44–1373 830070). In the United States the principal auctioneers are Butterfield and Butterfield, in San Francisco and Los Angeles (Tel: 1–415 861 7500; Fax: 1–415 861 3171); The Chicago Wine Company (Tel: 1–847 647 8789; Fax: 1–847 647 7265); Davis and Co, in Chicago (Tel: 1–312 587 9500; Fax: 1–312 654 1800); Morrell and Co, in New York (Tel: 1–212 307 4200; Fax: 1–212 247 5242); Phillips, in New York (Tel: 1–212 570 4830; Fax: 1–212 570 2207); Sherry Lehmann-Sotheby's, in New York, Los Angeles and Chicago (Tel: 1–212 606 7207; Fax: 1–212 606 7127) and Zachys-Christie's, in New York (Tel: 1–212 546 5830; Fax: 1–212 888 3274).

There are a few specialist madeira wine merchants who will mail madeira worldwide. Of the following four, Patrick Grubb Selections and The Rare Wine Company not only stock vintages still for sale in Madeira, but also sell vintages and old soleras (often sourced from private cellars) which are otherwise unobtainable.

In Britain: **Patrick Grubb Selections,** Orchard Lea House, Steeple Aston, Bicester, OX6 3RT. (Tel: 44–1869 340229; Fax: 44–1869 340867.) On average, there are over 200 vintage wines in stock.

The Madeira Selection, CWCL, 78 Shillitoe Avenue, Potters Bar, Herts EN6 3HR. (Tel. and Fax: 44–1707 646987.) On average, there are over 30 vintage wines in stock.

In Europe: **Madas n.v.,** Graspolderlaan 8, B-2660 Hoboken, Belgium. (Tel: 32–3 830 59 07; Fax: 32–3 828 27 24.) On average, there are over 100 vintage wines in stock.

In the USA: **The Rare Wine Company,** 21468 Eighth Street East,
Sonoma, California 95475. (Tel: 1–707 996 4484 or
1–800 999 4342; Fax: 1–707 996 4491.) On average,
there are over 40 vintage wines in stock.

In Britain there are a few wine brokers who, while not in any way
madeira specialists, often have old vintage and solera madeiras on
their lists. Stocks at any one time can vary greatly. Orders can be
sent abroad. Of these, the following four are worth trying:

Berry, Bros & Rudd, Fine Wine Broking Department, Hamilton
Close, Houndmills, Basingstoke, Hants RG21 6YB. (Tel: 44–1256
340154; Fax: 44–1256 340149.)

Corney and Barrow (Broker Services) Ltd, 12 Helmet Row, London
ECIV 3QJ. (Tel: 44–171 5122; Fax: 44–171 9371.)

Reid Wines, The Mill, Marsh Lane, Hallatrow, Bristol BS18 5EB.
(Tel: 44–1761 452645; Fax: 44–1761 453642.)

Turville Valley Wines, The Firs, Potter Row, Great Missenden,
Bucks HP16 9LT. (Tel: 44–1494 868818; Fax: 44–1494 868832.)

Notes

Introduction

1. Saintsbury, pp. 18–19. Saintsbury rated madeira higher than either port or sherry: 'The very finest Sherries of the luscious kind . . . cannot touch it' (p. 18); '[Red port] has not the . . . transcendental qualities of Burgundy and Madeira' (p. 32).
2. See also p. 162.
3. In 1986 the island provided 10,996 beds and recorded 319,419 visitors. In 1995 there were 17,492 beds and 649,132 visitors. See Anon. (6), p. 125.
4. Mayson (1), p. 222.

Chapter 1

1. Albuquerque and Vieira, p. 1.
2. Silva and Meneses, II, p. 171a.
3. *Ibid.*, II, p. 172b.
4. See, for a case in point, the Torre Bella family, pp. 97–9.
5. Albuquerque and Vieira, p. 56.
6. Silva and Meneses, II, p. 241b.
7. Albuquerque and Vieira, p. 38.
8. The Italian original is quoted in Henderson, footnote to pp. 248–9. Alvise da Mosto is known in Portugal as Cadamosto.
9. Silva and Meneses, III, p. 406a.
10. Tavares, p. 7.
11. Silva and Meneses, I, p. 37a.
12. *Ibid.*, I, p. 14b.
13. *Ibid.*, II, p. 281a.
14. Ribeiro, p. 49.
15. *Ibid.*, p. 48.
16. Simon, II, p. 217.

17. An Italian wine made from a noble grape variety of Greek origin.
18. Quoted in Italian in Aragão, pp. 63–4.
19. *Ibid.*, p. 126.
20. *Voyage of Lopes*, 1588, in *Purchas' Pilgrimages*, quoted in Johnson, p. 81.
21. Ribeiro, p. 51.
22. *Ibid.*, p. 52.
23. See Map No. 2 on pp. 228–9.
24. See pp. 250 ff.
25. This river runs between the Rua 5 de Outubro and the Rua 31 de Janeiro.
26. It seems likely, for geographical reasons, that this is the *fajã* which later became famous as the Fajã dos Padres. See also Silva and Meneses, II, p. 446a, where Manuel de Noronha is mentioned as owning *in sesmaria* the land which later became the Quinta of the Fathers of the Society [of Jesus] – i.e. Quinta Grande.
27. Canhas.
28. Extracted from Fructuoso, pp. 58–134.
29. Duncan, p. 48, though note the reservations about his methods expressed in the next chapter.
30. Cossart, p. 23.
31. Jeffs, p. 23.
32. Simon, III, p. 322.
33. Henderson, p. 301.
34. *Ibid.*, p. 303.
35. *Ibid.*, p. 194.
36. Quoted in Lemps, p. 37.
37. See Croft, p. 23; Henderson, p. 250; Redding, p. 230; and Driver, Appendix, p. xiii.
38. See p. 123.
39. See Bolton (1), p. 17; Croft, p. 23.
40. Croft, p. 24.

Chapter 2

1. Duncan, pp. 46–7.
2. Ibid., pp. 46–8.
3. Mauro gives different figures for this year, derived from different sources, which illustrates clearly the risks incurred by relying on any one set of figures. See p. 18.
4. Jeaffreson, pp. 171–2.
5. Ovington, pp. 9–10.
6. Aragão, pp. 66–7.

7. Ovington, p. 14.

8. Duncan, pp. 54 and 58.

9. See Simon and Craig, pp. 9–18.

10. Ovington, pp. 12–13.

11. Bolton (1), pp. 15–16, and Duncan, p. 71.

12. See Bolton (2), p. 32.

13. *Ibid.*, p. 23.

14. Duncan, pp. 40–1.

15. See under *milreí* in the glossary for an explanation of Portuguese currency.

16. Duncan, p. 39.

17. *Ibid.*, p. 45. Note, however, that Mauro, using different sources, asserts that out of a total of 2,619 pipes exported, 238 were Malvazia (p. 356, quoted in Lemps, p. 32). According to Mauro, therefore, Malvazia amounted to 9 per cent of the wine exported, which is two and a half times the amount suggested by Duncan. Clearly, more research is needed.

18. Bolton (1), pp. 91, 144 and 151.

19. *Ibid.*, p. 78.

20. Bolton (2), p. 75.

21. *Ibid.*, pp. 23–4. André Simon in his transcript of the letters also suggests that 'the richest Old wine', offered by Bolton as a substitute for Malvazia, is in fact Vidonia. See p. 74. He may have suggested this, however, because he regarded Vidonia – I think erroneously – as a sweet wine. Whereas Bolton always refers to Malvazia as 'rich' (and never as 'sweet'), Redding describes Vidonia (quoted in Appendix 6 on p. 250) as 'of good body'.

22. *Ibid.*, p. 78. Cf. pp. 47, 60 and 72.

23. Sloane, I, p. 10.

24. Ovington, pp. 8–9. This passage is perhaps better known from the quotation André Simon gives of it in his introduction to his edition of the Bolton Letters (see (1), pp. 19–20) from the English edition of Savary's *Universal Dictionary of Trade and Commerce* published in 1755. Simon does not indicate that he knew Savary had virtually transcribed this passage word for word from Ovington, and that it had been published more than sixty years earlier.

25. Bolton (1), p. 160.

26. *Ibid.*, p. 17.

27. Bolton (2), p. 45. He also reports (Bolton (1), p. 87) that, of a consignment sent to America, 'an abundance of wines have turned vinegar'.

28. Croft-Cooke, p. 66.

29. Duncan, p. 38.

30. Bolton (2), p. 50.
31. See p. 99.

Chapter 3

1. Lemps, pp. 34–5.
2. Biddle, II, p. 194, lists total annual shipments from 1774–1896 with some gaps. These figures appear to be based on customs house totals, but the already mentioned unreliability of the figures as a basis for calculation remains.
3. Atkins, p. 24.
4. Lemps, p. 52.
5. Cossart, p. 31.
6. See de Sousa, p.65. Lemps quotes (p. 45) from Castro e Almeida: *Arquivo da Marinha e Ultramar: Inventário: Madeira e Porto Santo* [2 vol., Coimbra, 1907–9] an annual average of 13,523 pipes for the period 1790–99.
7. Ibid.
8. Silva and Meneses, II, p. 36b.
9. The information in this paragraph is from the de Freitas MS.
10. Anon. (1), p. 9.
11. Anon. (2), II, p. 392.
12. Forster, p. 24.
13. Barrow, p. 20.
14. Staunton, p. 69.
15. Detailed figures for each parish are given in E. de Castro e Almeida, *op. cit.*, 1, p. 93, and quoted in Lemps, p. 44.
16. *Ibid.*, p. 56.
17. Silva and Meneses, III, p. 414a.
18. The de Freitas MS. The document is preserved in the Arquivo da Marinha e Ultramar, Funchal, Caixa II, Documento No. 311. I am indebted to Dr Ricardo de Freitas for drawing it to my attention.
19. Vieira (2), p. 91.
20. See *ibid.*, pp. 34–5.
21. *Ibid.*, pp. 39–44. See especially sections 13–18.
22. Silva and Meneses, III, p. 414b.
23. Vieira (2), pp. 86–7.
24. The de Freitas MS.
25. Lemps, p. 46.
26. Silva and Meneses, III, p. 414b.
27. Barrow, p. 21.
28. Ibid., pp. 38–9.
29. Croft, pp. 24–5.

30. Vieira (2), p. 59.
31. Anon. (1), pp. 5–6.
32. Apart from 1771, these figures are taken from Cossart, p. 167.
33. Other firms which do not now exist, even in name, but which survived into the twentieth century were: Shortridge, Lawton & Co., founded in 1757; and Welsh and Cunha (latterly Welsh Brothers), founded in 1794.
34. Vieira (2), p. 19.
35. Staunton, p. 70.
36. See Robertson, p. 28.
37. Cossart, p. 103.
38. *Ibid.*
39. Anon. (1), p. 8.
40. Croft, p. 23.
41. Cossart, p. 103.
42. Croft, p. 23.
43. Croft-Cooke, p. 66.
44. Jullien, pp. 232–3.
45. Vieira (2), p. 321: cf. Vieira (1), pp. 49–51 and Silva and Meneses, I, p. 425b.
46. Leacock's way of writing 5 milréis, I presume.
47. Quoted by kind permission of William Leacock.
48. *Ibid. Particular* was one of the qualities of wine shipped to England. See p. 37 below.
49. Penning-Rowsell (1), pp. 12–13. See also Penning-Rowsell (2), p. 819. Further fascinating information about sales of madeira at Christie's from 1777–81 can be found in *Christie's Wine Review* for 1977–80 and in *Christie's Wine Companion* for 1981.
50. Anon. (3), p. 14.
51. Hawkesworth, II, p. 133.
52. Vieira (2), p. 25.
53. *Ibid.*, p. 26.
54. Anon. (1), p. 8.
55. Anon. (3), p. 15.
56. Forster, p. 23.
57. Anon. (3), pp. 15–17.
58. Vieira (2), p. 31.
59. See *ibid.*, pp. 40–42.
60. Lemps, p. 53.
61. *Ibid.*
62. Bolton (2), pp. 42 and 43.
63. Croft-Cooke, p. 136.
64. Staunton, p. 69.

65. See Cossart, p. 109.
66. Croft-Cooke, p. 60.
67. Cossart, p. 109.
68. MWC MSS.
69. Croft-Cooke (p. 59) says that he took on board 3,032 gallons of wine, which Cossart (p. 27) works out to be a ration of 200 bottles per man for a voyage of some 900 days. This is repeated by Lemps (pp. 38–9), but is quite untrue and based on a misreading of the text, which is 'we took in . . . 3,032 gallons of *water*, and ten tuns of wine'. The italics are mine and the quotation is from Hawkesworth, II, p. 11.
70. Dunmore and Brossard, I, p. 244a; compare II, p. 17.

Chapter 4

1. Driver, p. 37.
2. Hodgson, p. 14.
3. Nash, p. 131.
4. See Silva and Meneses, III, pp. 40–1, and Gregory, pp. 103–4.
5. Condell Innes Notebook, p. 220.
6. Gregory, pp. 30–1.
7. See Appendix 7, p. 256.
8. Biddle, p. 194.
9. According to Alvaro de Azevedo, exports rose to an *average* of 20,000 pipes a year between 1810 and 1815 (Silva and Meneses, II, p. 156b.), but this is a huge over-estimate.
10. Condell and Innes Notebook, p. 147. Most of this appears to have gone to India.
11. *Ibid.*, p.176.
12. *Ibid.*, pp. 174–5.
13. Alternative round figures are provided by Taylor, but as they cannot in general be reconciled to what the Condell Innes Notebook tells us, they are probably inaccurate. See Taylor, p. 74.
14. Condell Innes Notebook, entry dated 31 December 1820, p. 261.
15. Vieira (2), p. 90.
16. *Ibid.*, p. 53.
17. Condell Innes Notebook, pp. 51–2.
18. Vieira (2), p. 219.
19. *Ibid.*, pp. 95 and 116.
20. See *ibid.*, pp. 49–51.
21. *Ibid.*, p. 120.
22. *Ibid.*, p. 59.
23. *Ibid.*, p. 98.
24. Holman, p. 23.

25. Vieira (2), p. 73.
26. *Ibid.*
27. *Ibid.*, p. 61.
28. *Ibid.*, p. 73.
29. *Ibid.*, p. 74.
30. Condell Innes Notebook, p. 220.
31. Anon. (4), pp. 53–4.
32. Vieira (2), pp. 137 and 141.
33. *Ibid.*, p. 278.
34. *Ibid.*, p.138.
35. *Ibid.*, p. 91.
36. See Vieira (4), p. 19.
37. Vieira (2), p. 107.
38. *Ibid.*, p. 89.
39. *Ibid.*, p. 97.
40. *Ibid.*, p. 87.
41. See Biddle, p. 194.
42. Hodgson, p. 3.
43. Cossart MS.
44. See Silva and Meneses, I, pp. 95–6. It is now known as ACIF, being a commercial *and industrial* association.
45. See Silva and Meneses, I, pp. 391–2.
46. The potato had first been planted in Madeira in 1760. See Silva and Meneses, III, p. 306b.
47. Quoted in Gregory, p. 106. Coincidentally, 1846 was also the year of the Irish potato famine.
48. Ibid., p. 176.
49. Silva and Meneses, II, pp. 329–30.
50. Alternative figures abound. According to Eduardo Dias Grande, the production between 1847 and 1852 was as follows. 1847: 19,572 pipes. 1848: 13,795 pipes. 1849: 14,508 pipes. 1850: 13,020 pipes. 1851: 9,217 pipes. 1852: 2,124 pipes. This gives an average production in the four years to 1851 of 12,635 pipes. (See Vieira, p. 304.) According to João Andrade de Côrvo, on the other hand, Madeira and Porto Santo had a combined production of 19,487 pipes in 1847 and 14,445 pipes in 1849. (See *ibid.*, p. 289.) Again, according to statistics published in the *Semanário Oficial* for 24 June 1854, the annual average of production for the years 1847 to 1852 was 13,690 pipes, contrasting with an average, according to Grande, of 12,039 pipes. In 1852 this number dropped to 2,110 pipes, and in 1853 to 690 pipes. These figures make for an even more sensational proportional drop in production. (See *ibid.*, p. 181.)
51. That is, 151 hectolitres, again according to Grande. (See *ibid.*, p. 303,

from which the production figures up to 1859 which are given below are also derived.)

52. Thudichum and Dupré, p. 694.
53. Burton, p. 71.
54. João de Andrade Côrvo, the investigator mentioned below. Vieira, p. 288.
55. Silva and Meneses, I, p. 392a.
56. Cossart asserts that the reduction was from seventy to fifteen British merchants (p. 86), stating in his Appendix IV (p. 169) that the number of British shippers had increased to seventy-one by December 1828. He lists only seventeen British firms as active in the year leading up to December 1828 – apparently implying that fifty-four new traders set up shop within a year. This is just incredible. Given the economic situation by 1828, there were no incentives for new merchants to come to the island, and the trade (reduced to average exports of 7,649 pipes a year) simply could not have supported such a number. Cossart previously claims that 'the wine-growing industry of the islands flourished until 1851'. Flourish it certainly did not.
57. Gregory, p. 104.
58. Printed in Vieira (2), pp. 280–302.
59. *Ibid.*, p. 302.
60. *Ibid.*
61. See Vieira (2), p. 187, and Anon. (5), pp. 11–13 and 72–3.
62. See Biddle, p. 147.
63. See Vieira (2), pp. 182–190.
64. Vizetelly, p. 201.
65. See Vieira (4), pp. 31–2 and 97.
66. Gregory, p. 108.
67. See p. 4.
68. Silva and Meneses, II, p. 33b.
69. Vieira (1), p. 61.

Chapter 5

1. For a detailed account of phylloxera, see Ordish. For a brief account, see the article on Phylloxera in Robinson(2), pp. 725–8.
2. Vizetelly, p. 202.
3. Some extracts from the minutes of the Commission's meeting are reprinted in Vieira (2), pp. 127–31. See also Silva and Meneses, II, pp. 32–3.
4. See Biddle, p. 147.
5. Vieira (2), p. 321.
6. Silva and Meneses, II, p. 159a.

7. See Biddle, p. 147.
8. See Gregory, p. 27. 'Madeiras' were, however, manufactured at Massandra in the Crimea during the period of the USSR, and in Australia, until quite recently.
9. See Vizetelly, p. 158.
10. See Vieira (2), pp. 281–3.
11. See p. 34.
12. *Ibid.*
13. Bowdich, pp. 110–11.
14. See Vieira (2), pp. 285–7.
15. White, p. 55.
16. Harcourt, p. 99.
17. See pp. 85–6.
18. Vizetelly, p. 173.
19. Taylor, p. 75.
20. See Vizetelly, p. 75.
21. See Vieira (2), p. 281.
22. White (1851), p. 56.
23. Vizetelly, p. 159.
24. See Anon. (3), pp. 18–19, and Harcourt, p. 99. A consequence of this use of gypsum would also have been to make the wine more acid. On this see p. 123, and Jeffs, pp. 270–1.
25. Thudichum and Dupré, pp. 692–3.
26. Johnson, p. 87.
27. Cossart (p. 100) says that Cossart Gordon were doing so in 1907.
28. See Simon and Craig, pp. 22–3.
29. See Cossart, p. 61.
30. Vizetelly, p. 96.
31. See Vieira (2), p. 326.
32. See *ibid.*, p. 172.
33. Vizetelly, p. 183.
34. For extracts of Portuguese texts of *A Brief Notice on the Treatment of Wine by Heat* (1882) and *The Three Systems of Treatment for Madeira Wine* (1900), see Vieira (2), pp. 313–27.
35. White (1851), p. 57.
36. Johnson, p. 90.
37. See p. 121.
38. Driver, Appendix, p. xii.
39. Holman, p. 18.
40. Bowdich, p. 109. Compare Driver, *loc. cit.*
41. Lyall, p. 363, and Redding, pp. 2301.
42. Vizetelly, p. 174.
43. See Harcourt, p. 98.

44. See for example Driver, Appendix, p. xiii.
45. White (1851), p. 61. It is also known as *vinho pálido* and *palhetinho*. Vizetelly, however, distinguishes Rainwater from *palhetinho*.
46. Driver, p. 75, and Wortley, p. 309.
47. See White (1851), p. 61. This may have been the liqueur mentioned by Bowdich (p. 111), made from the first pressing of the grapes after treading with the addition of an equal quantity of brandy.
48. Vizetelly, p. 190.
49. See Cossart, p. 57.
50. See Harcourt, p. 98.
51. Vieira (2), p. 316.

Chapter 6

1. See Tavares, p. 34.
2. Pestana, II, p. 233.
3. For this account I am indebted to Chapter 9 of Gregory's book, in which a more detailed account of the matter may be found.
4. See Gregory, pp. 127–8.
5. Quoted *ibid.*, p. 125.
6. See Silva and Meneses, II, pp. 405–6.
7. See *ibid.*, I, p. 292a. The provisions of the law of 18 September 1908 are printed in *Monarchia*, No. 226 (7 October) for 1908, and the regulations for Madeira in No. 59 (16 March) for 1909.
8. *Ibid.*, II, p. 160b.
9. See Pereira, I, p. 565.
10. Cossart, p. 81.
11. See Silva and Meneses, I, p. 99b.
12. See Tavares, pp. 34–5.
13. See *ibid.*, p. 35.
14. Here is a complete list of members of the 1934 Association, with dates of joining: Vinhos Viúva Abudarham & Filhos, Lda (1934); Aguiar Freitas & Cª Sucrs Lda (1936); A. Nobrega (Vinhos da Madeira), Lda (1953); A. Pries Scholtz & Co (not known); Barros, Almeida & Cª (Madeira), Lda (1936; this company had been set up in 1935 by the Madeira Wine Association and Barros, Almeida & Cª, the port firm in Vila Nova de Gaia, the latter transferring its shares to Sr José T. de Freitas a week later); Bianchi's Madeira, Lda (1953); Blandy's Madeiras, Lda (1934); Cossart Gordon & Co Lda (1953); Casa dos Vinhos Vasconcelos, Lda (1951); E. A. Cunha (not known); F. F. Ferraz & Cª Lda (1937; having been founded in 1915 and dissolved in 1931, it was reconstituted in 1937 by the Madeira Wine Association and Turquands, Barton, Mayhew & Co); Funchal Wine Company, Lda

(1934; the date on which it was constituted by the Madeira Wine Association and Turquands, Barton, Mayhew & Co); Freitas Martins, Caldeira & Cª Lda (1960; Martins, Caldeira & Cª Lda being dissolved and reconstituted under the new name); Gibbs & Co (not known); J. B. Spinola, Lda (1936); Krohn Bros. & Cª Lda (1951); Leacock & Co. (Wine), Lda (1934); Luiz Gomes (Vinhos), Lda (1953); Madeira Victoria & Co Lda (1936; having been constituted in 1934 by the Madeira Wine Association and Sr José T. de Freitas); Miles Madeiras, Lda (1969; although the right to use its trademarks was ceded to the Association in 1951); Power Drury (Wine), Lda (1934); Royal Madeira Company, Lda (1936; the company having been constituted in 1934 by The Madeira Wine Association and Sr José T. de Freitas); Rutherford & Miles, Lda (1951); Sociedade dos Vinhos Madeira Menéres, Lda (1936); Sociedade Agrícola da Madeira, Lda (1937; this company, founded in 1928 by Salomão da Veiga França and Maurílio Ferraz e Silva, should not be confused with the Sociedade Agrícola Madeirense of the previous century, long since defunct); Tarquínio T. da Câmara Lomelino, Lda (1936; the company joined the Association in two stages, when separate shareholders ceded their shares to it in 1934 and 1936 respectively, although the second Association had been given the right to develop the name and trade of the company in 1933); Vinhos Donaldson & Co Lda (1934); Vinhos Shortridge Lawton & Co Lda (1934); Welsh Bros (Vinhos), Lda (1934). Turquands, Barton, Mayhew & Co was the firm of accountants which audited the Association's accounts. It had a token shareholding in each of the companies to make up the minimum of two shareholders required by Portuguese law, and these were ceded to the Royal Madeira Company in 1982.

15. See Tavares, p. 35.
16. *Ibid.*
17. The other Dukes used for brands, all extinct dukedoms – Sussex, Cambridge and Cumberland – made their appearance on the market in the 1950s.
18. Writing in 1933, even André Simon had to report that Boal 'is not, as a matter of general practice, made from one kind of grape alone, and that grape the Boal'. See Simon and Craig, p. 40.
19. Cossart, pp. 111–12.
20. See Lemps, p. 119.
21. See p. 141.
22. Pereira, I, p. 588.
23. See Lemps, p. 119.
24. From 15,000 hectolitres in 1973 to 37,000 hectolitres in 1980. See Cossart, p. 82.

25. A more detailed description of the structure of the Regional Directorate of Agriculture and the Madeira Wine Institute is given in Appendix 2: see p. 239. The JNV continued in being until 1986, when it was renamed the Instituto da Vinha e do Vinho. Because Madeira is an autonomous province, however, the Instituto da Vinha e do Vinho has no jurisdiction over the IVM.

26. See pp. 139–42.

27. This norm properly applies only to quality table wines; the rules for quality liqueur and fortified wines have not as yet been finalized.

28. See Mayson (2), p. 210.

Chapter 7

1. See p. 114 for details of the scheme for restructuring such vineyards.
2. See p. 94.
3. See Cossart, p. 72.
4. Brazão, p. 7.
5. Lemps appears to have used old reference books rather uncritically, just as Cossart appears to have been rather uncritically used as a source for Robinson (1).
6. See under 'Vinhas' in Silva and Meneses, III, pp. 406–12.
7. These figures appear in Brazão, p. 7.
8. Silva and Meneses, III, p. 412a.
9. Cossart, p.73.
10. Cossart, p. 121, says that John Atkins traded two half-worn suits and three second-hand wigs for two pipes of Terrantez in 1720; following Cossart, this date is quoted by Lemps (p. 98). This, however, is erroneous: Atkins simply mentions wine without specifying the type.
11. Viala and Vermorel, VII, p. 316.
12. Silva and Meneses, III, p. 412a.
13. Cossart, p.72; Robinson (1), p. 218.
14. Anon. (3), p. 15.
15. Cossart, p. 72.
16. It is described in detail in Silva and Meneses, III, p. 410b.
17. See also p. 154.
18. Silva and Meneses, III, p. 410a.
19. *Ibid.*
20. Viala and Vermorel, VI, p.376.
21. Cossart, p. 75.
22. See p. 118.
23. Cossart, p. 76.

Chapter 8

1. Redding, C., *History and Description of Modern Wines*, 2nd ed., Whittaker & Co., London, 1836, p. 234.
2. The latest (1989) agricultural census figure is 14,098, but after nine years of rapid development this must be somewhat out of date.
3. See p. 29. Gordon apparently kept meticulous records of the results of the vintage of all his vineyards, but sadly these appear to have disappeared.
4. See p. 4.
5. See p. 76.
6. See p. 236 for an explanation of the term *Fajã*.
7. See p. 259, note 26.
8. Bowdich, p. 59.
9. Driver, p. xii. *Fazenda* is another word for 'farm' (note that *Fajã* is not an abbreviation of *fazenda*). 'Giram' is an anglicized version of Girão.
10. See p. 22.
11. *Ibid.*
12. Vizetelly, p. 174.
13. Silva and Meneses, II, pp. 6b–7a.
14. Cossart, p. 143.
15. Pereira, p. 563. On Dermot Bolger, see above.
16. Anon. (6), p. 70.
17. The other, at Ponta Delgado, belongs to Ricardo França, and was constructed at the same time. See p. 108.

Chapter 9

1. See pp. 34–5.
2. See p. 60.
3. 1 tonne=1,000 kg (1 ton=1,016 kg). The amount of must obtainable from 1 tonne depends on many variables: type of grape, amount of juice, degree of pressure in pressing, etc. In general, 130 kg of red grapes and 150–160 kg of white grapes are needed to produce one hectolitre of must (see Robinson (2), pp. 1080–2.) This means, for example, that one hectare of Sercial produces around 65 hectolitres of must.
4. Cossart, p. 77.
5. For further information see under 'Pruning' in Robinson (2).
6. See p. 201. A table wine made from Verdelho, sold under the name 'Atlantis', has been in production since 1994 by the MWC.
7. See pp. 35–6.
8. *Contas correntes* came into being under the legislation of 11 March 1901 (Art. 13). Shippers had to inform first the Customs, then the

Delegation of the JNV, of their purchases during the vintage and of their sales. Only the total amount of wine in stock was monitored. In 1973 the Delegation introduced *contas correntes* for bulk wines by variety but without date of making, and for vintage (*garrafeira*) wines. The present detailed system was introduced by the IVM in 1980.

9. See p. 139.

Chapter 10

1. As late as 1985 the MWC was purchasing *mosto* from the north of the island.
2. Since 1989 vinification sufficient to produce 4° of alcohol must take place before fortifying alcohol is added.
3. Cossart, p. 98.
4. Mayson (2).
5. The use of concentrated must has been carefully regulated by the IVM since 1991.
6. See p. 139 for the official sweetness tolerances for each type.
7. The lowest legal limit is 15.5°.
8. See Cossart, p. 104.
9. Cossart, however, indicates (pp. 99 and 113) that vintage madeiras used to be given *estufagem*.
10. For technical explanations of maderization, oxidation, rancio, acetobacter and the effect of oxygen on wine, see under these headings in Robinson (2).
11. If this were not done the wine would become a kind of *solera*.
12. Cossart, p. 142.
13. For an explanation of this term see note 6 of Chapter 11.

Chapter 11

1. Proposta de Alterações á Portaria 40/82.
2. Article 6 of Portaria 40/82, quoted in *Jornal Oficial* for 18 March 1994.
3. See p. 221.
4. See, on Listrão and on Moscatel, p. 87.
5. The principal legislation controlling the madeira wine industry is as follows. Decreto-Lei 41 166/57: norms for the commercialization of wine. Portaria 610/72: chemical tolerances for madeira. Decreto Regional 7/79: creation of IVM and its terms of reference. Portaria 40/82: norms for the production of madeira. Decreto Regional 20/85: norms for vineyards, vinification and sale of madeira. Decreto-Lei 326/88: definition of madeira as a VLQPRD, and further norms for the sale

of madeira. Portaria 16/94: permitted levels of acidity in madeira.
Decreto Regional 4/95: revised terms of reference for the IVM. The
technical wine specifications incorporated in the above laws have been
supplemented by EU regulations (published in the *Official Journal* of
the European Community), notably on 16 March 1987 and 19 June
1989.

6. Some of these terms may require a little explanation. Volatile acidity is
measured as acetic acid. When this measurement is converted into
tartaric acid, it can be added to the measurement for fixed acidity, and
this gives a reading known as 'total acidity'. In a similar way, non-
reducing extract is what you are left with when you subtract the
measurement for reducing sugars from the measurement of total
extract.

7. Decreto-Lei No. 41 166/57. These regulations make references to the
JNV and other government organs which no longer exist, but are
interpreted by the courts as references to the IVM. Moreover, certain
provisions (such as the official fixing of the price of grapes) are now
redundant. A legal tidying-up operation to relate these provisions
to organizational realities seems long overdue.

8. For *partidistas* the minimum is 75 hectolitres.

Chapter 12

1. Most of the wines shown to Vizetelly in 1877 were less than 10 years
old.

2. One occasionally comes across older bottles which are stencilled but
do not necessarily show the grape variety. Thus one may find *Vinho
Velho* (Old Wine), *Vinho Velhissimo* (Very Old Wine) or simply and
rather unhelpfully, just *Madeira*.

3. See Cossart, pp. 60–1.

4. See pp. 258–9.

5. Simon and Craig, p. 29.

6. See p. 92.

7. The reader will notice that one of the wines awarded a rosette for
quality in the next chapter is, although very old, not a vintage wine.

8. Cossart, p. 146.

Chapter 13

1. This information, confirmed by Avery's, is taken from the catalogue
of Christie's wine sale on 29 September 1977, Lot No 364.

2. Cossart, p. 138.

3. See p. 160.

4. See Cossart, pp. 137–8.
5. See *ibid.*, p. 120.
6. *Ibid.*, pp. 124 and 126.

Chapter 14

1. The name Barros e Sousa does not indicate the combination of two family names for business purposes (like, for example, Marks & Spencer), but is a single surname – rather like a double-barrelled family name such as Abel Smith.
2. See Silva and Meneses, II, p. 281b.
3. The family still maintains a remarkable private cellar. See pp. 172–3.
4. Cossart Gordon acquired a Terrantez 1846 from him in 1900. See p. 168.
5. See p. 70 and pp. 71–2.
6. This is the name of the company founded in 1925 as one of the components of the revamped MWA (see p. 71) to represent specifically Blandy's wine, as distinct from their other, wider commercial interests.
7. It would be impossible to do justice to all the firms that have been part of the MWC without turning this profile into a complete history of the company and thereby unbalancing the book. The history of Cossart Gordon – though not the rather sad way its London branch was absorbed into the MWC – is adequately dealt with in Noël Cossart's book, and that of Leacock in Croft-Cook's book. Henry Price Miles, aged one and a half, arrived in Madeira with his mother in 1852. At twelve he was apprenticed to a firm called Rutherford and Brown. Shortly thereafter the Browns went to South Africa and the Rutherfords decided to return to England. They sold the business to Henry Miles, then nineteen, on condition that exports to London would be exclusively to them. Thus in Madeira, Rutherford and Brown became H. P. Miles, later (in 1935) H. P. Miles & Co, while in London the name of Rutherford & Miles was registered. H. P. Miles & Co joined the MWA in 1969. Rutherford and Miles' most famous brand, Trinity House Bual, is now owned by the MWC but is no longer in production. The Miles family's activities are now centred on brewing, being part owners of the Empresa de Cervejas da Madeira, which produces the excellent Coral beer.
8. Already in existence in Fructuoso's time.
9. See Vieira (3), pp. 105 and 172.
10. The other firms are: Afonso & Irmão, Lda, Antonino da Côrte, Expovinhos, Francisco A. Costa; Gonçalo dos Santos and Pereira Ferraz, José Pita, José Procopio Gomes de Andrade and Manuel Eugénio Fernandes Lda.

Chapter 15

1. Brazão, p. 4.
2. Decreto-Lei 7/79, Art. 3 (e).
3. See pp. 136–7.

Appendix 1

1. Ribeiro, p. 22.
2. *Ibid.*, p. 36. Much of this account is directly derived from Ribeiro, but with more up-to-date values derived from Anon (6) – see Bibliography.
3. *Ibid.*, p. 111.

Appendix 2

1. See pp. 115–6.
2. Its members are the council of directors, government representatives from the departments of agriculture, commerce, industry, tourism and finance, and five trade members (*aguardente*, spirits, cane sugar, viticulture and the wine trade).

Appendix 5

1. This point is elaborated by Cossart: 'The wine was considered hardly ready for drinking . . . so it was only bottled . . . in 1840' (Cossart, p. 118). Apart from the unlikelihood of Napoleon being offered a wine that would only reach maturity at best in his extreme old age, the wine would have been 33 years old when it returned to Madeira (if the story is true) – which by the standards of the time, when madeira was still sold the year after the vintage, would have been a very old wine indeed.
2. Simon and Craig, pp. 35–6.
3. This and Walter Grabham's letter are quoted, by kind permission of Richard Blandy, from the originals in his possession.
4. Cossart, p. 136, footnote.
5. Vizetelly, p. 191.
6. See Cossart, pp. 125 and 146.
7. Cf. these entries from Christie's catalogues. 1 December 1977: Lot 411, 'Bual – Believed Vintage 1792. Blandy'. 25 September 1980: Lot 385, 'Believed Bual – Vintage 1792'. 18 June 1992: Lots 469–73, 'Bual Vintage 1792', with a note referring back to Lot 433, which is Blandy's Vintage 1792, itself with a note about the Napoleonic association.

8. Croft-Cooke, p. 126.
9. Cossart: cf. p. 67 with p. 125.
10. Cossart, p. 162.
11. Broadbent, I, p. 397.

Appendix 6

1. Redding, p. 194.
2. Vizetelly, pp. 206–7.
3. See, for example, Costa and Meio's *Dicionário da Língua Portuguesa*.
4. Vieira (2), p. 305.
5. Frutuoso (1), p. 104. Note that Frutuoso is the modern spelling of Fructuoso.
6. *Ibid.*, p. 117.
7. Frutuoso (2), p. 51.
8. Mauro, p. 443.
9. *Ibid.*, p. 415.
10. Bolton (2), pp. 23, 24 and 64.
11. *London Gazette*, No. 6173/3: quoted in the OED entry for Vidonia.
12. Condell Innes Notebook, p. 69.
13. Jullien, p. 231. Of the Canaries Vidonia he says, on page 229, that it 'is made with raisins before they are ripe, whence their harshness and dryness' and adds that 'they improve much by age, and become similar to *Madeira* wine, particularly when imported into warm climates'.
14. Redding, p. 229.
15. Thudichum and Dupré, pp. 692 and 693.
16. André Simon appears to suggest that Vidonia was sweet when he writes (Simon and Craig, p. 19.): 'Madeira produced mostly red wines and some white wines . . . as well as a very limited quantity of Malvasia or Malmsey, and even less Vidonia or Vidogna, sweet dessert wines'. I know, however, of no other evidence to support this view. In any case, the export figure of 2,381 pipes for 1650 quoted above hardly accords with 'even less' Vidonia than the 'very limited quantity' of Malvazia, given that in 1650 only 238 pipes of Malvazia were exported; see Mauro, p. 415.
17. Viala and Vermorel, VII, p. 341b. 'Vidonho. Portuguese grape variety from Beira Baixa, very extensive on the island of Madeira, according to certain authors identical to Vidogne or Chasselas, according to others different and very special.'
18. *Ibid.*, II, p. 7.
19. Silva and Meneses, III, p. 411a.
20. Cossart, p. 73.
21. Lemps, p. 96.

22. Robinson (1), p. 248.
23. Cossart, p. 109.
24. Redding, p. 229.
25. Vizetelly, p. 207.
26. Bolton, p. 17.
27. See p. 21 and note 16 above.
28. A dessert Malvazia is still produced in small quantities at La Palma, but it is not a fortified wine.
29. See p. 85.

Glossary

ACIF Associação Comercial e Industrial do Funchal. Local trade association which has a *Mesa dos Vinhos*, a sub-section to which shippers who export wines generally belong.

Adega Winery.

Agua pé Light refreshing drink made by mixing water with *bagaço* (q.v.).

Aguardente Strictly speaking a word for spirits, but universally used in Madeira to indicate the type of rum made from sugar cane. Wine spirits are *aguardente do vinho*.

Americanos American vines, or more specifically the variety called *Isabela* (*Vitis labrusca*).

Armazem Store or lodge.

Armazem de calor A form of *estufa*, being an artificially heated store.

Arrobo Boiled-down must used for sweetening.

Bagaço Grape skins, pips and stalks after fermentation and/or pressing.

Balseira Method of growing vines up trees common in the north of Madeira until the twentieth century.

Bardos Fences made from the branches of shrubs – normally *urze*, a giant heather – to protect the vines from wind damage and sea spray.

Baumé The name for the most generally used scale of measurement of the sugar content of a solution whose values are determined by using a hydrometer at a temperature of 15°C.

Bentonite An absorbent clay compound used for fining (i.e. clarifying and stabilizing) wine.

Bica aberta Method of fermenting wine in open-topped wooden casks.

Borracheiro Man who carries a *borracho*.

Borracho Sack made from a goatskin and retaining the shape of the animal, used for transporting must and wine.

Cadastro Register. In a wine context, a census of vineyards recording, *inter alia*, area and grape varieties.

Calda Syrup made from boiled-down sugar.

Canteiro Trestle upon which a cask rests. See *Vinho de canteiro*.

Carvão Charcoal.

Castas boas Former name for recommended varieties of grape.

Castas nobres Former name for classical varieties of grape.

Cepa Grape variety.

Concelho Local council.

Contrato de colonia Type of land leasehold whereby the lessor pays a proportion of the land produce in rental.

Cuba de calor Tank, often of concrete lined with epoxy resin, used for heating wine during *estufagem*.

Cuba de fermentação Tank, often of concrete lined with epoxy resin, used for fermenting wine.

Direct producers Ungrafted vines of American origin, not authorized for use in making madeira but used to make *vinho seco* (q.v.).

Espaldeira System of training vines on wires between posts.

Estágio Period of time during which wine is stored and rested.

Estufa Room or building in which *estufagem* takes place.

Estufagem Process of heating wine to simulate ageing.

Frasqueira Private store or cellar for wine. Alternative name for *garrafeira* in both the senses given (q.v.).

Freguesia Parish.

Garafão Glass demijohn, generally covered with wicker, used for storing wine; of varying capacities up to 25 litres.

Garrafeira Private store or cellar for wine. The name by which madeira which has been cask aged for at least twenty years is known. See *Frasqueira*.

Granel Youngest and cheapest type of madeira, exported in bulk.

IVM Instituto do Vinho da Madeira (Madeira Wine Institute), government body which controls the wine trade in Madeira.

Inox Stainless steel.

JNV Junta Nacional do Vinho. The controlling body which preceded the IVM.

Lagar Tank or trough, in Madeira often made from wood, in which the grapes are trodden at the vintage.

Latada Trellis, generally low-lying, which supports vines.

Levada A channel with a gentle gradient cut into hillsides in Madeira to collect water for irrigation. Small levadas feed larger levadas at lower altitudes, and combine to form an extensive water-supply network.

Lodge cask Cask holding 600 litres used for storing madeira.

Lote Specific parcel of wine; in English, a 'lot'.

Maderization Oxidation of wine through exposure to air, more generally applied to table wines which have oxidized than to those aged in cask.

Malvina Substance thought to be injurious to health found in American hybrid vines.

Mangra Madeiran word for *oïdium* or powdery mildew.

Mercaptan Evil-smelling substance produced by bacteria after fermentation.

Milréi Basic unit of Portuguese currency until the twentieth century. The relevant money table is as follows: 1 conto = 1,000 escudos; 100 centavos = 1 escudo; 10 réis = 1 centavo; 400 réis = 1 cruzado; 1,000 réis = 1 milréi (now 1 escudo).

Morgado Estate which is entailed and descends as a unit to whoever inherits it.

Mosto Must, or grape juice before fermentation.

MWA Madeira Wine Association, former name of the Madeira Wine Company.

MWC Madeira Wine Company.

OIV Office International de la Vigne et du Vin.

Organoleptic An adjective applied to tests on wine carried out by means of the senses (smell, taste, etc.), as opposed to chemical analysis.

Partidista Trader who buys or makes wine in order to mature it and sell it on to a shipper or other trader.

Patamars Vineyard terraces without retaining walls that have been constructed by bulldozing the soil.

Pipa Wooden cask or pipe. A shipping pipe contains in Madeira 110 'old' gallons, 92 imperial gallons, or 418 litres. A lodge pipe, used for maturing or storing wine, is half as big again.

Poio Terrace with retaining stone wall.

Produtores direitos 'Direct producers': American and hybrid vines not authorized for madeira production.

Quinta Farm: often used in Madeira to signify an estate with a large house.

Solera A system of fractional blending whereby a small amount is drawn from a reserve and replaced with younger but similar wine, which is then allowed to blend and mature with the remainder of the reserve before subsequent repetitions of the sequence.

Tetrahybrid A hybrid generated from three varieties.

Tornaviagem 'Round trip'. See *Vinho da roda*.

Vinha da pé Vineyard in which the vines are grown on the ground with minimal or no support.

Vinho abafado Literally 'smothered wine': wine to which alcohol has been added before fermentation has stopped.

Vinho claro Madeira after fermentation but before fortification.

Vinho da roda From the seventeenth to the twentieth centuries, wine that had been shipped on a round sea voyage. Much esteemed because of the improvement this treatment made to the wine.

Vinho de canteiro Wine matured in cask without *estufagem* (q.v.).

Vinho seco Table wine made for local consumption from direct producers (hybrid vines), so called because it has been fermented dry.

Vinho surdo Grape must to which alcohol has been added before the start of fermentation. Formerly a sweetening agent.

Bibliography

This bibliography is very selective, for the most part containing only books that are referred to in the text or which may be useful to the reader.

Albuquerque, L. de, and Vieira, A. *The Archipelago of Madeira in the XV Century*. Funchal, 1988.

Anon. (1) *A Journal of a Voyage Round the World in His Majesty's Ship Endeavour in the Years 1768, 1769, 1770, and 1771*. London, 1771.

(2) *A Collection of Voyages round the World performed by Royal Authority, Containing a Complete Historical Account of Captain Cook's First, Second, Third and Last Voyages*. 6 vols. London, 1790.

(3) *A Guide to Madeira, containing a short account of Funchall*. London, 1801.

(4) *An Historical Sketch of the Island of Madeira*. London, 1819.

(5) *125 Anos de Cerveja na Madeira* [by José Adriano Ribeiro]. Funchal, 1996.

(6) *20 Anos de Autonomia e Desenvolvimento*. Funchal, 1996.

Aragão, A. *A Madeira Vista por Estrangeiros*. Funchal, 1981.

Atkins, J. *A Voyage to Guinea, Brasil and the West-Indies*. 2nd. ed., London, 1737.

Barrow, J. *A Voyage to Conchinchina in the Years 1792 and 1793*. London, 1806.

Biddle, A. J. *The Land of the Wine, being an account of the Madeira Islands*. 2 vols. Philadelphia, San Francisco and London, 1901.

Bolton, W. (1) *The Bolton Letters. Letters of an English Merchant in Madeira 1695–1714*. Edited by A. L. Simon. London, 1928.

(2) *The Bolton Letters. The Letters of an English Merchant in Madeira*. Vol. II, *1701–1714*. Produced by G. Blandy, Funchal, 1960. Reprinted in 1976 and 1980.

Bowdich, T. E. *Excursions in Madeira and Porto Santo*. London, 1825.

Brazão, João do S. *Análise ao Sector Vitivinícola da Região Autonoma da Madeira*. Madeira, 1994.

Cossart, N. *Madeira the island vineyard*. London, 1984.

Croft, J. *A Treatise on the Wines of Portugal*. York, 1787.

Croft-Cooke, R. *Madeira*. London, 1961.

Dillon, F. *Sketches in the Island of Madeira*, London, 1850.

Driver, J. *Letters from Madeira in 1834*. London and Liverpool, 1838.

Duncan, T. B. *Atlantic Islands. Madeira . . . in Seventeenth-Century Commerce and Navigation*. Chicago and London, 1972.

França, I. de *Journal of a Visit to Madeira and Portugal (1853–1854)*. Funchal, [1970].

Forster, G. *A Voyage Round the World in His Britannic Majesty's Sloop RESOLUTION, commanded by Capt. James Cook, during the Years 1772 . . . 2 vols*. London, 1777.

Frutuoso, G. (1) *Livro Segundo das Saudades da Terra*. Ponta Delgado, 1968.

(2) *Las Islas Canarias (de 'Saudades da Terra')*. La Laguna de Tenerife, 1964.

Gonçalves, A. B., and Nunes, R. S. *Ilhas de Zargo. Adenda*. Parte I. Funchal, 1990.

Gregory, D. *The Beneficent Usurpers*. London and Toronto, 1988.

Harcourt, E. V. *A Sketch of Madeira*. London, 1851.

Hawkesworth, J. *An Account of the Voyages undertaken by the order of his Present Majesty for making Discoveries in the Southern Hemisphere*. 2 vols, the second vol. being *An Account of a Voyage Round the World in the Years 1768, 1769, 1770 and 1771 by Lieutenant James Cook, Commander of his Majesty's Bark the Endeavour*. 4th ed., Perth, 1787.

Henderson, A. *The History of Ancient and Modern Wines*. London, 1824.

Hodgson, S. *Truths from the West Indies*. London, 1838.

Holman, J. *Travels in Madeira . . . 2nd ed.*, London, 1840.

Jeaffreson, J. C. *A Young Squire of the Seventeenth Century*. 2 vols. London, 1878.

Jeffs, J. *Sherry*, 4th ed., London, 1992.

Johnson, J. Y. *Madeira, Its Climate and Scenery*. 3rd ed., London, 1885.

Jullien, A. *The Topography of all the known Vineyards*. London, 1824.

Lemps, A. H. de *Le Vin de Madère*. Grenoble, 1989.

Lyall, A. *Rambles in Madeira and in Portugal in the early part of M.DCCC.XXVI*. London, 1827.

Mauro, F. *Le Portugal, Le Bresil, et l'Atlantique au XVII Siècle (1570–1670)*. Paris, 1983.

Mayson, R. (1) *Portugal's Wines and Wine Makers*. Chapter 17. London, 1992.

(2) 'Does anyone know how to make madeira?' Article in *Decanter*, May 1991.

Nash, R. *Scandal in Madeira*. Lewes, 1990.

Ordish, G. *The Great Wine Blight*. London, 1972. New ed., London, 1987.

Ovington, J. *A Voyage to Suratt In the Year, 1689*. London, 1696.

Pamment, D. 'An Intricate Art.' Article in *Decanter Magazine's Guide to Madeira*, 2nd ed., 1987.

Penning-Rowsell, E. (1) 'Christie's wine auctions in the 18th century.' Article in *Christie's Wine Review 1972*. London, 1972.

(2) 'Auctioning Wine in the 18th Century.' Article in *Country Life*, 6 October 1966.

Pereira, E. C. N. *Ilhas do Zargo*. Vol. I, 4th ed., Funchal, 1989.

Pestana, E. A. *Ilha da Madeira*. 2 vols. Funchal, 1965, 1970.

Redding, C. *History and Description of Modern Wines*. London, 1833.

Ribeiro, O. *A Ilha da Madeira até Meados do Século XX*. (This is a geographical study.) Lisbon, 1985.

Robertson, G. *Port*. London, 1978.

Robinson, J. (1) *Vines, Grapes and Wines*, London, 1986.

(2) ed. *The Oxford Companion to Wine*. Oxford and New York, 1994.

Saintsbury, G. *Notes on a Cellar-Book*, London and Basingstoke, 1978.

Silva, F. A. da, and Meneses, C. A. de *Elucidário Madeirense*. 3 vols. Funchal, 1922. Reprinted 1940 and also in facsimile, Funchal, 1984.

Simon, A. L. *The History of the Wine Trade in England*. 3 vols. London, 1964.

Simon, A. L., and Craig, E. *Madeira – Wine Cakes & Sauce*. London, 1933.

Sloane, H. *A Voyage to the Islands Madera . . . and Jamaica*. 2 vols. London, 1707.

Sousa, J. J. A. de 'O Porto do Funchal e a Economia da Madeira no Século XVIII.' Article in *Das Artes e da História da Madeira*, Vol. VII, No. 37, 1967.

Staunton, G. *An Authentic Account of An Embassy from the King of Great Britain to the Emperor of China . . .* London, 1797.

Tavares, J. *Subsídios para o Estudo da Vinha e do Vinho na Região da Madeira*. Funchal, 1953.

Taylor, E. M. *Madeira: Its scenery and how to see it*. London, 1882.

Thudichum, J. L. W., and Dupré, A. *A Treatise on the Origin, Nature and Varieties of Wine*. London, 1872.

Various. *Decanter Magazine's Guide to Madeira*, 2nd ed., 1987.

Viala, P., and Vermorel, V. *Ampélographie*. 7 vols. Paris, 1901–10.

Vieira, A. (1) *Breviário da Vinha e do Vinho na Madeira*. Ponta Delgado (Azores), 1990.

(2) *História do Vinho da Madeira*. Funchal, 1993.

(3) *A Rota do Açúcar na Madeira / The Sugar Route in Madeira*. Funchal, 1996.

Vizetelly, H. *Facts about Port and Madeira*. London and New York, 1880. Reprinted in facsimile, Baltimore, n.d.

White, R. *Madeira Its Climate and Scenery*. London and Madeira, 1851. 2nd ed., rewritten with the addition of much new matter by J. Y. Johnson. Edinburgh, 1857.

Wortley, E. S. *A Visit to Portugal and Madeira*. London, 1854.

Manuscript sources

References to these unpublished sources are indicated in the text by means of the abbreviations shown here in square brackets.

Cossart, P. *Journal. From leaving Madeira 14 July 1833 to my return to it 15 May 1835*. In the possession of John Cossart, Esq. [Cossart MS]

Freitas, R. D. V. de. *Madeira no Século XVIII (1759–1779) Economia e Sociedade*. Dissertation, University of Lisbon. [de Freitas MS]

Newton, Gordon & Murdoch account books, ledgers, etc. in the archives of the Madeira Wine Company. [MWC MSS]

Anon. Manuscript account of the trading of Condell, Innes & Co (later Innes, Duncan, Lewis & Co), a firm of madeira wine-shippers, 1789–1821. 235 pp. In the possession of Blandy's Madeiras, Lda. [Condell Innes MS]

Index